Personal and Public Interests

Frieda B. Hennock. Photograph courtesy of The
Schlesinger Library, Radcliffe Institute, Harvard University.

Personal and Public Interests

Frieda B. Hennock and the Federal Communications Commission

Susan L. Brinson

Westport, Connecticut
London

Library of Congress Cataloging-in-Publication Data

Brinson, Susan L., 1958–
    Personal and public interests : Frieda B. Hennock and the Federal Communications
Commission / by Susan L. Brinson.
      p. cm.
    Includes bibliographical references and index.
    ISBN 0–275–97322–0 (alk. paper)
    1. Hennock, Frieda B. 2. United States. Federal Communications
Commission—Biography. 3. Women public officers—United States—Biography. 4.
Telecommunication policy—United States—History—20th century. I. Title.
HE7781.b74 2002
384'.0973—dc21   2001032906

British Library Cataloguing in Publication Data is available.

Library of Congress Catalog Card Number: 2001032906
ISBN: 0–275–97322–0

First published in 2002

Praeger Publishers, 88 Post Road West, Westport, CT 06881
An imprint of Greenwood Publishing Group, Inc.
www.praeger.com

Printed in the United States of America

The paper used in this book complies with the
Permanent Paper Standard issued by the National
Information Standards Organization (Z39.48–1984).

10 9 8 7 6 5 4 3 2 1

Copyright Acknowledgments

The author and publisher gratefully acknowledge permission for use of the following material:

Excerpts from Eleanor Roosevelt's correspondence to Frieda Hennock and from Thomas Corcoran are from Eleanor Roosevelt's Personal Letters file. Courtesy of the Franklin D. Roosevelt Library.

Excerpts from the Mary Dewson Papers (Woman's Rights Collection). Schlesinger Library, Radcliffe Institute, Harvard University. Detailed citation information appears in the text.

Excerpts from the Frieda Hennock Simons Papers. Schlesinger Library, Radcliffe Institute, Harvard University. Detailed citation information appears in the text.

Excerpts from the statement of Frieda Hennock on FCC Panel at NARTB; from the letters of Fred Weber and Seymour Krieger to Frieda B. Hennock; and from the letters of Edward Flynn, Robert Hannegan, India Edwards, and Frieda B. Hennock to Harry S. Truman, courtesy of The Harry S. Truman Library, Independence, Missouri. Detailed citation information appears in the text.

Excerpts from the Burt Harrison interviews, National Public Radio Oral Interview Project, courtesy of National Public Broadcasting Archives, University of Maryland-College Park. Detailed citation information appears in the text.

Excerpts from interviews with Keith Tyler, Richard Hull, and Morris Novik by James Robertson of Robertson Associates, Inc., from "Public Television's Roots Collection." With permission from the State Historical Society of Wisconsin. Detailed citation information appears in the text.

Excerpts from Susan L. Brinson, "Missed Opportunities: Frieda Hennock and the UHF Debacle," *Journal of Broadcasting and Electronic Media* 44 (2): 248–267. With permission of JOBEM and Broadcast Education Association.

Excerpts from the letters of Thomas G. Corcoran, Sr., to Eleanor Roosevelt with permission of Thomas G. Corcoran, Jr. Detailed citation information appears in the text.

For the independent women in my family,
Merlin Wienberg Brinson, my mother
Carol Brinson, my sister
Cari Morgan Wood, my niece

For my father,
Noah Frank Brinson, Jr.
Who taught me self-discipline and
the importance of a sense of humor

And for my husband,
J. Emmett Winn
Whom I admire and cherish

Contents

Acknowledgments

In my doctoral program, I was trained to do textual analysis and criticism. Over the years I learned that this methodology is, essentially, an isolating experience. Conducting historical research, on the other hand, requires the help of an enormous number of people. I would like to thank the following people for their contributions to both my research and the production of this book.

I worked with a variety of libraries and archives around the country and was continually astonished by the helpfulness and generosity of the women and men who work in them. At the Auburn University Library, I would like to thank Barbara Bishop, Boyd Childress, and Joyce Ledbetter for their considerable help in finding government documents and statistical information. Liz Safly, Carol Briley, and Dennis Bilger at the Harry S. Truman Library were similarly very helpful in locating useful documents. At the National Archives in College Park, Maryland, Dave Pfeiffer and Tab Lewis were indispensable in helping me navigate the voluminous and, at times overwhelming, FCC collection. There were three venues to which I was unable to travel and I am indebted to three individuals who researched their holdings for me and sent very useful information to me, particularly Nancy Snedeker at the Franklin D. Roosevelt Library, Spencer Waller at the Brooklyn Law School, and Susan Ravdin at Bowdoin Library.

Conducting historical research is financially costly. Without the financial support of the following groups, the research for this book would have been much more difficult to manage. My home Department of Communication at Auburn University generously provides annual financial support for faculty improvement. My home College of Liberal Arts supported this research in two ways, first through a Humanities Development Grant and then through the Summer Research Grant Program. The Truman Library and Institute provided me with grant money to support a research trip to their Library, as did the Radcliffe Institute. I am deeply grateful for everyone's sponsorship.

I would also like to take this opportunity to thank several individuals who, along the journey of this research project, provided me with intellectual and/or emotional support. Dr. John Heilman, both as Associate Dean for Research and Dean of the College of Liberal Arts, consistently demonstrated faith in this project. Dr. Mark Stegmaier and Dr. Lynn Musslewhite, professors of History at Cameron University, provided editorial feedback for early chapter drafts. Several of my colleagues in the Department of Communication demonstrated interest in my research and provided encouragement, particularly Dr. Susan Fillippeli, Dr. George Plasketes, Dr. Roger Myrick, and Dr. Mary Helen Brown. Similarly, my research assistants, most importantly Mary Henderson Taylor, were godsends.

I was fortunate to have the opportunity to interview three people who knew Frieda Hennock and generously shared their memories and insights with me. Mr. Arthur Stambler and Mr. Stanley Neustadt patiently answered many questions regarding Hennock's years at the FCC, while Mrs. Selena Sheriff shared family memories of her aunt. I appreciate their time and support very much.

As I mentioned previously, my doctoral training focused on media analysis and criticism. In the early stages of this project, I feared that my lack of training in historical research would result in a significant oversight. I am convinced that Frieda Hennock's spirit was protecting me, for at the same time I happened to be reading Elisabeth Israels Perry's book on Belle Moskowitz. With nothing left to lose except a bit of academic pride, I contacted Dr. Perry and asked her, in effect, to be my mentor. Over the course of several months and many e-mail messages, Elisabeth encouraged me to explore some ideas more fully and calmed my fears of inadequacy. And she always, always responded with kindness and generosity. Her answer to my call for help represents the true meaning of sisterhood in the academy, and I will be forever indebted to her.

Throughout the long haul of researching, writing, and finding a publisher for this book, five dear friends remained in the wings, always encouraging me to continue. Bill Benoit and Pam Benoit are, and always have been, stalwart supporters who sometimes have more faith in my abilities than I do myself. Marsha Vanderford is the kind of superior role model that every woman entering the academy should be so lucky to have. John and Kathy Tamblyn are great friends, always ready for a night of food, drink, and laughter. All five selflessly helped me through difficult periods involved in this project. I was extremely fortunate to receive their support.

I am especially indebted to Pamela St. Clair, who supported publication of my book, and Eric Levy and Jane Lerner, who shepherded it through the publication process at Praeger.

When the stresses of researching, writing, and publishing get to be too much, I always have my family in whose protective arms I may metaphorically fall. My parents, Merlin Wienberg Brinson and Noah Frank Brinson, Jr., give me loving shelter to escape the academy and its demands. My sister, Carol Brinson, helps me loosen up and stop taking everything so seriously, and reconnects me to the "real world" outside the rarefied atmosphere of academe. And my niece, Cari Morgan Wood, a wonderful, independent, protective, nurturing, funny, fun-loving young woman, reminds me of the importance of a youthful attitude toward life. It doesn't always have to be about hard work and seriousness; there's room for laughter and fun.

Finally, I offer my deepest, most heartfelt thanks to my husband, J. Emmett Winn, for his unrelenting encouragement during this project. He patiently awaited my return from research trips, ignored stacks of documents and books, shared my revelations, listened to my ideas as they took shape and were revised, and calmed my fears during the search for a publisher. We have created an intellectually and emotionally nurturing relationship, and still, sometimes, I can't believe I'm so lucky. Thank you, Emmett, for sharing your life with me.

Introduction

It was a sunny summer Thursday on 1 July 1948, the day that Frieda Hennock took the oath of office installing her as the newest commissioner on the Federal Communications Commission (FCC). It was a meaningful moment for Hennock, the culmination of the many hopes and dreams she nurtured for the fifteen years since she started working in the Democratic Party. Although she never envisioned a position on the FCC, whose responsibilities she knew little about as she swore to honorably discharge her duties as a commissioner, she longed for the opportunity to step up to the national political stage and prove herself capable and worthy. As the first woman appointed to the FCC, indeed the first woman appointed to any federal agency,[1] the opportunity she wished for now faced her. She was becoming a commissioner on one of the most powerful and controversial agencies in Washington, D.C., and she would play a role in creating and administering government policy to regulate powerful industries in the United States, including broadcasting, telephone, and telegraph.

Hennock had achieved considerable success in a "man's world," as FCC Chair Wayne Coy made clear when he welcomed Hennock to the commission by affirming that the FCC "has had 'rectitude, fortitude, solemnitude, but never before pulchritude.' "[2] Few women were allowed the opportunity to achieve success in both the legal and political arenas, as Hennock had done, and from society's perspective women may have been competent but they were still expected to fulfill both pre– and post–World War II definitions of *women*. From all outward appearances, Hennock satisfied society's demands. Image was always very important to her. She used her clothing, and especially her myriad array of hats, to communicate both personal style and set her male counterparts at ease. In the twenty-five years since she started practicing law she used femininity to assuage the sexist fears of male clients, lawyers, judges, and eventually politicians; the stylish dresses and suits, tastefully selected jewelry, smart hats, attractive perfumes, and intermittent spurts of extreme feminine emotional behavior were counterpoints to the steely, direct, occasionally ruthless, invariably successful attorney. It was the culture of the times that required Hennock to construct herself in such a way.

So here she was, looking very fashionable in her black suit and chic white hat with black feathers, in the reception room of the Post Office Building standing before Wayne Coy, Attorney General Tom Clark, and a crowd of other government officials and employees, giving a speech about what she hoped to accomplish at the commission. Initially intending to make comments about both radio and television, at the last minute Hennock deleted all comments about television from her installation speech and instead focused on radio; "radio and television are the vital media of entertainment" became "radio broadcasting is a vital medium of entertainment," and "when television and radio have had their full growth, the minds of men will no longer be earthbound" was changed to "when radio has had its full growth."[3] If she'd known the next seven years of her life would be consumed with the development of television in the United States and, moreover, that she would rest her political future on the development of educational television, she would have deleted the remarks about radio instead. The truth was, however, that she really did not know what she was getting into. As she told one of her closest friends, "perhaps I will come out with something new, or I might be a complete flop—who knows."[4] In true Hennock style, however, she continued with the determination that "I want to give myself a chance."[5]

Frieda B. Hennock served on the Federal Communications Commission from 1948 to 1955, and participated in many critical decisions regarding both the television and radio industries. Usually the lone dissenter, she consistently challenged policies created by the majority. Although charged with regulating in the public's interest, historically the FCC was more likely to make decisions favoring corporate interests, judgments that Hennock opposed. In many cases she simultaneously argued that the majority opinion did not serve the public, in whose interest the Commission was charged with serving, and explained the long-term implications of the majority decision. Unlike her colleagues, Hennock's positions stood the test of time and appeared to prove her more foresighted in her understanding of the television and radio industries.

Among her notable positions during the infamous 1948 "freeze," a four-year period during which the FCC stopped licensing television stations, she led the campaign to reserve channels for educational television and was the lone supporter of a color television technology that was compatible with existing black-and-white television technology. Her positions made her unpopular at the FCC, particularly with her fellow commissioners who disliked her perpetual defiance. The passage of time reveals that Hennock's opinions prevailed. In many of the most significant cases of the time period, her positions proved to be correct.

In spite of her position as one of the early female members of the executive branch of government and her central role in the development of the modern broadcasting landscape, very little academic research has been done on Frieda Hennock or her participation on the FCC. Only two articles have been published about her. The first, written in 1968, concentrates on Hennock's role in the reservation of educational television (ETV) channels from the perspective of colleagues who, I eventually learned, had a personal interest in disavowing Hennock's indispensability to the creation of ETV. Further, the article neither considers her written opinions nor does it address the larger context of FCC decisions made between 1948 to 1955. The second significant article, published in 1992, is an impressionistic piece written by a personal acquaintance of Hennock's. It is a tantalizing essay, offering much "inside" information about Hennock and her role as a commissioner. Other than these two articles, only an essay in the *Notable American Women, The Modern Period: A Biographical Dictionary* and another in a collection of commissioner's biographies have been located.[6]

Yet assessment of Hennock's role in FCC decisions is significant for a variety of reasons, principally because she represents the intersection of women's history, broadcast history, and federal policymaking. First, while a considerable body of research elucidates the historical development of radio and television in the United States, very little has focused on the contributions of women, other than celebrities, to these enterprises. Hennock was the first woman appointed to the FCC and she served during a time when the federal government attempted to assert considerable regulatory authority over the broadcasting industries. Add to this the fact that she was unlike many of the prominent women in politics who preceded her. Many of the women who were politically active and prominent during the 1920s, 1930s, and 1940s, such as Belle Moskowitz, Eleanor Roosevelt, and Frances Perkins, engaged in what Elisabeth Israels Perry calls "feminine politics,"[7] working behind-the-scenes to promote the policies and candidacies of prominent men such as Al Smith and

Franklin Roosevelt. While these women certainly agreed with the political philosophies they advanced, they did not promote themselves or their personal ambitions. Frieda Hennock did not subscribe to this type of self-sacrificing political work, and while she was certainly an avid supporter of Franklin Roosevelt and the New Deal, she did so with one eye on the public and the other eye on her own political future. She was, in every sense, a *politician*. Consequently, the evidence suggests that she requires a closer inspection regarding her role in broadcast regulation.

Second, just as legal scholars analyze majority and minority opinions developed by judges who shaped judicial philosophy and law, so may the positions of other government officials such as Federal Communications commissioners be the subject of analysis and critical evaluation. Many women and men have served on powerful agencies such as the Federal Communications Commission or the Federal Trade Commission and developed policy to regulate industries in the United States. In so doing, they played a considerable role in the evolution of those enterprises. In no small measure these politically appointed commissioners participate in the development of industries, consequently it makes sense to analyze their personal and/or political motivations for taking specific positions. Understanding the historical role public servants played in the regulatory development of the broadcast industry, and particularly the motivations for their decisions, may help us better understand the pressures faced by current communications regulators. Thus, Frieda Hennock represents an excellent case study for understanding the role of women in the development of national policy regarding one of the most powerful forms of mass communication: television.

I have been intrigued by Frieda Hennock since I "met" her in the spring of 1988. I was a doctoral student enrolled in a seminar on the history of American broadcasting when I read Erik Barnouw's three-volume history of broadcasting. Students interested in women's history get little information regarding the contributions of women in broadcasting from Barnouw's text, consequently I was both surprised and intrigued when I came across a succinct explanation of Hennock's rise to the FCC. Mr. Barnouw's account was tantalizingly brief; I suspected there was much more involved in Hennock's FCC appointment. She sounded fascinating, reminding me of the kind of pioneering woman I enjoyed reading about as a kid, like Amelia Earhart and Annie Oakley, independent women who challenged the status quo and found fame and social acceptance in doing so. I was hooked. The term paper I produced only whet my appetite for more information about Hennock, and I vowed to return to her "some day."

The realities of being an assistant professor prevented me from returning to Hennock for a few years after graduation. The Communication discipline is dominated by social scientific research methodologies and concerns, consequently my possible tenure and promotion were based on the ability to publish a quantity of articles. I knew I could not accomplish this goal if I devoted the time necessary to doing a proper history of Hennock and her FCC career, so I put her on the "back burner" and hoped that nobody else would discover the lack of academic attention paid her. Twice a year I researched whether new articles were published about her and, until 1992, was relieved to find there were none. That year, however, Henry Morgenthau published an essay in *Television Quarterly* explaining Hennock's role at the FCC and her activities regarding educational television in particular. I was devastated. Although Mr. Morgenthau's article is essentially accurate, the journal in which it was published did not require him to cite any of the sources on which he based his explanations of Hennock. Although temporarily "saved," I knew that chances were growing more likely that Hennock would be "discovered" by another researcher. In the summer of 1995 I began my work in earnest.

Although self-imposed barriers prevented me from researching Frieda Hennock, other research and teaching pursuits gave me the opportunity to develop the knowledge and skills I needed to tackle this project. My doctoral research training in textual analysis provided the foundation for analyzing Hennock's speeches, radio and television broadcasts, and hearings testimony and interrogations. Moreover, I was able to develop courses at Auburn University in media law, women and the mass media, minorities and the mass media, and history of American broadcasting, all of which played a fundamental role in helping me understand the contexts of Hennock's position at the FCC in the late 1940s and early 1950s. While my inability to turn full research attention to Hennock frustrated me, the seven years of working on other projects and developing classes were enormously beneficial to understanding the bigger picture.

During those seven years I pieced together intriguing facts about Hennock. The only woman on a commission of seven, she consistently held the lone dissenting opinion; she was the only one who disagreed with the creation of the Fairness Doctrine, who voted against establishing the CBS color system as the standard for the television industry, and was the champion of developing educational television in the United States. She took a strong stand against industry giants such as David Sarnoff and RCA, Frank Stanton and CBS, AT&T, and others. The more I learned about Hennock's public positions the more I wanted to know "why?" What were Hennock's positions regarding key FCC questions during the "freeze" and how did they serve the public interest? What was the regulatory context in which they were made? Why did she dissent so consistently? Why did she take the positions she did? These became the research questions guiding this book. Eventually the answers proved disarmingly straightforward. Several years of research revealed two facts about Hennock: she was a woman guided by two personal truths, the desire to serve both public and personal interests. Her desire to serve the public was the result of her upbringing in both feminine and Jewish contexts, both of which encouraged and prepared her to respond to the needs of others. The contexts of her personal ambitions are more difficult to pinpoint. Revealing why an individual manifests societal expectations seems fairly straightforward; understanding why they challenge them is a more difficult undertaking. In the final analysis, Hennock's predisposition to contradict sociocultural expectations by becoming a successful lawyer and politician and forgoing marriage and children was the result of, as a colleague put it, a "personality quirk."

This book employs both historical and critical analyses of Hennock's positions and opinions, both of which led to an understanding of a woman who figured prominently in creating modern broadcast regulations and the context in which those policies were created. Chapters 1 and 2 set the stage for understanding both Frieda Hennock as an individual and the context in which she developed her regulatory opinions. Chapter 1 introduces Frieda Hennock's biography from her immigration to the United States in 1910 to the eve of her nomination to the Federal Communications Commission. Hennock arrived at her post with a strong sense of commitment to the public welfare. After immigrating to the United States from Poland in 1910, she excelled in academic pursuits. She received her law degree in 1924 at the age of nineteen but was unable to start practicing law until she turned twenty-one. Once allowed to practice she chose the extraordinarily unlikely path for a female attorney and began practicing criminal law in New York City, where she became known as a tenacious defense attorney for her frequently underprivileged clients. By the early 1940s she moved to corporate law and was actively involved in Democratic politics in New York City. Both her personal and professional experiences reveal an abiding concern for the general public.

Chapter 2 concentrates on the political intrigue surrounding Hennock's appointment to the Federal Communications Commission, then briefly details the commission itself and the regulatory context in which Hennock participated, particularly regarding the infamous 1948 "freeze" in which the FCC artificially halted the development of television in the United States. The period 1948 to 1952 was critical for the development of the television industry. Although television was introduced to the public prior to World War II, its development was halted during the war. Immediately following the end of the war, however, television began to grow at a faster pace than anyone in the industry or the Federal Communications Commission might have anticipated. Between 1945 and 1948 it became increasingly clear to the FCC that it would have to resolve significant technical problems in order for television to become available to the entire American public. Chief among these problems was the insufficient frequency space set aside for the transmission of television signals. In other words, there weren't enough television channels to assign to the growing number of people requesting licenses. Hence in 1948, with only fifty television stations on the air and another fifty under construction, the FCC "froze" the issuance of any more television licenses until the technical problems could be resolved.

The Communications Act of 1934 granted the FCC the power to make such sweeping decisions as these. Philosophically speaking, the Act requires that all regulatory decisions regarding the broadcast industry must ultimately meet one significant test: the effects of the decision must serve the "public interest." Regulators, in the form of the FCC, are expected to administer the industry as the representatives of the public, although the concept is never clearly defined in the Act. Willard Rowland argues it is subject to two interpretations.[8] The first argues that the public is best served by protecting the business interests of the regulated industry, while the second asserts that the public's interest is served by forcing the industry to make business decisions with the public immediately in mind, particularly regarding broadcast programming. Historically, the FCC has adopted the former interpretation of "public interest" and has been more likely to make decisions favoring the commercial broadcast networks (ABC, CBS, and NBC) and their relationships with affiliate stations. Under ordinary circumstances, the development of policies regarding the 1948 Freeze might have been a smooth process toward their almost inevitable ends of favoring the networks. Ordinary circumstances did not exist, however, after Frieda Hennock joined the commission, where she rapidly distinguished herself as a commissioner who defined "public interest" as directly serving the needs and interests of the public. Unlike many of her predecessors, and the commissioners with whom she served, Hennock truly approached regulatory decisions with the *public's* interests in mind.

Chapters 3, 4, and 5 are detailed analyses of Hennock's positions on the three issues before the FCC during the "freeze": color television, frequency allocations, and educational television. The positions she took on these issues are evidence of her abiding commitment to serving both personal and public interests. Within a year of joining the FCC Hennock decided to champion the development of educational television (ETV) in the United States. It was the perfect issue for her. ETV served public interests in its potential ability to provide quality, educational, noncommercial programming with the sole intent of educating viewers. It was a perfect political vehicle as well. It was considered an "appropriate" issue for a female politician, it was considered "safe" during the Red Scare years, and its successful establishment would enable Hennock to establish a national political reputation. Once she set her sights on ETV Hennock analyzed and evaluated every other "freeze" issue according to its calculated effect on her pet project. Chapter 4 analyzes Hennock's participation in the color television debate and reveals her lone support of RCA's "compatible" color system was motivated by the threat the CBS "incompatible" system posed to ETV. Chapter 5 exposes Hennock's significant failure in understanding and possibly mitigating the inherently flawed development of UHF television in the United States, a miscalculation that seriously damaged the development of ETV. Finally, Chapter 6 concentrates on Hennock's considerable efforts to reserve channel allocations strictly for the development of educational, noncommercial television. Her efforts were successful and many of the stations originally reserved for educational use in 1951 became affiliates of the Public Broadcasting System (PBS) in the 1960s and 1970s. These three issues, both individually and taken together, resulted in some of the most important and controversial decisions made by the FCC and they fundamentally created the television landscape still before us today. Chapter 6 explains other significant decisions in which Hennock participated, her failed appointment as a federal district judge, her post-FCC career and, finally, concluding remarks.

Frieda Hennock was an unusual woman for her time period. She rose in Democratic Party politics as a result of her complete devotion to both her legal and political career and to the virtual exclusion of a personal life. Her campaign efforts were rewarded with an appointment to the FCC in 1948 where she became the first woman to participate in guiding federal policy regarding the communications industries. Her positions were significant, not only because she was the first to participate in such weighty policy rulings, but because history so consistently proved her minority opinions to be correct.

NOTES

1. It should be noted that Frieda Hennock was the first woman appointed to a federal *agency*, and that Frances Perkins was the first woman appointed to a *cabinet* position.

2. "Washington Briefs," 1 July 1948, newspaper clipping in Brooklyn Law School file on Hennock.

3. Installation speech, 1 July 1948, card #7, Frieda Hennock Simons Collection (FHS) 7/95.

4. FBH to Fraser, 6 September 1948, FHS 1/18.

5. Ibid.

6. R. Franklin Smith, "Madame Commissioner," *Journal of Broadcasting*, 12 (1967–1968): 69–81; Henry Morgenthau, "Dona Quixote: The Adventures of Frieda Hennock," *Television Quarterly*, 26 (2): 61–73; Maryann Yodelis Smith, "Frieda Hennock," in *Notable American Women, The Modern Period: A Biographical Dictionary*, ed. B. Sicherman and C.H. Green (Cambridge, MA: Harvard University Press, 1980), pp. 332–333; Gerald V. Flannery and Peggy Voorhies, "Frieda Hennock," in *Commissioners of the FCC: 1927-1994*, ed. Gerald V. Flannery (Lanham, MD: University Press of America, 1994), pp. 96–98.

7. Elisabeth Israels Perry, *Belle Moskowitz: Feminine Politics and the Exercise of Power in the Age of Alfred E. Smith* (New York: Oxford University Press, 1987).

8. Willard D. Rowland, "The Meaning of 'The Public Interest' in Communications Policy, Part I: Its Origins in State and Federal Legislation," *Communication Law and Policy*, 2: 309–328; Willard D. Rowland, "The Meaning of 'The Public Interest' in Communications Policy, Part II: Its Implementation in Early Broadcast Law and Regulation," *Communication Law and Policy* 2: 363–396.

CHAPTER 1

"Girl Lawyer Wins Point": Immigration to Political Prominence, 1910–1948

INTRODUCTION

Frieda Hennock was a remarkable woman. She was born into a Jewish family living in Poland in 1904 and lived her first six years in a politically repressive and religiously discriminatory society. When she died in Washington, D.C., in 1960 she was one of the most politically influential female policy-makers in the country. Throughout her life Hennock was recognized as "the first woman" to accomplish a seemingly "improper" role: the youngest woman to join the New York Bar Association, the first woman to practice criminal law in New York City courts, the first woman to join a prestigious New York law firm, the first woman appointed to the Federal Communications Commission and, indeed, the first woman appointed to a federal agency. Her letters and speeches reveal no particular concern or interest in her public "firsts." Rather, they reveal an intelligent, competent, politically savvy woman who set personal goals and met them, despite the fact that, as a Jewish woman, there were plenty of socio-cultural and political barriers to impede her success.

It is difficult to resist the temptation to paint Hennock's as a feminized Horatio Alger, rags-to-riches life. Her story is not one of a woman of privilege who negotiated her way through the ranks of political power to assume a position of national influence. As significant as their contributions were, many of the "New Deal" women who were Hennock's political prototypes came from positions of cultural, financial, and/or educational privilege, particularly Eleanor Roosevelt, Mary "Molly" Dewson, and others. Nor did Hennock fit within the ranks of working-class women such as Rose

Schneiderman, Mary Anderson, and Jo Coffin, who through trade union activities made connections with upper-class women who gave them *entre* to federal government positions. Hennock, instead, is a hybrid of the two. As a member of a middle-class Jewish immigrant family in New York City, she successfully avoided the factory and sweatshop experiences of her sister immigrants. Further, she extended the boundaries of white-collar employment by putting herself through law school. She fashioned herself into a professional, wealthy, politically powerful woman.

Indeed, Hennock's life resists easy definitions; it represents a series of contradictions and intersections of Jewish and gender socialization. Throughout her life she manifested the twin desires of serving both public interests and her own pursuits, particularly regarding political power and the accumulation of wealth. Her desire to help others was the result of a combination of both Jewish and feminine socialization. The Jewish value of *menschlichkeit*,[1] or "the readiness to live for ideals beyond the clamor of self, a sense of plebian fraternity," taught her the importance of community. The feminine sensibilities of nurturing and caregiving bolstered her Jewish instruction and resulted in a strong sense of responsibility to helping others. These other-oriented values were countered, however, by Hennock's strong sense of ambition and independence, characteristics borne of a strong desire to prove that she was more than just "another girl."[2] Like many second-generation immigrants, Hennock found herself torn between the traditional definitions of womanhood as embodied by her mother, and the teachers and role models she encountered in public life who represented "American womanhood."[3] Too ambitious to confine herself to the more traditional roles of wife and mother, yet nonetheless responsive to them, Hennock's Jewish and feminine sensibilities found voice and action in her unconventional and highly successful legal and political activities. Inherently aware of the challenges her legal and political careers represented to the gendered status quo, she inevitably involved herself in projects considered "appropriate" for women. Hennock, then, was a woman guided by conflicting impulses. As a Jewish woman she was taught to help others, preferably as wife and mother. As an intelligent and ambitious person, however, she was drawn toward the "masculine" domains of law and politics. The conundrum was resolved through her ability to develop a successful legal career which, in turn, led to an imminently notable political career. In both cases, however, she often directed her energies in "appropriately" feminine ways. Hence, Frieda Hennock was a woman shaped by the contexts of her life whose significant professional accomplishments were the result of both personal and political interests.

The bulk of this chapter analyzes the contexts of Frieda Hennock's life and concludes with the political activities that led to her position at the Federal Communications Commission. Such a framework provides an understanding of both how Hennock personified sociopolitical contexts as well as how she challenged them. Second, it contextualizes and offers theoretical premises for her FCC opinions. Chapter 2 explains Hennock's assumption of the commissionership as well as the historical and political contexts of the organization she joined. Chapters 3, 4 and 5 analyze three key cases in which she participated while at the commission. The present chapter sets the foundation for why she arrived at the positions she did in those three cases, each of which had long-term effects on the development of television broadcasting in the United States.

IMMIGRATION

Frieda Barkin Hennock was born on 27 September 1904 in Kovel, Poland, to Sarah Barkin and Boris Henoch.[4] Family history, revealed by Sarah Barkin Henoch to her grandchildren,[5] explained that the Henoch family went bankrupt after the Czar refused to pay them for their leather goods. Since it was considered shameful to go bankrupt, the family decided to immigrate to the United States and start a new life. Thus, together with her parents, five sisters and two brothers, six-year-old Frieda immigrated to the United States in 1910 and settled in New York City. Her family was not alone. Their immigration experience was duplicated by millions of Jewish women, men, and children in the period between 1800 and 1924. Historians estimate that one-third of eastern European Jews emigrated between 1880 and 1930.[6] By 1910 the entire Hennock family journeyed to the "new world" of America and settled in New York City.

The "old world" they left behind was inhospitable to Jews who, for several decades, lived under discriminatory and increasingly dangerous circumstances.[7] The pogroms advocated by Czars Alexander III and Nicholas II legitimated the physical attacks against both Jewish men in the form of beatings and Jewish women in the form of rape, and were becoming increasingly prevalent by the turn of the 20th century. The "overriding cause" of emigration was Jews' "fear for their lives."[8] While there is no evidence to suggest Frieda Hennock experienced this terror herself, it is clear that the family lived within a larger context of systematic and potentially brutal discrimination against people who shared their religious faith. However, it is possible that Hennock, at the age of six years when she emigrated from Poland, endured similar experiences as many "five- and ten-year-olds who subsequently became Americans, [and who] lived their earliest, formative years in the shadow of the pogroms [sic], in the shadow of fear, oppression, and terror."[9] At the very least, she was likely old enough to understand, at a rudimentary level, the rampant discrimination against Jews in her homeland, a perception that may have contributed significantly to both her desire to help others as well as her political activity.

Arrival in the New World deposited the Hennock family into a socio-cultural milieu with which they were unfamiliar, partially because the large Jewish immigrant population combined with increasing numbers of Irish and Italian, Protestant and Catholic immigrants, many of whom settled first on Manhattan's Lower East Side. The living conditions in which most immigrants found themselves were cramped, crowded, and filthy. Although ethnic neighborhoods quickly developed, these enclaves were surrounded by "unknowns."

Such living conditions could only be relieved through the accumulation of wages earned outside the home and, to that end, every member of the household was put to work. In this regard Jews were little different than other immigrant communities. Hennock's father became a banker and real estate broker,[10] thereby quickly establishing a somewhat more privileged position for his family within the Jewish community. While her mother did not work outside of the home, at least two of Hennock's sisters (who were considerably older than she) were employed, one as an accountant. Like most immigrant families, it became quickly apparent that even female family members had to seek employment, as their earnings potential were simply too valuable for the family's survival to indulge in the luxury of maintaining "old world" attitudes against women working outside the home. Immigrant families, and particularly women, quickly developed an understanding that "life in the United States meant an ever more inescapable confrontation with the capitalist world of wage-earning, money, and commerce."[11] Children were important sources of family income as well and a child's education was frequently deemed less important than the chance to earn wages. Between 1904 and 1913 children could legally leave school at the age of twelve or upon completion of the fifth grade, but many families found ways around this law and put their children to work earlier.[12] After 1913, when the legal school-leaving limit was raised to 16 years of age or completion of the sixth grade, large numbers of children failed to fulfill these basic educational requirements. In fact, "only a third of all children entering public school in New York in 1913 advanced as far as the eighth grade,"[13] and some immigrant children did not attend school at all.[14] In a climate such as this, it was certainly much more likely that Frieda Hennock would follow the same educational path as most of her sister immigrants than the likelihood that she would complete high school.

EDUCATION: "THE NEW JEWISH WOMANHOOD"

Enjoying a somewhat more comfortable economic position than most immigrant children, upon arrival in the United States Hennock immediately began attending public schools in Brooklyn, and far exceeded the average by graduating Morris High School in the Bronx in June 1921.[15] The role of public schools in the lives of immigrant students was profound, particularly those such as Hennock who received their entire education in U.S. public schools that focused on "Americanizing" immigrants. Policymakers in the New York City school system, confronted with an unprecedented influx of foreign-born students, redefined their roles as educators to include the responsibility of teaching immigrants of all ages the attitudes, values, and behaviors of "proper" United States' citizens.[16] The educational structure was retooled to Americanize immigrants, to initiate them "into the society of Americans, teach[ing] them the national myths and symbols . . . [and forming] their tastes and discriminations."[17] As such, the educational process became much more than learning the core principles of language use, mathematics, and science. It was transformed into a means of sociocultural and political indoctrination. The potential threat to the status quo represented by an ever-growing population of foreign-born people with widely divergent belief systems was understood by social and political leaders. The principal solution to the problem was to educate the foreign masses to the "American way."

Jewish immigrants accepted the educational opportunities presented by the United States more favorably than did their Irish and Italian counterparts. A variety of explanations account for the positive Jewish attitude toward schooling. Berrol explains that "traditional reverence for the learned man [sic] probably led many Jewish immigrants to view education favorably."[18] Similarly, having an education was considered by Jews to be a sign of both wisdom and "good character,"[19] and was clearly perceived as one of the most important paths to a "better" life.[20] As a result, "Jewish parents embraced a school system that was hospitable and free of costs, making every effort to enable their children to continue school as long as possible."[21]

While the availability of an education was generally accepted, the Americanization efforts of the public schools were met with varying degrees of tolerance by Jews. Some recognized and lamented the dilution of traditional Jewish lifestyles and attitudes by the Americanization of their children.[22] Others, however, viewed the Americanization process as important to their children's development and future in the United States and did not challenge the process.[23] In any case, having immigrated at the age of six and immediately enrolled in public school, Hennock was young enough to eagerly accept the Americanization efforts of her schoolteachers in the United States.

The fact that Hennock was a young female seeking education was irrelevant in the public schools of the United States, but this was not the case in the "old world" where it was a gendered experience ordinarily considered appropriate for males only.[24] The reasons for this attitude are numerous and are based in both Judaic law and custom. In the homeland, attendance at the *cheder*, religious school for learning the Talmud, was exclusively the province of males, usually beginning between the ages of four and six. Females were expressly forbidden to attend *cheder*. Indeed, the traditional Jewish lifestyles of women in the "old world," which concentrated on home, family, and economic support, encouraged the perception that religious education was wasted on them; there was nothing in their future that required such training. Accordingly, "Jewish girls, whom Judaic law had barred, for many centuries, [were prevented] from occupying the one social role their culture favored above all others—the good student."[25] In the "old world," receiving an education was a dream most women never achieved.

The "new world" literally opened the doors of education to Jewish women. As previously mentioned, New York City law required that *all* children attend school; there were no barriers erected to prevent the education of females at the elementary or secondary levels.[26] Most Jewish women responded to this freedom with the kind of passion usually experienced by people finally able to realize a long-held dream. Indeed, "upon discovering that learning was not the prerogative of males alone [in America], [Jewish females] took to the schools with a zest unmatched by other groups."[27] Girls and women alike flourished in the secular schools.

Receiving an education was not easily accomplished by Jewish women, and the endeavor was a controversial issue within the Jewish immigrant community. While many mothers, still grieving the loss of an education denied to them, insisted that their daughters take full advantage of the educational opportunities available to them in the United States,[28] some Jewish women found their fathers particularly opposed to their studies.[29] The economic necessity of earning a wage prevented most Jewish women from getting the education they desired, although many women took full advantage of the many night schools to acquire an education.[30] Birth order also played a role in determining whether a Jewish woman would receive an education. Females who were the last born in a family, as was Frieda Hennock, were more likely to be educated than their older sisters (and, in some instances, older brothers), largely because they were the youngest and presumably had older siblings to contribute to the family purse, or because family finances had stabilized by the time she arrived at school age.[31] These young daughters, who presumably entered the American educational system in kindergarten and remained there until high school, "tended to be among the best and brightest of its students."[32] The family's economic position and her rank as the youngest of eight children benefitted Frieda, who experienced life in ways very different than most young Jewish immigrant women. She was not forced to work as a laborer. Indeed, her proficiency at playing the piano enabled her to offer piano lessons while she was in high school,[33] clearly a much different encounter with employment than that faced by women in factories and sweatshops. She was afforded considerable educational opportunities, passing through the entire school system and graduating high school.

While most Jewish women did not enjoy a complete educational experience, Hennock was among a growing number of women who devoted themselves to achieving that goal. As early as 1918 twenty percent of Jews attending college were women,[34] and by the 1920s and 1930s increasingly larger numbers of Jewish women attended high school, colleges, and universities.[35] For many of these women, "education became . . . a metaphor for Jewish New Womanhood—a tool in the struggle for integration into civic life, a means to become . . . 'a person.' "[36] This was the tool that Hennock used to help her avoid the fate of many of her Jewish sisters who labored long hours for wages.

The fact that Hennock successfully graduated high school in 1921, and eventually law school in 1924,[37] reveals as much about her own character as it does the context of her times. In the face of significant odds she pursued her public education to its conclusion, revealing a strong personal belief in the importance of education. Hennock was undaunted by the fact that "old world" values discouraged female education, and took great advantage of "new world" educational opportunities. Her public schooling was complimented by extracurricular lessons as well. Young Frieda's family was able to afford piano lessons for her and she demonstrated a gift for music and the piano. Although she chose not to follow a career as a musician, she was a lifelong devotee of classical concerts and would often be found at the piano at dinner parties. Her devotion to cultured tastes was countered by a practical understanding of how to make her way in the world, as she demonstrated at the early age of twelve when she took lessons in "Rapid Legible Business Writing."[38] Living in the United States for barely six years and not yet a citizen, Hennock already defined herself as a white-collar worker. Each of these educational experiences figured prominently in her life, and a friend later said of Hennock that as "a first-generation immigrant . . . she really believed" in the value of education.[39] Recognizing the significant role education played in transforming her own life, Hennock became a strong supporter of the power of learning.

IMMIGRANT WOMEN AND THE WORKPLACE

An education was often the determining factor regarding the Jewish woman immigrant's wage-earning occupation. Women lacking educations generally held manual or skilled labor jobs, while educated women found "white-collar" positions. The relatively unattainable luxury of an education coupled with the financial necessity of earned wages resulted in a preponderance of women who toiled long days in "blue-collar" jobs that relied heavily on their labor, particularly the garment industry and, to a lesser extent, domestic work. Within the immigrant community nonprofessional occupations were divided according to status. Domestic work was available, but was considered appropriate only for "greenies," or greenhorns, newly arrived immigrants. Among the immigrant population, most women found employment in the garment industry.[40] Working conditions in factories were deplorable. Women garment workers labored in filthy rooms with inadequate lighting, no ventilation (which increased the spread of communicable diseases such as tuberculosis), poor facilities, and little relief from winter's cold or summer's heat. The authority exercised by supervisors ranged from timing the duration of a woman's visit to the bathroom ("excessively long" visits would result in wage deductions) to bosses' demands for sexual favors in return for jobs. Much of the work done for the garment industry was done outside of factories, however. Sweatshops, in which contractor's homes were turned in to miniature factories, flourished in New York City. Women in sweatshops turned out piecework, such as artificial flowers to decorate clothing and hats, caps, or handkerchiefs; women were paid per piece. Working conditions were equally as appalling as factory conditions, sometimes worse. It was common for women to work twelve to fourteen hours a day. Working conditions such as these prompted the creation of labor unions such as the International Ladies' Garment Workers' Union (1900) and the Women's Trade Union League (1903), which campaigned for better wages, working conditions, and led strikes against companies. Women leaders such as

Pauline Newman, Rose Schneiderman, and Clara Lemlich were prominent union organizers. All three, and many more activists like them, were
Jewish women.

The social and economic climate in which Frieda Hennock was socialized left life-long impressions on her. Throughout her school-age years
she likely watched the numbers of female classmates dwindle as many
were forced to leave the classroom and join the workroom. She may have
heard stories of the wretched working conditions from her parents, her
sisters, her friends, or read of them in newspapers such as *The Jewish
Daily Forward*. These stories may even have prompted her to become cer-
tified as proficient in "Rapid Legible Business Writing," an early indication of her desire to both avoid factory life and pursue a white-collar
career. Moreover, Hennock grew up in an atmosphere in which women
such as Newman, Schneiderman, and Lemlich were prominent leaders
who taught young Hennock lessons regarding the political power of
women and their abilities and responsibilities to help less powerful and
less fortunate people. Growing up in New York City during the 1910s, she
was enveloped in a climate supportive of women's activities in the public
sphere. The efforts of women like Schneiderman, Newman, and Lemlich
were no doubt reported upon in the *Jewish Daily Forward*, a newspaper
with a very large Jewish audience, and one that strongly supported progressive attitudes about women.[41] By 1916 Lillian Wald and her nurses,
through the auspices of the Nurses Settlement and the Visiting Nurses
Service, brought health care to hundreds of thousands of immigrant families throughout New York City. Women such as these, and many more
who didn't achieve the same level of notoriety, were representative of the
changing definitions of Jewish women's roles; women were no longer
necessarily expected to confine their interests to hearth and home.[42]

Contradictory attitudes about women existed, however, both beyond
and within the Jewish community. Working for wages and/or getting an
education were acceptable for unmarried women, but young Jewish
women were expected to marry and devote primary attention to having
children and nurturing the family. Moreover, until 1920 Jews lived within a larger political context that refused to grant women the right to vote,
thereby strictly limiting their political effectiveness. Frieda Hennock,
therefore, came of age in a sociocultural, political, and economic milieu
that communicated discordant messages. On the one hand, there were
important Jewish role models to whom she could look for direction. On
the other hand, there were clear lessons regarding traditional positions.
Her experiences in both the traditional culture of the "old world" and her
Americanized socialization helped her to negotiate the boundaries

between the two and investigate the opportunities for women during this Progressive era.

Virtually the only path out of the factories, and the drudgery and danger they represented, was education. With an education, a Jewish woman could significantly expand her occupational horizons. The largest percentage of educated women moved into the "white-collar" jobs considered appropriate for women: teaching, clerical work, salesgirl, and social work; occupations that became known as "the 'Jewish professions'" for women.[43] Although few Jewish women were able to complete high school and college, those that did overwhelmingly became teachers.[44] By 1920 Jewish women comprised 26% of the teachers in New York City public schools; by 1930 they were 44%, and by 1940 they were 56%.[45] The move into white-collar jobs was particularly evident in second-generation women, who were "much more likely to be employed in clerical, teaching, and sales" occupations than first-generation immigrant women.[46]

Consequently, it is significant that Hennock experienced her formative years very differently than most young female Jewish immigrants growing up at the same time. Family circumstances allowed her to complete the entire course of studies offered by the public schools of Brooklyn and the Bronx. Unlike most immigrant women, she was not forced to quit school to earn a living to help support the family, thereby escaping a working-class life. Her comparatively advanced curricular studies prepared her to navigate a position within the "white-collar" world of employment, a direction she intended to follow as early as twelve years of age. At some point, however, she decided to eschew even these "appropriate" career paths for young, educated Jewish immigrant women. Perhaps it was the Americanization efforts of her educators, or the influence of women like Schneiderman and others, or the Jewish value of education, or Progressive politics, or even passage of the Nineteenth Amendment in 1920 which granted women access to political power, or a combination of these influences and more that emboldened Hennock to follow a much different path. The sociocultural, political, and economic atmosphere of the 1910s called for a change, and Hennock answered that summons by deciding to pursue the legal profession.

The Law: An Unusual Career

In 1922 Hennock astonished and disappointed her parents when she announced her intention to become a lawyer.[47] She began her schooling without the financial help of her parents, particularly her father, who did not approve of her career path.[48] Undaunted, Hennock enrolled in the Brooklyn Law School, attended classes at night, and paid for them by clerking in a variety of law offices during the day.[49] An otherwise average student, Hennock scored her highest marks in constitutional law and graduated with an LL.B. on 5 June 1924.[50] Since the minimum age for taking the bar exam was twenty-one, Hennock, who was only nineteen years old upon graduation, was unable to take the exam and begin her law career until 1926.[51]

Hennock's professional choice was unconventional. By the 1920s the occupational choices Jewish women had were clearly demarcated. It is clear that the great majority of Jewish working women were employed in the garment and domestic industries. Comparatively few Jewish women completed both high school and college and, among those who did, the most common occupational choice was teaching. This leaves remarkably few Jewish women who entered the professions considered to be "properly male": physicians, dentists, accountants, and lawyers.

The legal profession was attractive to many immigrant Jews; it was an esteemed profession in the immigrant's new home, offered considerable social mobility, and was a direct path to civic and/or political activity. But the mainstream profession itself was not receptive to Jews, male or female. Applications to law schools increased along with immigration, much to the horror of well-to-do Protestant lawyers who feared the "pollution" their ranks would suffer once the "undesirables" graduated.[52] Consequently, many law schools (particularly those in the Ivy League) altered admission standards in ways that excluded immigrants. Refusing to be ostracized from their envisioned future, many Jewish immigrants turned to studying law in night schools.[53]

Jewish involvement in the profession soared. Between 1920 and 1930, the number of foreign-born lawyers in New York increased 76%.[54] Ability to practice law did not necessarily constitute acceptance, however, and a hierarchy of positions quickly developed. Indeed, "the distribution of wealth, status, clients and power within the profession, with Wall Street practice at one level and solo practice at another, correlated closely with ethnic stratification that separated white Protestant from [Eastern European] Jew."[55] With similar motivations in mind, bar associations revised admission requirements in ways that made it difficult for Jews to meet.[56] As a result of exclusionary tactics such as these, the Jewish community created its own "middle-class institutions" that included Jewish law firms.[57]

Just as their brothers chose the legal profession as the avenue for social and/or political success, so Jewish women elected to follow the same route. They experienced more obstacles, however. Law schools that only grudgingly accepted Jewish men were loathe to accept Jewish women. Upon graduation, women faced the twin evils of the difficulty of finding a job and pervasive sexual discrimination; "few women lawyers were being hired; those who found employment generally did office rather than court work, performing routine jobs such as bill collection, title searches, and other tasks."[58] Susan Brandeis, who was the first woman to argue a case before the Supreme Court in 1925 (and was the daughter of Supreme Court Justice Louis Brandeis), lamented the discrimination women lawyers faced, as it was common practice for women to be restricted to practicing limited types of law, usually the less lucrative forms.[59] Despite these obstacles, Jewish women joined the legal profession in relatively high numbers. Role models for success existed as early as the 1920s and 1930s. Justine Wise Polier earned a law degree from Yale University and went on to become the first woman to serve as a Municipal Judge in New York City. Similarly, Susan Brandeis graduated from the University of Chicago law school and ultimately became the first woman to serve as a special assistant to the U.S. Attorney in New York.[60] Nonetheless, in 1920 less than one percent of the attorneys in the United States were women.[61]

FRIEDA HENNOCK, ESQUIRE

Already the beneficiary of more life choices than most of her peers enjoyed, Frieda Hennock chose a legal career for herself. At a time when most professionally-oriented young women chose to be teachers, it is unclear why Hennock chose the more difficult and distinctly unconventional path toward a law career. Her motivations may have been similar to those of her male Jewish colleagues; a legal career offered financial security, social mobility, and access to civic and/or political activity for intelligent and ambitious people. It is also possible that she chose this career because, like other Jewish women who chose the law, it provided an effective means for satisfying both personal, Jewish, and gendered expectations by being "useful to others,"[62] a way to fuse the personal desire for independence and accomplishment with religious and sociocultural expectations for nurturing and care-giving but with higher pay and considerably more social status.

Hennock's legal career began quietly but progressed rapidly. Exchanging legal services for desk space, Hennock began practicing law in 1926.[63] She was among the extreme minority of Jewish women practicing law, as well as "the youngest woman lawyer" in New York City.[64] In 1926 she used $3000 from personal funds to defend "Red" McKenna, an accused murderer who escaped from jail and committed suicide the day before the trial was to begin.[65] She received notoriety early in her career and displayed a propensity for both accepting and winning difficult criminal cases. In 1928 she received acclaim as the first woman defense attorney in a murder trial in New York and subsequently received greater attention for "winning seven acquittals in murder cases."[66] Her clients were frequently the socially disadvantaged, such as immigrants,[67] social outcasts,[68] and bootleggers,[69] the representation of whom satisfied her need to help those who were less fortunate. Hennock displayed an early propensity for matching altruistic motivations with self-serving ones, as the cost of representing underprivileged clients was subsidized by the high fees she charged for practicing administrative law for wealthy clients, who simultaneously increased her personal financial affluence.

The complications of being a female within the male-dominated legal profession began to take their toll on Hennock, however. Unable or unwilling to follow the masculine model of objective and dispassionate defenses, Hennock became emotionally involved to the point of exhaustion defending her clients. Moreover, she faced incessant professional discriminations. By her own admission, Hennock's work in criminal trials was both educational and exhausting, particularly since "as a woman she had to work doubly hard to win criminal cases."[70] The prejudice she faced is evident in a *New York Times* article reporting her encounter with Judge Collins during the Benedetto brothers' trial. Chastising Hennock for her request to see the District Attorney's information regarding her clients, Judge Collins claimed that she knew "the information was there because, woman like, you have been peeking. You'd be very much offended if the District Attorney were to do that."[71] When Hennock tried to explain herself, the Judge admonished her not to "inject sex into this case."[72] She experienced sexist inequities at the hands of client's wives, too, who refused to allow their husbands to be represented by Hennock.[73]

The fact that Hennock was a woman working in a male-dominated profession had a significant impact on both her ability to practice her craft as well as the personal choices she made in doing so. She remained single through most of her professional life.[74] When she began her professional life in the mid-1920s, roughly 54% of working women were single.[75] The percentage of single women in the workforce declined steadily, however, during Hennock's most productive years. When she joined the FCC in 1948, only 35% of the female labor force was single, and by 1955, when she left the FCC, only 25% of working women were single.[76] Hennock was ambivalent about remaining single, as she alternately questioned its wisdom and appreciated the contributions of what she euphemistically called "the career girl."[77]

But Hennock chose to be a "career girl," despite the fact that she had opportunities to follow the more conventional feminine expectations of marriage and family. She was a very attractive woman in a variety of ways. She enhanced her physical attractiveness with designer dresses, an impressive array of hats, fur coats, expensive jewelry, and a devotion to dying her hair blonde. She was an athletically active woman who enjoyed swimming, golfing, tennis, and horseback-riding. She was clever and fun-loving. She described the results of a day at the beach as "stiff muscles, sprained wrists, loss of atti-post [sic] tissue (reduction of fat) and a coat of tan with swarms of mosquito injections."[78] Indeed, one of the most engaging photographs of Hennock, taken in the 1930s judging by her clothing and hairstyle, shows her in the midst of a full-fledged, knee-slapping belly laugh.

Not surprisingly, men found Hennock irresistible. In 1922 "Nat" sent her a black silk sweater. Another suitor called her his "sweet 'little dream girl,' " despite the fact that she rejected his advances. Yet another suitor chastised her rejection in a heart-wrenching love letter written on Western Union telegraph paper, expressing both his "holy love" for her while patronizingly cautioning her to re-evaluate her priorities. Yet another man claimed that he didn't wash his hands for two days after shaking hands with Hennock because he didn't want to lose the scent of her perfume. Apparently Hennock had a confusing effect on James Lawrence Fly, one-time prominent chair of the FCC, who exclaimed "woman, I don't know what you did to me! But . . . January becomes August and Tuesday is only Thursday, [and] Summer's made for Winter" since he met her.[79] Despite all of this attention, Hennock chose to remain single. Perhaps she believed, as many women did and still do, that a professional career and married life were incompatible. While her reasons remain unknown, Hennock rejected traditional expressions of nurturing directed toward husband and children and replaced them with caring for family members and the public.

Personal costs aside, Frieda Hennock proved herself to be an able and successful attorney. The practical realities of being a female attorney, which she described as "the difficulties in the way of success for a woman lawyer," prompted Hennock to form a partnership with Julius Silver in 1927,[80] thereby following a similar path as many other Jewish attorneys who created their own law firms. During this period she gradually turned to the more lucrative practice of corporate and administrative law. Readily admitting that her early criminal law career drew attention, Hennock conceded that "when I started making money I dropped out of sight."[81] Her income increased markedly. At a time when much of America suffered the economic impact of the early years of the Great Depression and the average yearly earnings of an attorney were less than $5,000,[82] Hennock earned $55,000 for arranging a single company merger.[83] By 1930 she was doing well enough financially to move to an apartment on Central Park West in Manhattan where she lived with her parents, a sister, and two nieces.[84] In 1936 she moved again to a penthouse apartment on Park Avenue.[85] In the late 1930s she became involved in a highly publicized child custody case involving a member of the DuPont family,[86] a case that likely drew a large fee. By the time she joined the FCC, her annual income was estimated at $40,000 per year,[87] she owned a home in New York City and at the beach, and lived in a "swanky suite in the Hay Adams hotel" in Washington D.C.[88]

Always guided by the need to satisfy the twin desires of serving both public and personal interests, this was an unfulfilling time for Hennock. While her professional life was successful and her bank account was healthy, she was not serving public interests. Her devotion to family members assuaged her feminine motivations for nurturing, but that alone did not satisfy a greater need to serve the public, especially during a time of economic and social depression when the public needed so much help. But what could a young lawyer do? In 1935 Hennock gave up her lucrative partnership with Julius Silver over a dispute regarding legal work for Edwin Land, a young inventor who had recently developed a new camera. She began exploring other avenues for her legal talents. Between 1935 and 1939 she worked as an assistant attorney on the New York Mortgage Commission, where her understanding of real estate law came into good use. More importantly, her work at the commission helped appease her desire to benefit the public, as her work helped untangle the legal mess left by the real estate market collapse in 1929. She also used her legal expertise to return to her alma mater, Brooklyn Law School, where she lectured on politics and the economy. These experiences helped Hennock develop an affinity for politics.

When the Mortgage Commission disbanded in 1939 Hennock began searching for employment and in 1941 she re-entered the corporate legal community. Her re-entry was extraordinary, though, as she joined the prestigious Wall Street law firm of Choate, Mitchell and Ely in 1941. At a time when most Jewish lawyers practiced within their own law firms, and were systematically excluded from the more prominent and powerful (and Protestant) Wall Street firms,[89] Hennock was invited to join one of the most respected firms in the country. In doing so, she became its first woman, first Jew, and its first Democrat. Her position at Choate, Mitchell and Ely was a significant accomplishment in many regards, but it was primarily self-serving. Her ability to advise "clients [in] how to make a lot of money"[90] was financially lucrative. While her work at Choate, Mitchell and Ely provided monetary wealth, her ardent support for, and growing influence within, the Democratic Party satisfied both her taste for influence and desire to help others.

A POLITICAL LIFE

While practicing as an attorney in New York, Hennock became active in Democratic politics, both statewide and within the City. Her activity was consistent with the political interest demonstrated by her contemporaries, who used their law profession to gain *entre* into political candidacies, and similar to a widespread political commitment evidenced by Jewish immigrants. This diligence was the result of a centuries-old recognition that Jews "depended for their lives on the authorities, on the persons and groups who exercised legitimate power."[91] Liberal political philosophies, which were not inherent to Jewishness, were a manifestation of the immigrant's encounter with the constitutionally-protected rights of American citizens. Among the immigrant arrivals during the early decades of the twentieth century were Jewish intellectuals carrying more leftist political philosophies than were generally found in the United States, and their liberal themes found receptive audiences among the mass of newcomers. Socialism, in particular, enjoyed extensive immigrant support.[92] Socialist philosophies that were popular between 1900 and 1920 were made more palatable, and thus received even greater support, in the philosophies of the New Deal.

The Jewish population solidly supported the Democratic Party's New Deal.[93] The social ideals pledged by the New Deal, such as adequate housing, support for unemployed workers, educational opportunities, and health care, struck a resonant chord with immigrants whose ethnic history consisted of extreme discrimination. This was particularly true for second-generation immigrants, many of whom lived with the contradictions of seeing all that America had to offer but facing systematic preventatives from achieving their dreams. The Democratic Party and the New Deal extended political recognition of and support for those aspirations in return for party loyalty.

Neither group was disappointed. Starting in the 1920s, the Jewish vote swung from the socialist and anarchist extremes to New Deal ideologies. As the decade progressed, and the popularity of Franklin D. Roosevelt increased, Jewish electoral support steadily grew. Indeed, support for both the New Deal and Roosevelt were inextricably intertwined; "a massive enthusiasm for Roosevelt [existed] within the Jewish community: the whole of it, from working class to bourgeois, from east European to German, from right to left."[94] Strong Jewish support helped Roosevelt win his first presidential bid in 1932. With each passing election, Jewish approval increased; between 1936 and 1945, Jews were the only voting block that consistently increased its patronage.[95] Roosevelt demonstrated his appreciation of this solidarity by opening the doors of government to Jews, large numbers of whom, particularly lawyers, followed the new President to Washington D.C. in 1933 to participate in the social revolution represented by the New Deal and, for the first time, "Jews became acceptable in Washington, and in some rare instances desirable."[96] Loyal support for Roosevelt and the New Deal, combined with an education, provided many Jews with both the recognition and legitimacy they craved from their adopted country.

The New Deal offered a "new deal" to women in particular. The same social ideals that were so appealing to Jews (educational support, health care, unemployment compensation, family services) were equally attractive to women. Eleanor Roosevelt appealed to these sensibilities when she wrote that "the basis of all useful political activity is an interest in human beings and social conditions, and a knowledge of human nature."[97] Moreover, since women had only recently been granted the right to vote, the Democratic Party, through New Deal channels, gave them a direct connection to political activity. As Molly Dewson wrote in the program for the 1936 Democratic National Convention program, "women's belief in their power to help and their determination to do so has been shown in many ways" and "the Democratic Party has made fresh recruits among women."[98] For some women, political activity came in the form of holding office in Washington D.C. Beginning with the Franklin Roosevelt administration, women held prominent and unprecedented positions of power in the capitol.[99] The most visible was Frances Perkins, who became the first female Secretary of Labor and remained in that post from 1932 until 1945, the duration of Roosevelt's presidency. Many other women filled less conspicuous, but influential, positions.[100]

Access to political jobs occurred through a process of networking. Eleanor Roosevelt encouraged women to become active in local politics. In her book *It's Up to the Women!*, published in 1933, Roosevelt instructed women on how to get politically involved and encouraged their opportunity "to render a permanent service to the general happiness of the working man and woman and their families."[101] Women who, by 1932, already demonstrated their commitment to the New Deal received political appointments through an effective networking system led by Mary "Molly" Dewson, who was the chair of the Democratic National Committee's Women's Division. Although hers was not a government position, it nonetheless provided her with considerable political influence which she skillfully used to place women in government jobs, a form of patronage that Dewson believed "should be utilized to reward women who were active workers in the campaigns."[102] Dewson and Eleanor Roosevelt, who contributed both strong political support and direct access to Franklin Roosevelt, helped create a political climate that welcomed women's viewpoints, hard work, and votes.

Hennock's political interests were motivated by equal parts of personal ambition and public service responsibility, and they allowed her to assuage three desires. First, working on behalf of the Democratic Party provided Hennock access to power and influence beyond that available to her as a practicing attorney. Second, as a woman, the Democratic Party encouraged her participation and welcomed her considerable abilities, while simultaneously providing an outlet through which she could express the feminine characteristics of nurturing and helping others by helping to enact legislation. Finally, politics provided an arena through which Hennock may have been able to respond to both the needs of Jewish people as well as the code of *menschlichkeit*.

Frieda Hennock, however, was a different sort of "political woman" than those who came before her. As Elisabeth Israels Perry explains, women such as Belle Moskowitz, Eleanor Roosevelt, and Frances Perkins worked behind-the-scenes to enact the ideals of political men, in these cases Al Smith and Franklin Roosevelt.[103] None of these women were career politicians. Hennock was fundamentally different and, although she certainly benefitted from the earlier political activities of these women, she developed and followed an agenda designed to meet her own personal and political goals.

Hennock's earliest political activities were expressed in 1934 through an interest in working with the New Deal administration when she applied for appointment as Assistant Attorney General.[104] Failing to receive the position, Hennock achieved her first political placement, with the help of Democratic National Committee Chair James Farley,[105] by joining the New York Mortgage Commission which was formed in 1935 to rehabilitate the mortgage industry following the stock market crash of 1929 and subsequent real estate market collapse. There she served as an attorney in the Appeal Bureau of the Mortgage Commission's Legal Department where she prepared legal briefs regarding the constitutionality of the Commission's authority.[106] Working at the Mortgage

Commission allowed Hennock to encounter prominent people already well-entrenched in national politics, such as Ferdinand Pecora.[107] It was during this period that she became involved in local Democratic politics, which she eventually supplemented with activity in the state Democratic organization. In 1938 Hennock actively campaigned for Herbert Lehman's successful gubernatorial race, for which he thanked her for her "very generous service in [his] behalf. As a result of [her] efforts," Lehman wrote, he was "sure that on Election Day we may all go to the polls feeling confident of another great victory."[108] Many women, before and since, were content to work behind the scenes of the Democratic machine. But Frieda Hennock forced her position within the political hierarchy. Having proven her commitment to the party through years of fund-raising and campaigning, she expected to be rewarded by the patronage system. Throughout most of her professional life her ambitions were defined according to accomplishments as an attorney. The more active and successful she became within the Democratic party, however, the more her ambitions became politically defined.

By 1941 she had attracted the attention of a variety of political and legal leaders, and her political aspirations took shape. She advanced herself in a number of ways. In that year Eleanor Roosevelt was the figurehead organizing a group of prominent American women who would study civilian defense in Great Britain, which was already engulfed in World War II. Frieda Hennock enlisted the help of several friends, who wrote letters to Mrs. Roosevelt suggesting Hennock as a candidate for the entourage.[109] Support came from William Richardson, Dean of the Brooklyn Law School, who attested to Hennock's legal expertise.[110] Edward Flynn, Chair of the Democratic National Committee, vouched for her contributions to Franklin Roosevelt's 1940 presidential campaign, and later described her as "one of the most valuable and industrious associates in the New York office of the National Democratic Committee and in that of the New York State Democratic Committee."[111] Similarly, Thomas Corcoran, a Washington D.C. attorney, confirmed Hennock's commitment to Democratic Politics. He wrote, "I have met her everywhere the New Deal was having a hard political battle, and I have admired her not only for her professional competence and her social conscience, but also for the realistic and devoted courage with which she undertook—where others shrunk—the hardest of political work; i.e., the raising of funds with all the unhappy implications of personal obligation which that kind of work involves."[112] Indeed, it appears as if Hennock's principal contribution to Democratic Politics was fund-raising. In a memo to President Roosevelt, Hennock was described as "a lawyer, raised money by giving luncheons and other things; received practically no cooperation from the State group."[113] Eleanor Roosevelt later recognized Hennock's contributions by asserting that she knew "how much time and work you gave to the re-election of the President. . . . I shall look forward to having an opportunity of thanking you in person and expressing the President's appreciation to you."[114]

By 1947 Hennock was recognized as a leader in Democratic politics,[115] and her political work began to pay dividends. The party and leaders for whom she worked diligently began advocating her candidacy for a variety of federal positions, positions that are indicative of her contributions to the Democratic Party. She joined the 38–member Executive Committee of the National Health Assembly, which was formed by the Federal Security Administration to develop a 10–year national health program.[116] Edward Flynn, former chair of the Democratic National Committee, urged President Truman to consider Hennock for "such important positions as a member of the Federal Communications Commission or as an Assistant Secretary of the Interior."[117] The stage was set.

CONCLUSION

Hennock was a woman of her time, the personification of the changing roles of women in American society. Like women before and since, Hennock felt the conflict between sociocultural demands for female behavior and individual inclinations and, like others before her, found ways to mediate between the two. Raised in both a personal and societal atmosphere that expected women to become wives and mothers, Hennock rejected these traditional nurturing roles by refusing to marry and, instead, becoming a "career girl." The desire to nurture was strong, however, so she found ways to express the gendered quality of caring for others. In her personal life she became the primary breadwinner in her family. Professionally, she successfully defended social misfits such as working-class immigrants, dance-hall women, and bootleggers. In civil practice, she studied low-cost housing and socialized medicine. By the time she was appointed to the FCC, her interests in serving the public were well-established.

Equally well-determined were her personal political interests, which were also tempered by gendered interests and expectations. Whether serving on the New York Mortgage Commission or campaigning for local, state, and national Democratic committees, Hennock was a politician. Again, however, her political activities were tempered by the fact that she was a woman. She restricted herself to "womanly" activities (luncheons, fund-raising, remaining within women's division activities). Nonetheless, her success in political activities culminated in her nomination for and appointment to the FCC.

This, then, is the woman who became the subject of considerable back-room political activity in late 1947 and early 1948. Frieda Hennock was an intelligent, capable woman lawyer, committed to serving both personal and public interests. An upbringing that followed Jewish and feminine value structures motivated her to make choices that helped serve public interests. An equally powerful personal ambition prompted her to take positions that would serve her own political goals. These interests ultimately figured into her daily activities at the Commission, and played a significant role in the positions she took on key cases. Throughout her tenure at the FCC her opinions and decisions were guided by both public and personal interests.

NOTES

1. Irving Howe, *World of Our Fathers* (New York: Harcourt Brace Jovanovich, 1976), p. 645.

2. Sarah Barkin Henoch explained to her granddaughter, Selena Sheriff, that Boris Henoch was very upset when Frieda was born, exclaiming that she was "just another girl" (at least the fifth daughter). The story was recounted often in the family, to the extent that family members believed that Hennock's ambitions were partly the result of wanting to prove to her father that she was more than "just another girl." Personal interview with Selena Sheriff, 7 April 1999.

3. Deborah Dash Moore, "Assimilation of Twentieth Century Jewish Women," in *Jewish Women in America: An Historical Encyclopedia*, Vol. 1, ed. Paula E. Hyman and Deborah Dash Moore (New York: Routledge, 1997), p. 92. See also Doris Weatherford, *Foreign and Female: Immigrant Women in America, 1840–1930* (New York: Facts on File, Inc., 1995).

4. "Frieda B. Hennock," *Current Biography-1948*: 278–280; "Frieda Hennock," *Cyclopedia of American Biography, Vol. H* (New York: James T. White and Co., 1952), p. 337; Patricia Sugrue, "Frieda Hennock, Attorney, Is Dead," *The Washington Post*, 21 June 1960, p. B4; "Frieda Hennock Simons Dead," *New York Times*, 21 June 1960, p. 33.

5. Sarah Barkin Henoch told her granddaughter, Selena Sheriff, of the family's reasons for immigrating to the United States. Personal correspondence with Sheriff, 15 March 1999; and personal interview with Selena Sheriff, 7 April 1999.

6. Neil M. Cowan and Ruth Schwartz Cowan, *Our Parents' Lives: The Americanization of Eastern European Jews* (New York: Basic Books, Inc., Publishers, 1989).

7. Cowan and Cowan, *Our Parents' Lives*; Helena Znaniecki Lopata, *Polish*

Americans: Status Competition in an Ethnic Community, (Englewood Cliffs, NJ: Prentice-Hall, Inc., 1976); Gerald Sorin, *A Time For Building: The Third Migration 1880–1920*, (Baltimore, MD: The Johns Hopkins University Press, 1992); Joyce Antler, *The Journey Home: Jewish Woman and the American Century* (New York: The Free Press, 1997); Kathie Friedman-Kasaba, *Memories of Migration: Gender, Ethnicity, and Work in the Lives of Jewish and Italian Women in New York, 1870–1924* (Albany, NY: State University of New York Press, 1996); Sydney Stahl Weinberg, *The World of Our Mothers: The Lives of Jewish Immigrant Women* (Chapel Hill, NC: The University of North Carolina Press, 1988); Susan A. Glenn, *Daughters of the Shtetl: Life and Labor in the Immigrant Generation* (Ithaca, NY: Cornell University Press, 1990).

8. Cowan and Cowan, *Our Parents' Lives*, p. 35.

9. Cowan and Cowan, *Our Parents' Lives*, p. 36.

10. "Frieda B. Hennock," *Current Biography-1948*, pp. 278–280; "Frieda Barkin Hennock," *Cyclopedia of American Biography*, p. 337.

11. Donna Gabaccia, *From the Other Side: Women, Gender, and Immigrant Life in the U.S., 1820–1990*, (Bloomington, IN: Indiana University Press, 1994), p. 46.

12. Selma Berrol, "Public Schools and Immigrants: The New York City Experience," in *American Education and the European Immigrant: 1840–1940*, ed. Bernard J. Weiss, (Urbana, IL: University of Illinois Press, 1982), pp. 31–43.

13. Sydney Stahl Weinberg, "Longing to Learn: The Education of Jewish Immigrant Women in New York City, 1900–1934," *Journal of American Ethnic History* 8(2) (Spring 1989): 110.

14. Berrol, "Public Schools and Immigrants," p. 32.

15. "Frieda B. Hennock," *Current Biography-1948*, p. 278.

16. For a detailed explanation of the development and importance of night school education see Selma C. Berrol, "From Compensatory Education to Adult Education: The New York City Evening Schools, 1825–1935," *Adult Education* 26(4) (1976): 208–225.

17. Stephan F. Brumberg, *Going to America, Going to School: The Jewish Immigrant Public School Encounter in Turn-of-the-Century New York City* (New York: Praeger Special Studies, 1986), p. 92.

18. Selma C. Berrol, "Education and Economic Mobility: The Jewish Experience in New York City, 1880–1920," *American Jewish Historical Quarterly* 65(3) (March 1976): 269.

19. Berrol, "Public Schools and Immigrants," p. 45.

20. Ruth Jacknow Markowitz, *My Daughter, The Teacher: Jewish Teachers in the New York City Schools* (New Brunswick, NJ: Rutgers University Press, 1993).

21. Markowitz, *My Daughter, The Teacher*, p. 5.

22. Weinberg, "Longing to Learn."

23. Berrol, "Public Schools and Immigrants," p. 39.

24. Henry L. Feingold, *A Time for Searching: Entering the Mainstream,*

1920–1945, (Baltimore, MD: The Johns Hopkins University Press, 1992).

25. Cowan and Cowan, *Our Parents' Lives*, p. 94

26. Ibid.

27. Weinberg, "Longing to Learn," p. 109.

28. Markowitz, *My Daughter, The Teacher.*

29. Weinberg, "Longing to Learn"; Weinberg, *The World of Our Mothers*; Charlotte Baum, Paula Hyman, and Sonya Michel, *The Jewish Woman in America* (New York: The Dial Press, 1976).

30. Gabaccia, *From the Other Side*; Weinberg, "Longing to Learn," *The World of Our Mothers*; Baum et al., *The Jewish Woman in America.*

31. Markowitz, *My Daughter, The Teacher.*

32. Ibid, pp. 9–10.

33. "Frieda B. Hennock," *Current Biography-1948*, p. 278.

34. Jacob R. Marcus, *The American Jewish Woman, 1654–1980* (New York: KTAV Publishing House, Inc., 1981), p. 132.

35. Antler, *The Journey Home*; Weinberg, "Longing to Learn"; Weinberg, *The World of Our Mothers*; Baum et al., *The Jewish Woman in America*; Markowitz, *My Daughter, The Teacher*; Marcus, *The American Jewish Woman.*

36. Weinberg, *The World of Our Mothers*, p. 220.

37. Hennock did not receive a college degree, but rather moved directly from high school to law school. I suspect that law schools such as BLS, which was open to women and minorities, did not require a college degree for admission.

38. A certificate recognizing Hennock's proficiency at "Rapid Legible Business Writing" may be found in Box 6, Folder 76, Frieda Hennock Simons collection (FHS).

39. Richard Hull to Jim Robertson, Series 1/Box 2/Folder 6, Jim Robertson Collection, Public Broadcasting Oral History Project, National Public Broadcasting Archives, University of Maryland, College Park, MD, (hereafter cited as Robertson Collection).

40. Glenn, *Daughters of the Shtetl*; Cowan and Cowan, *Our Parents' Lives*; Baum et al., *The Jewish Woman in America*; Elizabeth Ewen, *Immigrant Women in the Land of Dollars: Life and Culture on the Lower East Side, 1890–1925* (New York: Monthly Review Press, 1985); Weinberg, *The World of Our Mothers.*

41. Berrol, "Public Schools and Immigrants," pp. 31–43; Rudolf Glanz, *The Jewish Woman in America: Two Female Immigrant Generations 1820–1929* (New York: KTAV Publishing House, Inc., 1976).

42. Henry L. Feingold, *A Time For Searching.*

43. Baum et al., *The Jewish Woman in America*, p. 125; Weinberg, *The World of Our Mothers*; Paula Hyman, "Culture and Gender: Women in the Immigrant Jewish Community," in *The Legacy of Jewish Migration: 1881 and Its Impact,* ed. David Berger (New York: Brooklyn College Press, 1983), p. 160.

44. Markowitz, *My Daughter, The Teacher.*

45. Ibid, p. 2.

46. Teresa Amott and Julie Matthaei, *Race, Gender, and Work: A Multicultural Economic History of Women in the United States* (Boston, MA: South End Press, 1991), p. 113; Hyman, "Culture and Gender," pp. 161.

47. In a 1950 interview Hennock claimed that she entered law school because she "found that the law school was the only one that had any good courses left. Teaching was already crowded with women—medicine was impossible—and so, that left law." Tex McCrary and Jinx Falkenburg, "New York Close-Up," *New York Herald-Tribune*, 15 June 1950.

48. Ibid, p. 278; Maryann Yodelis Smith, "Frieda Hennock," in *Notable American Women, The Modern Period: A Biographical Dictionary*, eds. B. Sicherman and C.H. Green (Cambridge, MA: Belknap Press of Harvard University Press, 1980), p. 332.

49. *Current Biography-1948*, p. 278.

50. Academic records (1921–1924) were courteously provided by the Brooklyn Law School.

51. *Cyclopedia of American Biography*, p. 337; Sugrue, 1960; "Frieda Hennock Simons Dead."

52. Jerold S. Auerbach, "From Rags to Robes: The Legal Profession, Social Mobility and the American Jewish Experience," *American Jewish Historical Quarterly* 66(2) (December 1976): 249–284; Jerold S. Auerbach, *Unequal Justice: Lawyers and Social Change in Modern America* (New York: Oxford University Press, 1976).

53. Auerbach, "From Rags to Robes," pp. 249–284.

54. Auerbach, "From Rags to Robes," p. 261.

55. Auerbach, "From Rags to Robes," pp. 264–265; Albert I. Goldberg, "Jews in the Legal Profession: A Case of Adjustment to Discrimination," *Jewish Social Studies 32* (1970): 148–161.

56. Feingold, *A Time For Searching*.

57. Daniel Stone, "Jewish Emigration from Poland Before World War II," in *Polish Americans and Their History: Community, Culture, and Politics*, ed. John J. Bukowczyk (Pittsburgh: University of Pittsburgh Press, 1996), p. 105.

58. Antler, *The Journey Home*, p. 189.

59. Susan Brandeis, "The Woman Lawyer in the United States," speech delivered in Washington, D.C. in 1929. Susan Brandeis Gilbert papers, Brandeis University.

60. Antler, *The Journey Home*.

61. Antler, *The Journey Home*, p. 182.

62. Antler, *The Journey Home*, p. 182.

63. *Current Biography-1948*, p. 278; John MacLeod, "The Woes and Triumphs of a Lady Advocate," *American Weekly*, 5 September 1948, p. 12.

64. "Frieda B. Hennock," *Current Biography-1948*, p. 278.

65. "Youngest Portia Uses Her Charm," *New York City American*, 24 June 1929.

66. *Current Biography-1948*, p. 278.

67. Such as the Benedetto brothers who were accused of murder. "Girl Lawyer Wins Point," p. 21; "Woman is Counsel for 2 As Slayers," *New York Times*, 3 May 1928, p. 7.

68. "Youngest Portia," 24 June 1929.

69. "New York Woman is Named to FCC, Would be first on the Board," *New York Herald-Tribune*, 24 May 1948, p. 1.

70. Smith, "Frieda Hennock," p. 332; Sugrue, "Frieda Hennock, Attorney, Is Dead," p. B4; "Frieda Hennock Simons Dead," p. 33.

71. "Woman is Counsel for 2 As Slayers," *New York Times*, 3 May 1928, p. 7.

72. Ibid.

73. MacLeod, "Woes and Triumphs," p. 12.

74. She married William H. Simons in 1956 when she was 51 years old.

75. "Marital Status of Women in Civilian Labor Force," *Historical Statistics of the United States, Bicentennial Edition, Part 1*, Bureau of the Census, Department of Commerce (Washington, D.C.: Government Printing Office, 1976), p. 133.

76. Ibid.

77. MacLeod, "Woes and Triumphs," p. 12; Hennock to Nash, 5 July 1956, 4/144, Ruth Cowan Nash papers, Schlesinger Library, Radcliffe College.

78. Hennock to Nat, 11 July 1922, Box 1, Folder 16, Frieda Hennock Simons papers, Schlesinger Library, Radcliffe College, Cambridge, MA, (hereafter cited as FHS).

79. Ibid; Solomon to "Sweet 'little dream girl,' " undated, FHS 1/16; "Howard" to "Fritzie," undated, 1/16, FHS; McCarty to Robertson, Series 1/Box 2/Folder 18, Robertson Collection; Fly to Hennock, January 1949, 1/16, FHS.

80. Untitled testimony of Hennock before the Senate Judiciary Committee regarding her nomination for Federal Judgeship, 19/155, FHS.

81. Ibid.

82. In 1941 the average annual net income of non-salaried lawyers was $4,794. Although similar figures are not available for 1930, it is likely that attorney earnings were less than this amount. "Earnings in Selected Occupations—Non-salaried Lawyers," *Historical Statistics of the United States, Bicentennial Edition, Part 1*, p. 176.

83. Martha Millspaugh, "Miss Commissioner Hennock," *Baltimore Sun*, 8 August 1948, p. A5; MacLeod, "Woes and Triumphs," p. 12; *Current Biography–1948*, p. 279.

84. Biographical information sheet completed by Hennock for the Federal Judge position, found in FHS 6/76. Family information provided by Selena Sheriff in a personal interview. Mrs. Sheriff was one of the two nieces who lived with Hennock.

85. Val Montanari, "First Woman Member of FCC Makes Impression on Senators With Frankness," *Washington Post*, 5 July 1948, p. 2; U.S. Congress, Senate, Committee on the Judiciary, Frieda B. Hennock: Hearings for the U.S.

District Judge for the Southern District of New York Before the Committee on the Judiciary, 82nd Congress, 1st Session, September–October 1951, (testimony of David Schenker, p. 380), (hereafter cited as Senate, Committee on the Judiciary).

86. Glendening v. Glendening, 29 NE 2nd 926 (1939), 19 NYS 2nd 693 (1939), 22 NE 2nd 169 (1939), 10 NYS 2nd 17 (1939).

87. An income nearly ten times that of the average lawyer's. Laurence Eklund, "Portia on the FCC," *Milwaukee Journal*, 1 September 1948, p. 18.

88. Ibid.

89. Susan Ware, *Holding Their Own: American Women in the 1930s* (Boston: Twayne Publishers, 1982).

90. Eklund, p. 18.

91. Ben Halpern, "The Roots of American Jewish Liberalism," *American Jewish Historical Quarterly* 66 (September 1976): 190–214. See also, Edward S. Shapiro, *A Time For Healing: American Jewry since World War II* (Baltimore, MD: The Johns Hopkins University Press, 1992).

92. Stone, "Jewish Emigration," pp 91–120.

93. Deborah Dash Moore, *At Home in America: Second Generation New York Jews* (New York: Columbia University Press, 1981); Shapiro, *A Time For Healing*; Feingold, *A Time For Searching*.

94. Howe, *World of Our Fathers*.

95. Ibid.

96. Feingold, *A Time For Searching*, p. 219.

97. Eleanor Roosevelt, *It's Up to the Women!* (New York: Frederick A. Stokes Co., 1933), pp. 210–211.

98. Mary W. Dewson, "Democratic Women in Politics," *The Democratic National Convention Program, 1936*, Mary Dewson papers, Schlesinger Library, Radcliffe College, Cambridge, MA.

99. Susan Ware, *Beyond Suffrage: Women in the New Deal* (Cambridge, MA: Harvard University Press, 1981); Frances M. Seeber, "Eleanor Roosevelt and Women in the New Deal: A Network of Friends," *Presidential Studies Quarterly* 20 (Fall 1990): 707-717.

100. Ware, *Beyond Suffrage*.

101. Roosevelt, *It's Up to the Women!*, p. 200.

102. Seeber, "Eleanor Roosevelt," p. 709.

103. Elisabeth Israels Perry, *Belle Moskowitz: Feminine Politics and the Exercise of Power in the Age of Alfred E. Smith* (New York: Oxford University Press, 1987).

104. Richardson to Cummings, 22 May 1934, courtesy of Brooklyn Law School, (hereafter BLS).

105. Farley to Hennock, 17 April 1935, 1/20, FHS.

106. Senate, Committee on the Judiciary, p. 339.

107. Ferdinand Pecora was a prominent lawyer and politician in the 1930s and 1940s. In 1933 he was hired by the U.S. Congress as an independent coun-

sel to investigate the Stock Market Crash of 1929, a position in which he achieved considerable notoriety. In 1935 he was appointed to the New York Supreme Court, where he remained until 1950 when he resigned in order to run (unsuccessfully) for mayor of New York City. Hennock and Pecora were close friends, as evidenced by numerous references to him throughout personal correspondence between Hennock and various friends. During closed-door sessions the propriety of the Hennock/Pecora relationship was questioned during her federal judgeship hearings in 1951.

108. Lehman to Hennock, 4 November 1938, 1/20, FHS.

109. Hennock's letter-writing campaign is an early example of a strategy that she used several times during her political career, in which she urged influential friends and colleagues to contact decision makers regarding a Hennockian cause.

110. Richardson to E. Roosevelt, 17 November 1941, BLS.

111. Flynn to E. Roosevelt, 28 November 1941, Box 432, Folder "Office of Civilian Defense," Eleanor Roosevelt Collection, Franklin D. Roosevelt Presidential Library, (hereafter ER); Flynn to Truman, 29 January 1948, Box 22, Folder 12, Edward Flynn Papers, FDR Library, (hereafter EF).

112. Corcoran to E. Roosevelt, 29 November 1941, Box 1595, Folder Co-Cy, ER.

113. "Memo for the P.S.," undated, Box 67, Folder 1932–1944 Campaign, President's Personal File, Franklin D. Roosevelt Library.

114. E. Roosevelt to Hennock, 10 November 1944, Box 1726, ER.

115. "Woman Nominated as Member of FCC," *New York Times*, 25 May 1948, p. 29; "Hennock Heard," *Broadcasting*, 14 June 1948, p. 21; "Hennock in Balance," *Broadcasting*, 22 June 1948, p. 22+; "Lady Commissioner," *Broadcasting*, 28 June 1948, p. 25.

116. National Health Assembly, *America's Health: A Report to the Nation, Official Report* (New York: Harper & Brothers Publishers, 1949).

117. Flynn to Truman, 29 January 1947, Box 22, Folder 12, EF. A copy of the same letter may be found in Box 645, Official Files (OF) 112–A (G-I), Harry S. Truman Library.

CHAPTER 2

Appointment and the Federal Communications Commission

The year 1948 was pivotal for Frieda Hennock. Since immigrating to the United States in 1910 she consistently achieved personal goals that set her apart from the vast majority of women in the United States, especially her sister Jewish immigrants. Her public schooling and legal education far exceeded the accomplishments of most Jewish women, and her success as a lawyer surpassed the aspirations of the majority of women in white-collar jobs. Passing from criminal to corporate law enabled Hennock to establish both personal wealth and access to influential people, both of which equipped her to become a prominent participant in the New York Democratic Party. She enjoyed a snug fit with the Democrats and their New Deal for America satisfied Hennock's two most valued motivations. Like her, the Democrats were committed to creating a better life for the average citizen. Equally important, the Democratic Party both encouraged women's participation in political life and happily accepted their campaign efforts.

By early 1948 Frieda Hennock had positioned herself as a leading member of the New York Democratic Party and a tireless supporter of the national party. Unlike most women who actively associated with the Democrats, Hennock expected to be rewarded for her efforts and 1948 was the year that her lifelong ambitions reached fruition. Her political clout confirmed, coupled with her desire to take both her personal and public interests to the next level, she began the process of lobbying for an appointment within the federal government. Her placement on the Federal Communications Commission (FCC) was improbable, due to a general Republican opposition to placing Democrats in long-term positions. Once there, she found herself in the midst of a relatively young bureaucracy facing monumental decisions, and helped shape the future of broadcasting in the United States. The seven years Hennock spent at the FCC, from 1948 to 1955, were the most exhilarating, exhausting, demanding, and fulfilling of her life.

APPOINTMENT TO THE FEDERAL COMMUNICATIONS COMMISSION

The path to appointment began in late 1947. The campaign to put Hennock on the FCC was led by three different groups interested in achieving her appointment: the Democratic Party machine, the Women's Caucus of the Democratic National Committee, and influential members of the politically conservative Jewish community. The Democratic leadership was intent on rewarding Hennock for her considerable party work and particularly her ability to raise campaign funds. Leaders from both the state and national organizations pressed President Harry Truman to appoint Hennock to the FCC position left vacant by Clifford Durr's retirement. Robert Hannegan, Chair of the DNC, expressed his belief that Hennock should be considered for the FCC: "I know Miss Hennock to be very capable, intelligent and loyal, and I personally think it would be well to give consideration to the appointment of a woman; I know of no better one than Miss Hennock."[1] Furthermore, Edward Flynn (former Chair of the DNC) and Paul Fitzpatrick (Chair, New York State Democratic Committee),[2] joined Hannegan in supporting Hennock. Following a different political agenda, the Women's Division of the DNC, led by Associate Director (and later Director) India Edwards, joined the campaign to place Hennock on the FCC in March 1948. Moreover, pressure to reward Hennock with an FCC appointment increased in April 1948 when she received further support from Doris Byrne (New York State Assemblywoman), and Oscar Ewing (Federal Security Administrator).[3] Responding to the advocacy of so many prominent members of the Democratic party, President Truman nominated Hennock to the FCC on 22 May 1948 to fill the vacancy left by Clifford Durr.[4]

Securing the nomination was only half the battle, however. At the same time Democrats lobbied Truman to appoint Hennock to the FCC, Republican congressional leaders were convinced that Truman's chances of winning the upcoming presidential campaign were slim. Controlling both the House and the Senate, they successfully prevented confirmation of any of Truman's pending appointments to a variety of government posts. Specifically targeting Hennock, legislators on the floor of the House responded to her nomination with outrage and intimated that she was a member of the Communist Party. One particular legislator expressed considerable relief that "fortunately the Republican controlled Senate will hold up confirmation until the next session of Congress."[5] Back room politicking, however, took her nomination through different corridors and she received support from an unlikely third group of influential Republicans who appealed directly to the Republican Party leadership on behalf of Hennock.[6] In June 1948 Hennock appeared before members of the Communications subcommittee of the Senate Interstate Commerce Committee.[7] While there were no records kept of this executive session hearing, information subsequently reported in the press indicated she responded to questions with unusual candor, which made a favorable impression on the members. She reportedly told the Republican-dominated subcommittee "I'm against you and always have been. I have done my best to collect money for Roosevelt and have probably taken a lot of good Republican money away from what you wanted to collect."[8] When asked what she knew about the radio industry, she responded "only that I've raised a lot of money for radio programs for Roosevelt."[9] On 14 June 1948 the entire Senate Interstate Commerce Committee unanimously approved her appointment,[10] probably due to the support of Senator Robert Taft.

The same week she appeared before the subcommittee, Hennock privately met with Senator Robert A. Taft (R-Ohio), known as "Mr. Republican" and the chair of the Republican National Committee. The meeting was not widely reported in the press, but figured importantly in Hennock's confirmation. As Taft later wrote to Brigadier General Julius Klein, "I appreciate very much your arranging for me to meet Miss Hennock personally, because it is fair to say that her confirmation grew out of that interview."[11] Taft also explained that, following the meeting, the Republicans "withdrew [their] general opposition to confirming anyone to a long-term job, because of [Hennock's] excellent recommendations as an attorney, in spite of the fact that she had been active in several Roosevelt campaigns."[12] Taft further told Hennock that she was "confirmed, in spite of the general policy against confirmation of long-term appointments, because of the very excellent recommendations of her legal ability."[13]

When her nomination came before the Senate on 19 June 1948, the secrecy with which her confirmation was considered drew heavy political fire. Senator Joseph Ball (R-Minnesota) was particularly incensed that:

the only investigation, the only hearing, regarding this nomination, was a brief executive session of the subcommittee of the Committee on Interstate and Foreign Commerce. For several weeks the reports were that the nomination would never get out of committee. Then all of a sudden it was reported, with, I may say, somewhat suspicious haste [that her nomination was approved]. So far as I can discover, [Hennock] has no experience in radio matters, and from what I can learn of her background, frankly I do not think she is qualified for the job, and I want to be on record as opposed to her confirmation.[14]

Senator Owen Brewster (R-Maine) responded to Ball's complaints by asserting that the subcommittee, on which he served as chair, believed the FCC needed "new blood, and it was the consensus of those of us who became familiar with this matter through contact with many who were acquainted with [Hennock], that she would be well qualified to fit into this position, and we believed her confirmation was warranted and wise."[15] Immediately following Brewster's comments, Hennock's appointment was confirmed. *Broadcasting* magazine described it as "tantamount to a legislative miracle"[16] and reasoned that Republican support resulted from both a fear of female retaliation at the election polls that autumn, as well as contradicting earlier GOP swipes against Democrats for failing to appoint women to prominent government positions.[17]

Hennock's confirmation was implausible for a variety of reasons. Most significantly, the fact that she was female certainly made it unlikely that she would achieve such a politically prominent and powerful position. Although the number of women employed in all federal positions increased dramatically during World War II,[18] the post-war period from 1944 to 1947 witnessed a 60.2% drop in federal employment of women and the vast majority of these positions were clerical. The same was true at the Federal Communications Commission where women represented 35.7% of employees in 1939, 40.8% in 1944, and 37.4% in 1947, mirroring the overall trend in which women's federal employment increased during the war then dropped postwar.[19] In 1947 women filled less than 3% of the highest ranking federal government positions.[20] As early as 1941 a pamphlet recognizing the contributions of women in the Federal Service cautioned that women in prominent Federal positions "are frequently publicized and thus give a perhaps too optimistic impression that such examples are commonplace. It is true and probably will be for many years to come that the number of women officials is small in comparison with the number of men of similar rank."[21] As Owen Brewster wrote, "Caesar's wife had a picnic compared with what women in public life must face today as they move to the upper levels [of government]."[22] The fact that Hennock was an intelligent, capable woman, likely played the largest role in her appointment, since her assignment opposed the trend.

In addition to her sex, it is possible that Hennock received Republican support as a result of a promise Senator Taft extracted from her during their private interview.[23] Concerned about the influence of FCC lawyers, their perceived liberalism, and recent investigations of suspected Communist sympathizers at the FCC,[24] Taft allegedly persuaded Hennock to "be independent—she would not come under the sway of the people . . . at the Commission. . . . And she promised Senator Taft, that if she was confirmed that she would indeed be independent."[25] Hennock and Taft made oblique references to such an understanding in correspondence with each other. Hennock wrote that she understood "the very high standards which [Taft] expressed as necessary for the commissionership," and Taft responded that "the basic problems [of the communications industry] should be passed on by members of the Board [sic] rather than by the Legal Department."[26]

Hence, against considerable odds and under unusual circumstances, Frieda Hennock took her oath of office on 1 July 1948 and became the first woman commissioner of the FCC and the first woman appointed to a federal agency. During her installation ceremony she asserted that "it seems fundamental that in this field—so peculiarly affecting women—the viewpoint of their sex should be represented."[27] She further appreciated the opportunity "to render a service to [her] country in a position where [she] could be of some use,"[28] and promised to make judgments based on the welfare of the people. She devoted herself to making decisions in the public interest. Her appointment was politically motivated, however, and she was a politician at heart. The positions she took while at the FCC were a powerful combination of both personal political interests and concern for the public. And so Frieda Hennock took her oath of office on a beautiful summer day and began her new job as a Federal Communications commissioner.

THE FEDERAL COMMUNICATIONS COMMISSION

The organization Frieda Hennock joined in 1948 had existed for only fourteen years as the Federal Communications Commission but its regulatory antecedents existed for at least thirty-eight years. Originally established as the Federal Radio Commission in 1927 then revised as the Federal Communications Commission in 1934, from its inception the agency acquired an uncomfortable middle position between the federal government and the broadcast industries.[29] As an authority of the federal government the FCC was expected to develop and administer policy that was consistent with both federal and public interests regarding broadcasting. Yet the commission similarly encouraged and expected the industries to carry out their own research and development which could, and probably would, be subject to FCC review and acceptance. The nature of the relationship between government and business was inherently tense and unstable. The political nature of commission appointments potentially exacerbated this relationship, as politically conservative or liberal commissioners attempted to sway commission decisions, and hence policy affecting the broadcasting industries, according to their political positions. Toss in the ability of both the House of Representatives and the Senate to oversee FCC activities and the importance of understanding the commission as an innately political agency becomes clear. Indeed, politics played a role from the inception of legislation regarding wireless technology.

Early Legislative Attempts

The first legislative attempt to regulate the technology of broadcasting occurred in 1910 with the Wireless Ship Act,[30] when the technology was called "wireless" and was primarily a form of point-to-point communication utilizing Morse Code rather than voice transmissions.[31] The Wireless Ship Act required that all ships leaving American ports must have wireless equipment on board. Two years later the Radio Act of 1912 was passed, partly in response to the Titanic disaster, which established requirements for wireless use,[32] specifically ordering both professional and amateur wireless operators to be licensed by the Department of Commerce and Labor in order to operate their equipment. It further set conditions by creating restrictions on use of wireless equipment such as location, purpose, wavelength assignments, and hours of operation.[33] The Act established the significant precedent of federal government intervention in the use of this technology.[34]

In 1920 the technology used primarily for point-to-point communication took a sudden turn when corporate engineers and amateurs alike began broadcasting programming to increasingly larger audiences.[35] Between 1920 and 1922 the Department of Commerce and Labor was deluged with license requests; in 1920 they licensed only one station, but by 1923 more than 500 broadcast stations were officially sanctioned by the government.[36] The department found itself faced with the growing dilemma of too many broadcasters and the inability to effectively control the foundling industry. According to the Radio Act of 1912 the government could do nothing more than issue licenses; it had neither the statutory power to deny anyone a license nor the authority to revoke a license for misconduct. The implications of that regulatory paralysis became apparent as more and more broadcasting stations went on the air. Broadcasters frequently found themselves competing with each other for use of the same frequencies to transmit messages; the interference problems became a serious threat to the development of broadcasting.[37] Unable to broadcast from the frequency assigned to them by the Commerce and Labor regulators, broadcasters simply jumped frequencies and attempted to transmit from there, which only worsened the channel interference. Although a violation of their licensing agreement, broadcasters got away with "wobbling" because the government did not have the authority to punish them.

The government certainly looked for ways to officially regulate broadcasters. Herbert Hoover, then the Secretary of the Department of Commerce and Labor, was especially active in a variety of attempts to more forcefully regulate the industry. Between 1922 and 1925 Hoover led the annual Radio Conferences in which members of both the federal government and the burgeoning broadcast industry, as well as amateurs, convened to discuss ways in which the interference problems would be resolved.[38] Hoover particularly advocated two ideas. First, the federal government should create a specific agency that would have broad administrative authority over the radio industry, and would be overseen by the Department of Commerce and Labor. Second, anyone utilizing the public airwaves for broadcast purposes would be required to operate in "the public interest."[39] Hoover was especially aggressive in demanding specific government regulation during the Third and Fourth Radio Conferences, held in 1924 and 1925. Despite public and industry requests for federal intervention in the broadcasting industry, the pro-business, anti-government regulation Congress invariably ignored the problems.[40]

While the proposals generated by the Radio Conferences met with routine government rejection, Hoover pursued another approach to taking administrative control of broadcasting. Through a series of court cases Hoover attempted to establish regulatory authority over the industry,[41] only to be met with consistent rulings that the Radio Act of 1912 did not give the government any authority to refuse or revoke broadcasting licenses. Frustrated by his apparent legal inability to govern, in 1926 Hoover asked U.S. Attorney General William J. Donovan to review the 1912 Act and specifically outline the government's administrative capabilities regarding the radio industry. Hoover did not receive good news. Attorney General Donovan concluded that the Radio Act of 1912 was "inadequate to cover the art of broadcasting. . . . If the present situation requires control, I can only suggest that it be sought in new legislation, carefully adapted to meet the needs of both the present and the future."[42]

By late 1926 the interference problems were overwhelming. It was clear that the radio industry would be unable to continue progressing until the twin problems of interference and wobbling were resolved, and it further appeared as if only a national legal authority could accomplish that goal. Major corporations were particularly anxious to resolve the problem, especially RCA and its newly formed subsidiary NBC, which established two national radio networks (NBC-red and NBC-blue).[43] Under pressure from Commerce and Labor, broadcasters, and the American public, President Calvin Coolidge finally requested Congress to enact legislation,[44] and in February 1927 the Radio Act of 1927 was passed.[45] It was landmark legislation.

Effective Legislation: The Radio Act of 1927 and the Communications Act of 1934

The Radio Act of 1927 was significant for many reasons.[46] It created the Federal Radio Commission (FRC), an agency led by five commissioners who were responsible for administering the radio industry. The FRC was charged with establishing and maintaining order within the radio industry, which would be accomplished through the power to grant, review, renew, suspend, and revoke licenses. Broadcasters were required to abide by all aspects of the Radio Act of 1927, which included giving the FRC the authority to assign frequencies and power levels. Every decision the FRC made was subject to both internal and federal judicial review. The FRC was granted quasi-judicial powers; it could be petitioned by a licensee to review a commission decision and it could hold hearings on important issues for which the agency could call and question witnesses. One of the most important aspects of the Radio Act of 1927, however, was its incorporation of Hoover's "public interest" theory. Throughout the act broadcasters were exhorted to operate their stations in the "public interest, convenience, and necessity" and the FRC itself was required to make decisions in the "public interest."[47] Although the concept was not clearly defined in the act itself, its meaning was clearly understood by all involved. "Public interest" was a concept that developed over the previous century with regard to government oversight of the transportation and utility industries.[48] Its commonly understood meaning, incorporated into legislation and daily administration, was to protect the business interests of industries which, in turn, would protect public interests. Such was the case with the Radio Act of 1927, in which "public interest" and protection of the developing commercial broadcast industry went hand-in-hand. Further, efforts to protect noncommercial interests were ignored. In short, "the public interest was therefore being interpreted . . . as . . . preference for commercial stations, particularly those in the burgeoning network operations."[49] The Radio Act of 1927 was effective legislation. It admirably met the challenge of cleaning up the interference and wobbling problems faced by the radio industry. Although many broadcasters who lost their licenses challenged FRC decisions, the federal judiciary upheld the agency's conclusions virtually without fail. As far as the federal courts were concerned, the Radio Act was constitutional legislation and the FRC invariably exercised its authority fairly and legally.

Indeed, the 1927 act was so effective at taking control of the radio industry that President Franklin Roosevelt succeeded in giving the agency more far-reaching authority under the auspices of the Communications Act of 1934.[50] The Federal Radio Commission was transformed into the Federal Communications Commission and was given broad regulatory control over all forms of communication, including the broadcasting, telephone, and telegraph industries. Furthermore, the FCC was increased from five to seven members, all of whom were political appointments but no more than four of whom could be from the same political party. The newly-formed commission also had the power to grant, review and revoke licenses, and the 1934 act placed similarly strong importance on the concept of "public interest," as it specifically asserted that the "Commission may, consistent with the public interest, convenience, and necessity, make reasonable regulations."[51] At least in the broadcasting area, the 1934 act focused all of its administrative authority on local radio stations only and allowed the corporate interests to develop free of direct government interference. This aspect of the act was an indication of the power struggle between the public and the industry with the government caught in the middle.

Public versus Corporate Interests

The conflict of public versus corporate interests in the use of wireless, and then radio, existed virtually from the beginning of the technology's development in the United States. Although wireless was used primarily as a form of maritime communication in its earliest years in the United

States, by 1906 amateur use of wireless was gaining ground.[52] Many in the wireless industry lamented the problems caused by amateur use of the technology. The popular press published stories supporting such criticisms, such as amateurs interfering with distress calls. Although there is ample evidence to suggest that amateurs were as likely to be helpful as harmful,[53] the growing perception of amateur-as-nuisance was sufficient to create a public versus corporate opposition. When the Radio Act of 1912 was passed, part of its motivation in requiring government licensing was the growing belief that amateur operators, the non-industry users, could not be trusted to use the technology properly, which also accounted, in part, for the act's provision allowing the federal government to seize all wireless equipment during times of national emergency.

The public versus corporate conflict was further manifested in early criticisms of the developing commercial nature of radio broadcasting. The concept of advertising was introduced with the now-famous ten-minute description of life at the Hawthorne Court Apartments on New York City's WEAF in 1922. Soon thereafter Herbert Hoover, speaking at the First Radio Conference in 1922, asserted that "direct advertising was to be curbed."[54]

The public versus corporate conflict was further illustrated in the struggle over the future of the industry. In the earliest years of broadcasting many of the radio stations were licensed to educational institutions, particularly colleges and universities, who envisioned themselves as public servants and devoted their programming to educational material.[55] These stations were noncommercial and generally supported by the institution itself. Many other radio stations were entirely commercial in nature, particularly after 1922 and WEAF's demonstrated success at making money by selling air time.[56] Usually owned by either local businesses or, increasingly, by major corporations such as Sears & Roebuck, Westinghouse, General Electric, or RCA, the goal of these stations was to turn radio broadcasting into a profit-oriented industry. The more money they made, the more corporate interests guided their decisions. After an intense struggle between public/noncommercial and corporate/commercial interests to determine the future of the broadcasting industry, the Communications Act of 1934 all but solidified corporate America's control of the industry.[57]

As a result, the FCC was placed in the awkward position of both supporting both an inherently capitalist broadcasting industry while serving "the public interest" in its decision-making. The tensions faced by the FCC in attempting to serve both interests were clear from virtually the moment the Communications Act of 1934 was passed. Two cases in particular represent the public versus corporate tensions faced by the Commission. Although the practice of broadcast networking existed prior to 1934,[58] the Communications Act did not attempt to exert legislative authority over the corporate interests who developed networks. Stations that affiliated with a network (by 1939 that accounted for 75% of radio stations[59]) usually found themselves at the complete mercy of network programmers who essentially controlled the affiliate's airwaves. This put radio stations in an impossible position. The FCC expected stations to broadcast in the "public interest," but their network affiliation contract required them to all but relinquish control of their airwaves. The FCC was similarly caught in a regulatory net, since the Communications Act of 1934 did not give them any authority to regulate the networks yet simultaneously required them to administer the broadcasting industry in the "public interest." The conflict continued to escalate until the FCC, under the leadership of the controversial activist and New Dealer James Lawrence Fly, passed the 1941 Chain Broadcasting Rule, which indirectly but effectively limited network authority over broadcasting stations by creating strict policies regarding the network contracts local stations were allowed to sign. NBC, which had the most to lose if the Rule was allowed to stand, challenged the decision to the Supreme Court which ruled in favor of the FCC in 1943.[60] In this case the conflict between competing corporate and public interests was resolved in favor of the public, at least theoretically.

The opposite was true in the case of FM radio, in which the tensions between public and corporate interests were settled in favor of big business. FM (frequency modulation) radio was developed by Edwin Howard Armstrong, whose experiments were subsidized by RCA and its autocratic leader David Sarnoff. Armstrong publicly demonstrated FM for the first time in 1935.[61] The clarity of the FM transmissions was a vast improvement over the static-laden AM transmissions and all who heard the experiment were astounded by the purity of the sound. Sarnoff, however, although initially supportive of FM, eventually perceived it as a threat to his newest technological god-child, television. Moreover, as the FCC became involved in the development of both FM and television it became increasingly clear that both media competed for the same frequency space. The struggle for limited frequency allocations resulted in "a deadly personal feud" between Armstrong and Sarnoff, who had once been close friends.[62] The power RCA represented regarding both manufacturing FM radio sets and developing FM networks was considerable, and RCA pressured patent licensees not to manufacture radio sets that would receive FM frequencies. As far as frequency space was concerned,

Sarnoff "meant for television to have most of what would be available"[63] and he actively worked against Armstrong and the development of FM networks, affiliates, and radio sets.[64]

The FCC was also involved in the early stages of FM development, which it termed "high fidelity broadcasting," although only to the extent that it reserved frequencies for FM experimentation. In 1937 the commission asserted that "the interest in stations of this class has not continued to develop, a fact which may be attributed to the lack of receivers in the hands of the public that can be tuned to these frequencies,"[65] an early indication of the conflict between FM stations and manufacturers who refused to produce radios that could tune in the frequencies to which FM stations were assigned. The following year the FCC recognized the superior sound quality of FM transmissions but likewise noted with concern the greater bandwidths the new transmissions required, a difficulty that precluded the commission from establishing final frequency allocations for FM radio.[66] Even a year later, "finding that [FM] had developed to a stage where a regular service could safely be inaugurated, [the FCC] was confronted with the problem of finding sufficient space in the radio spectrum to accommodate this new service."[67] Finally in 1941 the commission established FM broadcasting in the 42 to 50 megacycle range of frequencies,[68] the frequencies that would have been Channel 1 in the VHF band. But the problem of FM was already clear. It required a considerable amount of frequency space to transmit a signal, which put it in direct competition with television for bandwidths. The FCC's obvious preference for the development of television was demonstrated when the commission reversed its ruling in 1945 and moved FM out of the 42 to 50 megacycle range and into the 88 to 108 megacycle range. The FCC then moved television in and issued the "go-ahead signal for expansion of black-and-white television service . . . in the 13 channels between 44 and 216 megacycles . . . allocated for commercial television."[69] The decision was a considerable blow to both Armstrong's Yankee Network of FM stations and, more importantly, to the thousands of listeners whose FM radio sets were rendered obsolete because they could not receive the new frequency range to which FM was assigned.

As the Chain Broadcasting Rule and the FM fiasco demonstrate, the FCC as an agency was deeply divided regarding its responsibilities. Commissioner Clifford Durr, whose position Frieda Hennock assumed in July 1948, expressed the dilemma well in a speech delivered to the National Lawyers Guild just prior to his departure from the FCC:

The beginning of all administrative agencies follows a somewhat similar pattern. An evil arises that needs correction and about which public feeling is aroused. . . . The legislative body moves in to correct the situation. It creates an administrative agency with power to act. It charges that agency with responsibility for seeing to it that the public's interest is protected. . . . The immediate evil is corrected. . . . The public sighs with relief and goes back to its daily business. . . , secure in the belief that it now has a champion and that its interests hereafter and forever more will be protected without further concern on its part.

The representatives of the industry that started it all reconcile themselves to their liking. . . . They have some problems of their own. Maybe their erstwhile enemy, the administrative agency, can be a friend after all and help them with their problems. . . . They begin to call on the agency more often—sometimes just for a friendly chat.

Gradually, somehow they begin to look a little like the "public" the legislature had in mind all along when it was legislating about the public interest, convenience and necessity. At least these are about the only members of the public the agency sees.[70]

When the FCC began to face the growing problems with the development of television broadcasting in the United States, they were an agency with divided loyalties. By federal law they were charged with serving public interests; with making decisions as the representatives of the public. In reality, however, the commission was inclined to allow the industry to play an active role in policy formation despite its responsibilities to both Congress and the American public. These were the kinds of pressures faced by the FCC as both the industry and America moved closer to the creation of a televised society. And this was the agency Frieda Hennock joined in June 1948.

The Development of Television

As early as 1935 the FCC began to struggle with the regulatory issues surrounding television. The first electronic television image was transmitted in 1927 when Philo T. Farnsworth, working without significant corporate support, produced the prophetic image of a dollar sign. Sarnoff and RCA attempted to wrestle the patent away from Farnsworth through litigation but were ultimately unsuccessful.[71] Failing that, RCA was forced to license the patent from Farnsworth and, at the 1939 World's Fair in New York City, demonstrated television in what was billed as "the first public demonstration."[72]

While the industry grappled with inventions and patents, the Federal Communications Commission struggled with setting basic standards for television broadcasting. Having simply established the seven channels in which television experimentation would take place, the FCC relied on the industry to experiment with and suggest transmission standards. The industry recommended standards as early as 1936,[73] but in 1939 the FCC continued to assert that the technology was not ready for standardization.[74] Finally in 1941 the commission established the technical standards of 525-lines of signal transmissions delivering 30 frames-per-second.[75] A small portion of the broadcast frequencies, channels 2 to 13 (54 to 216 MHz) in the very high frequency (VHF) range, were set aside for television broadcasting (the frequencies that would have been channel 1 were reserved for FM). Although early attempts were made to establish color television standards, the commission was convinced that color technology was insufficiently developed and, hence, standards were premature.[76] Television appeared to be well on its way to establishment when the United States entered World War II in December 1941 and the commercial development of the medium was halted.

When the war finally ended in 1945, television skyrocketed. The rapidity with which the medium was accepted in the United States was breathtaking. Four events had to happen simultaneously for the industry to fully develop: manufacturing, purchasing, programming, and licensing. Three of the four took place. Manufacturing was led by RCA, who held most of the significant television patents, and other smaller companies who licensed the patents through RCA and, hence, were dependent on the giant for their own manufacturing. The FCC estimated that by June 1947 approximately 300,000 television sets had been manufactured.[77] One year later the commission estimated that 50,000 television sets rolled off the production lines *per month*.[78] Early television sets were expensive, costing between $250 and $2500 a piece, with an average cost of around $300.[79] The cost of the average television is significant to understanding the unparalleled popularity of the new medium, since $300 represented *ten percent* of the average income of $3031 in 1947.[80] Nonetheless, postwar consumers purchased TV sets in droves. In the four-year-period from 1946 to 1950 the number of television sets in American homes increased from 8,000 to 3.8 million.[81] Yet, the TV sets were only useful if there was something to watch. Beginning in 1946 the four television networks,

ABC, CBS, DuMont, and NBC, began extremely limited network programming. The combination of these three events and the swiftness with which they occurred resulted in a virtual television explosion.

The weak link that endangered television was the lack of local television stations. Only six television stations were on the air in the United States in June 1947, with only 60 more companies granted construction permits (CPs).[82] One year later the FCC found itself coping with an "unprecedented surge in the number of applications for new TV stations."[83] One more station had gone on the air, 102 construction permits were on file, and 294 were pending.[84] The lack of television stations on the air had a domino effect. Although the networks owned and operated most of the television stations on the air in the so-called "TV cities,"[85] (those cities with licensed television stations, particularly New York City, Los Angeles, Washington, D.C., and Chicago), there were no television stations in the rest of the country with which to affiliate, which meant they could not adequately distribute their programming on a nationwide basis. Consumers in the "TV cities" eagerly bought television sets but found little to watch on them. Potential viewers in the rest of the country read about the antics of Milton Berle and impatiently waited to buy sets, but no local stations meant no programming. Manufacturers became concerned that television sales would slow once the saturation point in the "TV cities" was reached. Moreover, advertisers cautiously bought air time on the networks since their ads would be viewed in limited portions of the country. The FCC admitted that the unavailability of "television receivers, transmitters, cameras, and other associated equipment" was matched by the "increased public interest in visual radio [sic]."[86] The significant dilemma faced by the commission, for which they were unprepared, was that "the demand for television facilities was so much greater than the available allocated channels."[87] In short, the twelve channels reserved for television broadcasting, 54 to 216 MHz in the VHF, were insufficient to meet the "unprecedented" demand for television station licenses.

In fact, the desire for television licenses mirrored the unexpected demand for radio licenses twenty-five years earlier. Just as the radio broadcasting industry grew at a phenomenal pace in the early 1920s, so the television industry grew in the late 1940s. Unlike the Department of Commerce and Labor, which could do nothing except distribute broadcast licenses and search for ways to control the growth of the industry, the Federal Communications Commission had the regulatory authority to both recognize, contain, and repair the growing debacle. The commission did all three when it issued an order that became known as the "freeze" on 30 September 1948, which stopped the processing of television licenses until two fundamental and related problems could be resolved: interference and lack of sufficient frequencies reserved for television broadcasting. As the commission's engineers discovered, television signal transmissions were subject to both co-channel and adjacent-channel interference. Two stations licensed to broadcast from the same channel would experience co-channel interference if there was insufficient distance between the two stations (the distance varied depending upon the channel). Similarly, two stations licensed to broadcast from adjacent channels (2 and 3, 3 and 4, 4 and 5, 6 and 7, 7 and 8, etc.) would experience adjacent-channel interference unless there was a comfortable distance between the stations. Theoretically the problem could have been easily resolved by simply establishing adequate mileage between stations. In reality, however, the problems of co-channel and adjacent-channel interference were exacerbated by the fact that the FCC had reserved insufficient amount of frequency space for television broadcasting. The increasing requests for television licenses made it impossible to put enough distance between channel assignments because there were not enough channels with which to work. In short, there was too little space for too many demands. Consequently, the commission decided to freeze the licensing process until it could "find" more frequency space.

The "freeze" became one of the most controversial actions taken by the Federal Communications Commission. Interested parties of the television industry initially applauded and supported the commission's decision to suspend licensing, particularly since FCC Chair Wayne Coy predicted that the "freeze" would last only six to nine months.[88] Coy's prediction proved to be wildly imaginative. Within a short period of time it became clear that the "freeze" would probably last well beyond the anticipated June 1949 deadline. Following an engineering review by both FCC staff members and an Ad Hoc Committee composed of FCC, government, and industry engineers, the commission issued a *Notice of Further Proposed Rule Making* on 11 July 1949.[89] What was initially expected to be a straightforward "technical study"[90] blossomed into a full-fledged, exhaustive review. In addition to undertaking "an extensive revision" of its frequency allocation tables with particular attention to the utilization of the VHF and UHF channels,[91] the commission further invited "interested persons . . . to submit comments concerning the utilization of color television,"[92] despite the fact that just nine months earlier the FCC was advised that color television had not yet been sufficiently developed for commercial introduction.[93] Moreover, the commission's failure to mention noncommercial, educational broadcasting in the *Notice of Further*

Proposed Rule Making prompted Frieda Hennock to both issue a dissent criticizing the majority's shortsightedness and launch a campaign to persuade educators to petition the FCC for a hearing.[94] Consequently, three hearings had to be scheduled, one each for the color television issue, the allocation of VHF and UHF channels, and educational television. The six-to-nine month "freeze" eventually lasted nearly four years, a period during which the development of the television industry was artificially halted.

The entire commission was absorbed with the "freeze," including Frieda Hennock who joined the Commission only three months before the "freeze" was instituted. Barely four months before the "freeze" Hennock told her Senate subcommittee inquisitors that the only thing she knew about the broadcasting industry was that she raised funds to buy radio programs for Roosevelt's presidential campaigns, and during her FCC installation ceremony she deleted remarks about television and focused entirely on radio. Now faced with participating in momentous decisions regarding the future of television, Hennock had neither knowledge nor understanding of megacycles, interference, bandwidths, frequencies, propagation effects, or the transmission of television signals, but she effectively taught herself about electronics and engineering.[95] Witnesses who filed past the Federal Communications Commission over the next two years of hearings found their assumptions of a woman's ability to understand complex engineering principles challenged by Frieda Hennock. Those same hearings taught her the power of corporations involved in the television industry, particularly RCA, whose influence she initially did not fully appreciate. As a skilled student, she taught herself electronics. As a competent politician, she became well-versed in the capacity of broadcast corporations to prompt particular policy decisions. In all cases, she had to both quickly learn the intricacies of broadcast regulation and how to manipulate them in order to protect the development of educational television. Her first examinations came with the color television hearings.

NOTES

1. Hannegan to Truman, 15 October 1947, Box 645, OF 112–A (G-I), Harry S. Truman Presidential Library, (hereafter HST).

2. Fitzpatrick to Truman, 12 May 1948, Box 645, OF 112–A (G-I), HST.

3. Edwards to McGrath, 26 April 1948, Box 2, General Correspondence-1948, India Edwards Collection, HST.

4. Dawson to Hopkins, 22 May 1948, Box 643, OF Folder 112

(1945–1948), HST. The nomination received extensive press attention, especially in Hennock's home state of New York. For examples, see "N.Y. Woman is Named to FCC, Would Be First on the Board," *New York Herald-Tribune*, 24 May 1948, p. 1; "Truman Picks Lady Lawyer For FCC Post," *New York Journal-American*, 24 May 1948, p. 1; "Woman Lawyer Named to Commission Post," *Radio Daily New York City*, 25 May 1948, p. 1; "Boro Woman Lawyer Named to FCC Post," *Brooklyn Eagle*, 25 May 1948, p. 1; "Woman Nominated as Member of FCC," *New York Times*, 25 May 1948, p. 29; "Madam Commissioner," *Broadcasting*, 31 May 1948, p. 44. Friends believed that Franklin Roosevelt promised Hennock a federal judgeship. Since no judicial positions became available, Truman upheld Roosevelt's promise by appointing Hennock to the FCC. Richard Hull to Burt Harrison, Box 5, Folder 16, Burt Harrison Collection, Public Radio Oral History Project Series, National Public Broadcasting Archive, University of Maryland, College Park, MD, (hereafter Harrison Collection); Richard Hull to Jim Robertson, Series 1/Box 2/Folder 6, Jim Robertson Collection, Public Broadcasting Oral History Project, National Public Broadcasting Archives, University of Maryland, College Park, MD, (hereafter Robertson Collection).

5. U.S. Congress, House, Representative Charles Vursell of Illinois speaking against Frieda B. Hennock nomination to the FCC, 80th Cong., 2nd Session, *Congressional Record*, 1 June 1948, p. 6816.

6. Events leading to Republican support for Hennock seem to have followed this sequence: Dr. Armand Hammer, the wealthy industrialist, contacted Brigadier General Julius Klein, the National Commander of the Jewish War Veterans of the USA and a strong supporter of Senator Robert Taft. Klein agreed to support Hennock and contacted senators who played a key role in the FCC appointment decision, including Taft and Owen Brewster, who then supported the nomination among their colleagues. Brewster to Klein, 29 June 1948, Box 1/Folder 19, Frieda Hennock Simons collection, Schlesinger Library, Radcliffe College, Cambridge, MA, (hereafter FHS); Klein to Hammer, 1 July 1948, 1/19, FHS; Hawkes to Klein, 6 July 1948, 1/19, FHS; Klein to Dahlberg, 6 July 1948, 1/19, FHS; Taft to Klein 10 July 1948, 1/19, FHS; Klein to Hennock, 19 October 1948, 1/19, FHS.

7. The subcommittee consisted of Senators Homer Capehart (R-Indiana), Edwin Johnson (D-Colorado), and Owen Brewster (R-Maine), and was formed to consider Hennock's nomination to the FCC. Brewster to Hennock, 28 May 1948, Senate Files 80B–A3 Interstate and Foreign Commerce Committee, Executive Nominations: Frieda Hennock, National Archives and Records Administration.

8. Val Montanari, "First Woman Member of FCC Makes Impression on Senators With Frankness," *Washington Post*, 5 July 1948, p. 2; Laurence Eklund, "Portia on the FCC," *Milwaukee Journal*, 1 September 1948, p. 18; *Current Biography–1948*, p. 278.

9. Montanari, "First Woman Member," p. 2; Eklund, "Portia on the FCC," p. 18.

10. U.S. Congress, Senate, Senator Albert Hawkes of New Jersey speaking for Frieda Hennock nomination to the FCC, 80th Cong., 2nd Sess., *Congressional Record*, 17 June 1948, p. 8619; and U.S. Congress, Senate, Senator Brewster of Maine speaking for Frieda B. Hennock's nomination to the FCC, 80th Cong., 2nd Session, *Congressional Record*, 19 June 1948, p. 9169; "Lady Commissioner," *Broadcasting*, 28 June 1948, p. 62.

11. Taft to Klein, 10 July 1948, Box 893, Folder "Appointments, Executive 1948," Robert A. Taft Collection, Manuscript Division, Library of Congress (Hereafter RAT).

12. Ibid.

13. Taft to Hennock, 9 July 1948, HST Official File, Box 782–Endorsements, HST.

14. U.S. Congress, Senate, Senator Ball of Minnesota speaking against Frieda B. Hennock's nomination to the FCC, 80th Cong., 2nd Session, *Congressional Record*, 19 June 1948, pp. 9168–9169.

15. U.S. Congress, Senate, Senator Owen Brewster of Maine speaking for Frieda B. Hennock's nomination to the FCC, 80th Cong., 2nd Session, *Congressional Record*, 19 June 1948, p. 9169.

16. "Lady Commissioner," p. 25.

17. Ibid, p. 62.

18. Women employed in federal jobs increased 540.4% between 1939–1944. *Women in the Federal Service, 1923–1947, Part 1: Trends in Employment* (Washington, D.C.: U.S. Civil Service Commission, 1949), p. 17.

19. Ibid, p. 36.

20. *Women in the Federal Service, Part 11: Occupational Information* (Washington, D.C.: U.S. Civil Service Commission, 1950), p. 69.

21. Lucille Foster McMillin, *Women in the Federal Service*, (Washington, D.C.: U.S. Civil Service Commission, 1941), p. 44.

22. Brewster to Klein, 29 June 1948, 1/19, FHS.

23. Neustadt to Robertson, Series 1/Box 2/Folder 20, Robertson Collection.

24. U.S. Congress, House, Committee on Appropriations, Hearings Regarding Goodwin B. Watson, William E. Dodd, Jr., and Robert Morss Lovett, 78th Congress, 1st Sess.

25. Neustadt to Robertson, Series 1/Box 2/Folder 20, Robertson Collection.

26. Hennock to Taft, 25 June 1948, Box 893, Folder-Appointments/Executive 1948, RAT; Taft to Hennock, 9 July 1948, Box 782, Folder 208I-Endorsements, HST Official File, HST.

27. Notecard #12 of Installation Ceremony Speech, FHS 7/95; and "The First," *Time*, 7 July 1948, pp. 92, 94.

28. Eklund, "Portia on the FCC," p. 18.

29. The Federal Communications Commission enjoys regulatory authority over all forms of broadcast and electronic communication, including the telephone, telegraph, broadcasting, cable, and satellite industries. For the purposes of this book I confined myself to the broadcast industry.

30. 36 Stat. 629 (24 June 1910); see also Susan Douglas, *Inventing American Broadcasting, 1899–1922*, (Baltimore, MD: The Johns Hopkins University Press, 1987); Frank J. Kahn, *Documents of American Broadcasting*, (Englewood Cliffs, NJ: Prentice-Hall, Inc., 1984).

31. Isolated experiments in voice transmissions occurred prior to 1910, most notably Reginald Fessenden's 1906 Christmas and New Years' transmissions, and the "Doc" Herrold's regular broadcasts in California. These were isolated experiments, however. The vast majority of wireless transmissions were point-to-point Morse Code.

32. See Erik Barnouw, *A Tower in Babel* (New York: Oxford University Press, 1966); Louise Benjamin, "Radio Regulation in the 1920s: Free Speech Issues in the Development of Radio and the Radio Act of 1927" (Ph.D. diss., University of Iowa, 1985); Douglas, *Inventing American Broadcasting*; Robert B. Horowitz, *The Irony of Regulatory Reform: The Deregulation of American Telecommunications* (New York: Oxford University Press, 1989); Kahn, *Documents of American Broadcasting*; Lucas A. Powe, *American Broadcasting and the First Amendment* (Berkeley, CA: University of California Press, 1987); Christopher Sterling and John Kittross, *Stay Tuned: A Concise History of American Broadcasting* (Belmont, CA: Wadsworth Publishing, 1990).

33. Radio Act of 1912, 37 Stat. 302 (13 December 1912); 47 USC 51, 52.

34. The legislators who passed the 1912 Radio Act likely did not realize the import of their decision; they had no way of knowing that the technology known as "wireless" would eventually transform into "broadcasting," consequently they did not know they were setting the stage for government regulation of a form of mass communication. In any case, the 1912 Act eventually proved problematic since the Department of Commerce and Labor could do nothing more than distribute licenses to virtually anyone who requested one.

35. Dr. Frank Conrad, an engineer with Westinghouse Corp., is historically credited with transforming "wireless" into "broadcasting," operating out of Pittsburgh, PA. He received the first commercial radio broadcasting license in 1920 and operated on station KDKA. Westinghouse eventually built a station for Conrad and took over operations of KDKA.

36. Barnouw, *A Tower in Babel*, p. 104.

37. Barnouw, *A Tower in Babel*; Louise Benjamin, "Working It Out Together: Radio Policy from Hoover to the Radio Act of 1927," *Journal of Broadcasting and Electronic Media* 42 (Spring 1998): 221–236; Thomas Hazlett, "The Rationality of U.S. Regulation of the Broadcast Spectrum," *Journal of Law and Economics* 33 (April 1990): 133–175.

38. Benjamin, "Radio Regulation," and "Working it Out Together;" Barnouw, *A Tower in Babel*; Daniel E. Garvey, "Secretary Hoover and the Quest for Broadcast Regulation," *Journalism History* 3 (Autumn 1976): 66–69; Robert W. McChesney, *Telecommunications, Mass Media, & Democracy: The Battle for the Control of U.S. Broadcasting, 1928–1935* (New York: Oxford University Press, 1993); Walter B. Emery, *Broadcasting and Government: Responsibilities and*

Regulations (Michigan State University Press, 1971); Willard D. Rowland, "The Meaning of 'The Public Interest' in Communications Policy, Part II: Its Implementation in Early Broadcast Law and Regulation," *Communication Law and Policy* 2: 363–396.

39. The concept of "public interest" was introduced during the First Radio Conference, was endorsed during the Third Radio Conference, and became the "basis for broadcasting" during the Fourth Radio Conference. See Benjamin, "Working it Out Together."

40. See Benjamin, "Radio Regulation" and "Working it Out Together;" Garvey, "Secretary Hoover;" and Emery, *Broadcasting and Government.*

41. See Hoover v. Intercity Radio, 52 AppDC 339, 286 Fed 1003; U.S. v. Zenith Radio Corp., 12 F2d 614.

42. 35 Ops Att'y Gen 126. See also Kahn, *Documents of American Broadcasting*, p. 34.

43. The patents pool created in 1919 and involving RCA, Westinghouse, General Electric, and AT&T, was dissolved in 1926. Out of the corporate rubble rose an even more powerful RCA, which undertook the operation of the new NBC radio networks. See Federal Communications Commission, *Report on Chain Broadcasting*, (Washington, D.C.: GPO, 1941); Robert Sobel, *RCA* (New York: Stein and Day, 1986).

44. Coolidge's message to Congress, H.R. Doc. 483, 69th Cong., 2nd Sess. (7 December 1926); see also Kahn, *Documents of American Broadcasting*, p. 36.

45. Radio Act of 1927, 44 Stat. 1162 (23 January 1927).

46. The explanation of the Radio Act of 1927 provided here is meant to serve as a general introduction to the Communications Act of 1934. For a more detailed explanation of the 1927 Act and its regulatory significance, see Barnouw, *A Tower in Babel*; Benjamin, "Radio Regulation" and "Working it Out Together;" R. Terry Ellmore, *Broadcasting Law and Regulation* (Blue Ridge Summit, PA: Tab Books, Inc., 1982); Emery, *Broadcasting and Government*; Garvey, "Secretary Hoover;" James Herring and Gerald Gross, *Telecommunications: Economics and Regulation* (New York: McGraw-Hill, 1936); Horowitz, *The Irony of Regulatory Reform*; McChesney, *Telecommunication*; and Powe, *American Broadcasting.*

47. 44 Stat. 1162

48. Willard D. Rowland, "The Meaning of 'Public Interest' in Communications Policy, Part I: Its Origins in State and Federal Legislation," *Communication Law and Policy* 2: 309–328.

49. Willard D. Rowland, "The Meaning of 'Public Interest' in Communications Policy, Part II: Its Implementation in Early Broadcast Law and Regulation," *Communication Law and Policy* 2: 328.

50. Communications Act of 1934, 48 Stat. 1064, 47 USC 151. Again, this is intended to be a review of the 1934 Act. For more detailed analyses and/or explanations, see Barnouw, *A Tower in Babel*; Ellmore, *Broadcasting Law and Regulation*; Emery, *Broadcasting and Government*; Horowitz, *The Irony of*

Regulatory Reform; McChesney; *Telecommunications*; and William B. Ray, *FCC: The Ups and Downs of Radio-TV Regulation* (Ames, IA: Iowa State University Press, 1990).

51. 48 Stat. 1064, 47 USC §302a. Several sections of the 1934 Communications Act further mandate regulation and operation in the "public interest, convenience and necessity" (PICN). See also, 47 USC §303 which outlines the powers and duties of the Commission, 47 USC §307a which stipulates that licenses must be granted in the PICN, 47 USC §309a asserts that the PICN must be considered when granting license applications, and 47 USC §316 requires the PICN be addressed when station modifications or CPs are granted.

52. Douglas, *Inventing American Broadcasting*.

53. Ibid.

54. Benjamin, "Working it Out Together," p. 222.

55. See McChesney, *Telecommunications*; Barnouw, *A Tower in Babel*.

56. Ibid.

57. For an excellent detailed analysis of the struggle between public and corporate interests in broadcasting, see McChesney, *Telecommunications*.

58. NBC operated two separate networks beginning in 1926 and the CBS network began operation in 1927. Federal Communications Commission, *Report on Chain Broadcasting*.

59. Ibid.

60. NBC v. U.S. 319 US 190 (1943).

61. Barnouw, *A Tower in Babel*; Don Erickson, *Armstrong's Fight for FM Broadcasting: One Man vs. Big Business and Bureaucracy* (Tuscaloosa, AL: The University of Alabama Press, 1973).

62. Kenneth Bilby, *The General: David Sarnoff and the Rise of the Communications Industry* (New York: Harper & Row Publishers, 1986), p. 4.

63. Sobel, *RCA*, p. 129.

64. Ibid.

65. Federal Communications Commission, *Third Annual Report of the Federal Communications Commission* (Washington, D.C.: GPO, 1937), p. 38.

66. Federal Communications Commission, *Fourth Annual Report of the Federal Communications Commission* (Washington, D.C.: GPO, 1939).

67. Federal Communications Commission, *Sixth Annual Report of the Federal Communications Commission* (Washington, D.C.: GPO, 1940).

68. Federal Communications Commission, *Seventh Annual Report of the Federal Communications Commission* (Washington, D.C.: GPO, 1941).

69. Federal Communications Commission, *Thirteenth Annual Report of the Federal Communications Commission* (Washington, D.C.: GPO, 1947), p. 25.

70. Clifford Durr, "The Voice in Democracy: Radio Frequencies Are Not Private Property," *Vital Speeches of the Day* 14 (1 May 1948): 444.

71. Bilby, *The General*.

72. Ibid.

73. Federal Communications Commission, *First Annual Report of the*

Federal Communications Commission (Washington, D.C.: GPO, 1936).

74. Federal Communications Commission, *Fifth Annual Report of the Federal Communications Commission* (Washington, D.C.: GPO, 1940).

75. Federal Communications Commission, *Seventh Annual Report*.

76. Ibid.

77. Federal Communications Commission, *Thirteenth Annual Report*, p. 23.

78. Federal Communications Commission, *Fourteenth Annual Report of the Federal Communications Commission* (Washington, D.C.: GPO, 1948), p. 39.

79. Ibid; U.S. Department of Commerce, Bureau of the Census, *Statistical Abstracts of the United States, 71st Edition* (Washington, D.C.: Government Printing Office, 1950), p. 818.

80. U.S. Department of Commerce, Bureau of the Census, *Historical Statistics of the United States, Part I* (Washington, D.C.: Government Printing Office, 1976), p. 296

81. U.S. Department of Commerce, Bureau of the Census, *Historical Statistics of the United States, Part II* (Washington, D.C.: Government Printing Office, 1976), p. 796.

82. A construction permit (CP) is the first step in starting a broadcast station. The FCC first issues a CP granting permission to build the broadcast facilities; then, once the station is built and outfitted, actually licenses the station for operation.

83. Federal Communications Commission, *Fourteenth Annual Report*, p. 37.

84. Ibid.

85. George Lipsitz, "The Meaning of Memory: Family, Class and Ethnicity in Early Network Television," *Cultural Anthropology* 4 (1986): 355–387.

86. Federal Communications Commission, *Fourteenth Annual Report*, p. 37.

87. Ibid.

88. Rufus Crater, "Television Freeze," *Broadcasting*, 4 October 1948, p. 22A. See also, "TV Freeze," *Broadcasting* (11 October 1948): 28; Rufus Crater, "TV Faces Crisis," *Broadcasting*, 13 September 1948, p. 21; Rufus Crater, "TV Processing," *Broadcasting*, 20 September 1948, p. 21; Rufus Crater and Larry Christopher, "TV Expansion," *Broadcasting*, 27 September 1948, p. 21.

89. *First Report of the Commission*, 41 FCC 4. (1 September 1950).

90. "TV Freeze," p. 28.

91. Ibid.

92. *First Report of the Commission*, p. 4.

93. Ibid.

94. *Notice of Further Proposed Rule Making*, FCC 49–948, 11 July 1949.

95. See Martha Millspaugh, "Miss Commissioner Hennock," *Baltimore Sun*, 8 August 1948, p. A5; and Eklund, "Portia on the FCC," p. 18.

CHAPTER 3

A Noteworthy Dissent: The Color Television Decision

There is a charming scene in the film *Avalon* in which a 1940s era family, surrounded by extended family members, eagerly brings home its first television set. So excited are they all to "watch television," they sit mesmerized in front of a black-and-white screen from which the Indian Chief test-pattern emanates. While America was just starting its love affair with television in the fall of 1949, government and industry leaders were looking to the future of the medium. Over the next year they met in New York City, Washington, D.C., and San Francisco to watch and evaluate color television. While a relatively small portion of the American public sat before their black-and-white sets and enjoyed the spectacle of Milton Berle, an even smaller coterie analyzed a model's "life-like" skin tones or the "realistic" hues of a vase of flowers. Within a year the government leaders made a momentous decision by selecting one of the three competing color television technologies as the industry standard.

The lone female among the appraisers was Frieda Hennock, who approached the color television decision with equal parts of devotion to serving both public and personal interests. Hennock had been at her post for only fifteen months when it began the color television hearings. When the decision was released in the *First Report of the Commission* (September 1950), she distinguished herself as the only dissenting opinion against selection of the CBS color system as the industry standard. Reactions to her position drew surprise. Shortly after release of the *Second Report of the Commission* (October 1950), in which Hennock took a stronger stand against the CBS color system, the *Boston Sunday Post* claimed that "there is no question but Miss Hennock has been some-

what of a surprise to her male colleagues on the commission."[1] Stanley
Neustadt, her legal assistant, was similarly astonished that she voted
against CBS.[2] Her position seemed to defy what most at the commission
believed was "common sense"; she appeared to support an industry attitude motivated by profitability. Her stand against the CBS color system
was prompted, however, by a commitment to both personal and public
interests.

It is tempting to valorize Hennock for being the sole dissenting voice,
for presciently recognizing that the "right" color system was RCA's compatible color technology, yet her motivations for supporting compatible
television had nothing to do with "taking sides" with RCA and most of
the television industry. Despite the fact that RCA lagged far behind CBS
in research and development, it was clear to Hennock that the "compatible" system was the only one that wouldn't disserve more than 7 million
television set owners. Equally as important, however, was the fact that the
CBS system threatened the possibility of educational television, the creation and development to which Hennock was deeply devoted and which
represented her political aspirations. So while her color television dissent
may appear, at first glance, to represent brilliant foresight, this is twenty-
twenty hindsight. She could not have known that hostilities in Korea
would temporarily slow the development of television technology, thereby giving RCA the time it needed for further theoretical development.
Nor could she have known that television manufacturers would simply
ignore the FCC's decision establishing incompatible color as the standard
and, in 1953, eventually force the Agency to recognize what the industry
used instead: RCA compatible color. Indeed, as Hennock later testified,
industry refusal to comply with the FCC color decision resulted in the
commission "spen[ding] many months of hearings [that were] worthless."[3] Instead, her position was motivated by the twin desires of representing public interests, as both her personality and the Communications
Act of 1934 directed her to do, and expressing her own political preoccupations.

THE FCC AND COLOR TELEVISION TECHNOLOGY

The path to the color television hearings began as early as 1940 when
CBS first demonstrated a color television prototype.[4] The following year,
during hearings to establish general television technical standards, the
FCC again considered, and withheld judgment on, color television.[5] In
1945, CBS requested that the FCC further evaluate its technology as the
standard for the industry. In response, the agency urged both CBS and

RCA, which joined the 1945 hearings, to continue with research and development, but again refused to establish color television standards.[6] Believing its color system was ready for implementation, CBS again requested that the FCC create color standards on 27 September 1946.[7] This time the agency seemed more inclined to acquiesce to CBS' demands, perhaps because of the encouragement of influential people. Two years later when the commission issued the "freeze,"[8] it asserted that among the decisions that must be made before the television industry could progress was the selection of a color television standard.

The urgency the commission suddenly placed on the color decision, evidenced by placing it first among the decisions to be made during the "freeze," was likely the result of a combination of events. In 1947 Wayne Coy was appointed as Chair of the FCC. Coy was formerly an executive with the Washington Post Company in charge of operating the organization's radio stations, some of which were affiliated with CBS.[9] It is possible that Coy joined the FCC with an inclination to help his former company, and equally possible that "as the commission's chairman, Coy began to give [CBS President Peter Goldmark] everything he had hoped for."[10] Coy's apparent eagerness to establish color television standards may have been matched by commissioner Robert Jones' enthusiasm for the technology. Following a trip to the Midwest where he witnessed a demonstration of the CBS color system, Jones became an enthusiastic supporter of color TV and "made enough of a fuss" about it to persuade his fellow commissioners to establish hearings to set a color standard. He was later described as "leading the group in the commission that favored the CBS color system."[11] Finally, Senator Edwin C. Johnson (D-Colorado), the chair of the Senate Interstate and Foreign Commerce Committee and known for playing an active role in the commission's affairs, was a particularly strong supporter of color television and frequently pressured agency members to make a decision as quickly as possible.[12] Attempting to jump-start the commission, which Johnson believed seemed "reluctant to indicate when and if it will act with respect to authorizing commercial licensing of color,"[13] into making a decision on color television, the Senator formed a committee to investigate the possibilities of color television. The so-called Condon Committee delivered its final report only six weeks before the FCC issued its decision in the *First Report and Order*, and did not provide any more information than that collected during the FCC's hearings. Nonetheless, Johnson made it clear, through the auspices of the Condon Committee, that he wanted color television *immediately*.

If Coy, Jones, Johnson, and CBS were ardent advocates of the FCC color hearings, there were opponents to them as well. One of the most vocal adversaries was RCA, whose color television technology, although theoretically promising, was far from ready for actual demonstration. Further, as RCA's critics loudly claimed, the company wanted to delay the development of color television as long as possible until the market for black-and-white sets was saturated.[14] Since RCA held the patent rights for nearly every aspect of television technology, it stood to make tremendous financial profits from both the sale of its own television sets as well as the royalties collected from other television manufacturers utilizing RCA patents. As an internal FCC document explained, RCA was in a sound position to recoup its research and development expenses for black-and-white television through patent licensing, but the company wasn't "ready to go forward with color television from a patent viewpoint."[15] Despite its unwillingness to participate, RCA was forced to respond to CBS' attempts to establish its color system as the standard.

Finally, there were some individuals—Frieda Hennock among them—who just didn't see what all of the fuss was about. When the color television hearings began in September 1949, television had been available to the general public for little more than three years. There was relatively little regularly-scheduled programming available, and that was generally confined to the evening hours. With only 7 million television sets in U.S. homes at the time of the "freeze," television viewing had not yet become the standard diet of virtually everyone in the country. Although the public clamored for television, they seemed perfectly satisfied with black-and-white reception, just as they were satisfied with black-and-white motion pictures despite the decades-old development of color in films.[16] Hennock may have been speaking for many people when she said, "Why they made such an issue of color, I do not know."[17] But an issue it became and, on 26 September 1949, the FCC opened hearings during which they listened to witnesses testify to the merits and/or shortcomings of the three color television systems from which the agency had to select a standard.

COMPETING COLOR TELEVISION TECHNOLOGIES

The fundamentals of the competing color television technologies must be investigated in order to understand many of the issues at stake during the hearings. Three color television systems received the lion's share of the FCC's attention during the hearings, developed by CBS (often referred to as the Columbia system), RCA, and CTI (Color Television, Incorporated, based out of San Francisco). Each system, by 1949, had its own merits and problems.

The CBS color system was the furthest developed and had been successfully demonstrated in tests throughout the country.[18] The CBS technology utilized a camera that sequentially scanned an image (or field) through a spinning disk composed of blue, red, and green filters.[19] Each scanned image was transmitted to a receiver. The transmissions occurred so rapidly, however, that the human eye never detected them, assuming the disk was properly synchronized. The so-called "field sequential" system reliably transmitted accurate color images, but there was one significant problem. It was incompatible with the existing television standards that were developed by the FCC in 1941, one of which established that all television images were to be composed of 525 lines of electronic visual information. CBS' field sequential system transmitted color images on 405 lines, thereby making it incompatible with all of the contemporary television technology (television sets, cameras, studio equipment, etc.). While this incompatibility became a significant issue during the hearings, the CBS color system was nonetheless the only one that consistently performed well during both public and FCC demonstrations.

RCA developed a much different color television system. Unlike the CBS system, which utilized a spinning disk that scanned sequential fields of color, the RCA system was entirely electronic. Color tubes and mirrors (blue, red and green) scanned images as "dots" of information, then transmitted them to a receiver which re-created the "dots" into a color picture.[20] Again, the transmission occurred so rapidly that it appeared as a "real" picture to the human eye. Better yet, the RCA system transmitted pictures at 525 lines, making it "compatible" with the existing television standards. As many engineers testified during the hearings, the RCA "dot sequential" system was elegant and technologically sophisticated. Perhaps it was a bit too complex for its own good, however. Indeed, calling it a color "system" assumes that an entire, workable electronic process existed, which was not the case. When the hearings began in September 1949, RCA's engineers successfully developed discrete parts of the whole, but were still unable to produce a color transmitter and receiver that would live up to its theoretical promise.

Finally, a third company often ignored in explanations of the entire color television debacle was CTI, Color Television, Inc. Unlike CBS and RCA, CTI was formed solely to develop color television technology. Under the CTI system, a color television image was created by a camera scanning entire lines of electronic information, hence the "line sequential" color system.[21] Although CTI's system was theoretically "compatible," since it transmitted a 525–line image, the company was further behind in research and development than RCA, being unable, during any of the public or FCC demonstrations, to transmit a clear, color picture.[22]

Regardless of which technology was selected to be the industry standard, the immediate potential financial impact on the American buying public was significant. The degree to which a consumer's finances would be strained varied between color systems, and depended upon how desperately the individual wanted color pictures. In this regard three terms became prevalent during the hearings: adaptability, convertibility, and compatibility. Adaptability allowed black-and-white receivers to receive a black-and-white picture from a color transmission, but required an adaptor. An adaptor was needed only if the CBS system was selected, since it was incompatible with existing television technical standards. Convertibility allowed black-and-white receivers to convert a black-and-white picture to a color one. Again, however, a special converter was needed to accomplish this until color television sets could be manufactured. Finally, compatibility meant that a black-and-white television set could receive a black-and-white picture despite the fact that the picture was transmitted in color. This is what the RCA system promised to eventually deliver, and what the CBS system could never achieve.

HENNOCK AND THE COLOR HEARINGS

The stakes were high, then, when the color hearings portion of Docket 8736 got under way on 26 September 1949. The commissioners, witnesses and their interlocutors, and interested spectators gathered in the wood-paneled room of the Department of Commerce building where daily hearings began around 10:00 a.m. Sessions recessed for lunch around 12:30 p.m. and resumed at 2:00 p.m. for an afternoon session that generally lasted until around 5:00 p.m. The congregants listened to engineers, executives, and other assorted experts profess their color system to be the best and their opponents' the worst.

By September 1949 Hennock had been on the commission for fifteen months. In that short period of time the two guiding principles of her life had already manifested themselves: a devotion to serving public interests and an equally powerful dedication to serving her own political interests. They were inextricably bound. The clearest manifestation of these inspirations was Hennock's campaign for educational television (ETV). Following a visit to the Institute for Education by Radio and Television (IERT) in May 1949, Hennock settled on ETV as the cause that would satisfy her personal drive to secure both public and political interests. In the July 1949 *Notice of Further Proposed Rulemaking*, she dissented from the majority opinion by asserting that television channels ought to be set aside for strictly educational use.[23] Immediately thereafter a flood of letters left her office encouraging educators to express their interests in educational television to the FCC. It was clear that Hennock would present herself as a vocal proponent of the public, and loudly proclaim herself to be their protector. As a result, the ETV campaign became central to Hennock's participation in the color decision. When the color hearings initiated in September 1949, Hennock's campaign for ETV was well underway and she was devoted to creating and developing noncommercial, educational television. As the "white horse"[24] that could establish her national political reputation, she zealously and jealously guarded ETV against all potential threats. And color television became a potential threat. Although the color hearings temporarily diverted Hennock's direct attention from ETV issues, they nonetheless remained central to her approach to the color television hearings, as is evident in her cross-examination of witnesses.

While her devotion to personal interests is evident in the hearings, the dominant theme of her concerns centered on the public and the impact the color television decision would have on "the grass roots."[25] The quintessential New Deal Democrat, she was most interested in communal interests rather than corporate or elitist ones. Attending nearly all of the hearings, Frieda Hennock focused her attentions on asking questions that would enable her to protect three things: the public interest, educational television, and her own political interests.

"Public Interest" and Color Television

Nearly everyone who attended the color hearings had an agenda. Some were overt, such as CBS, RCA, and CTI who wanted to persuade the FCC to select their color technology to be the industry standard. Others were covert, such as the possibility that commissioners Coy and Jones were predisposed to select the CBS system. Frieda Hennock's principal agenda was representing and protecting the one group that had no direct voice in the hearings, but in whose interest the commission was charged to serve: the public. She consistently served as the voice of public concerns by seeking answers to a series of specific questions: (1) When will color be ready, (2) Is color television important enough to warrant the significant changes demanded of the industry and public, (3) What are the problems and costs involved with adaptors and converters, (4) What are the issues involved with compatibility and incompatibility, and (5) Why can't the competing companies work together? In each instance, Hennock frequently questioned witnesses for lengthy periods of time, alternately cajoling and badgering them to explain how the system they supported would serve the public. The answers often displeased her.

Such was particularly the case when she tried to learn from witnesses when color TV sets would be available for the public to buy. Witnesses, especially those associated with RCA, were loathe to answer this question. They did not want to commit either themselves or their company to setting a date when color would be ready, especially since many people believed television manufacturers wanted to saturate the market with black-and-white television sets first. Hennock, of course, wanted to know how quickly consumers would be able to buy sets after the commission established standards. Her questions were largely motivated by the knowledge that 7 million television sets were already in American living rooms and, as the hearings progressed, it became very clear that manufacturers were producing hundreds of thousands more TVs every month. At that rate, millions more black-and-white sets would be glowing in a relatively short period of time. Since there was a possibility that the CBS system might be selected as the industry standard, every set that rolled off the assembly line compounded the incompatibility problem. Consequently, she asked probing questions, such as those she directed toward W.B. Sullinger during a lengthy session. "I just want to know how soon you will get [color TV] built and how soon the broadcasters will have the service if you are serious about it. If you are, that is all I want to know, and just give me some dates. That is all I am trying to get out, I made that clear. We just want dates."[26]

As frequently happened when Hennock questioned witnesses, the relationship became tense. Hennock's well-developed cross-examination abilities, honed from her years as both a defense attorney for underprivileged clients and a litigator for corporate interests, were effective strategies to elicit information from witnesses. As a friend later explained, "she would take in the bottom line and know the man's weakness and keep on asking the hard questions."[27] Such was the case when she pressed David B. Smith of Philco to reveal "how many [color] sets will you produce in the next six months? How many are you planning to produce?"[28] Dissatisfied with his responses, her questions became protracted and pointed. Finally, Smith proclaimed that "If I have not been able to reassure you by this time, Miss Hennock, I don't believe I can." She responded, "You have not."[29]

During the several months through which the color hearings were held, Hennock asked the same question repeatedly: "when will color be ready?" Whether the witness was an individual representing his own small company, such as S.W. Gross, or someone representing an association of television manufacturers, such as R.M. Baker of the Radio Manufacturers Association (RMA), or an engineer such as Elmer Engstrom of RCA, or the head of a major corporation such as David Sarnoff of RCA,[30] her question remained the same. Deeply suspicious of their responses to provide color television in "the future" and the motivations for those answers, in exasperation she claimed that "There are various definitions of future here. Columbia says they have color today. RCA says next year, and DuMont says ten to twenty years."[31] Despite her persistence, she was dissatisfied with industry responses to her insistence on knowing when color would be ready. She remained convinced, however, that color had to be made available as quickly as possible. As she wrote in her separate opinion when the commission made its decision, "it is imperative that the problem posed by the great number of black-and-white receivers . . . be contained at its present level,"[32] which could be accomplished by producing color television sets quickly.

While Hennock pressed hard to find out when color would "be ready," she was unconvinced that the technology was important enough or sufficiently developed to warrant either the color hearings or the logistical nightmare of switching from a black-and-white standard to a color one. The color hearings, she believed, were an unnecessary distraction from the more important tasks of allocating television channels nationwide, reserving 25% of those channels for noncommercial educational use and ending the "freeze."[33] She was likewise skeptical that color television was important enough to cope with the problems and costs of converting to a color broadcasting standard, and was likely speaking for millions of people when she later explained, with a small measure of sarcasm, that "I had a small apartment, I paid for my black and white set . . . I was minding my own business when CBS came along with their great color system."[34] The black-and-white set, it seems, was sufficient for her viewing needs. Consequently, she occasionally asked witnesses such as Leopold Kay of CBS whether color television was "sufficiently superior to a black-and-white to warrant the cost of conversion?"[35] Engineers and executives waxed eloquent in their descriptions of the visual wonders of color television. Their rhetoric fell on deaf ears, however, as Hennock continued to believe that color television was highly overrated. As far as she was concerned, "the public cannot want what they have not seen yet, can they?"[36] Finally, to illustrate her point that the industry clamored for a technology about which the public may have been ambivalent, Hennock turned to FM radio for example. Although introduced in 1933, the general public seemed only marginally interested in the technology. During the hearings,

Hennock declared that she was "worried about what happened to FM, for instance. Is that what is going to happen to color?" [37]

Hennock's concerns regarding public interest were demonstrated in her demands to know when color would be ready and whether the switch was really that important, and this was equally the case with queries regarding the problems and costs involved with adapting and/or converting existing black-and-white television sets. At the time of the hearings, more than 7 million television sets had taken up residence in American homes. Regardless of which color system was selected, consumers would likely have to purchase an additional apparatus to continue to watch their TV. If the CBS system was selected, whose 405-line transmission would not be received by existing television sets, viewers would have to buy an adaptor which would modify the 405-line transmission to a 525-line television. In other words, the adaptor would enable their black-and-white TV set to broadcast a monochrome picture. Without the adaptor, it was a useless piece of 1950s high-tech junk. A converter was necessary if the viewer wanted a color picture, since it would convert a black-and-white television set into a color set. Without a converter, the picture would remain monochrome. Clearly the selection of a color system would require the public to spend more money, in addition to the cost of the television set, to adapt and/or convert it.

Hennock focused considerable attention on this issue while cross-examining witnesses during the color hearings. She asked C.P. Cushway of CBS whether he or his organization "consider[ed] the public demand for these converters? Did you think they were something that the public would be interested in?"[38] George Sleeper of CTI, who admitted that converters would be expensive, motivated Hennock to question him whether "in view of the high cost of your converter, what is to happen to the . . . television sets there will be in circulation by the end of this year?"[39] Drawing an analogy from FM radio again, for which converters were necessary to enable AM radios to receive FM signals as well, Hennock asked Milton Shapp of CBS whether he remembered "the many complaints that we brought home to you people in the trade about converters . . . and their inefficiency?" and continued that "What I am concerned about is that perhaps this adaptor you speak of will cause the same kind of trouble [as the FM adaptor caused] to the present [TV] set owner."[40] Finally, thinking in practical terms and making the point that crystallized the adaptor/converter dilemma, Hennock explained that "If we have one converter to take UHF into a VHF set, that is one. Then if we have to have color converters, that is 2."[41]

Although the problems inherent to adaptors and converters were significant, and certainly were relevant to public concerns, the issue of compatibility became central to Hennock's questioning. Compatibility was a term used throughout the hearings to refer to whether a color system was congruent with the existing television standards. The CBS system was considered incompatible since its color signal was transmitted through 405 lines of electronic information. As a result, all 7 million television sets in the country would be unable to receive the CBS transmission. The RCA system was compatible, consequently a black-and-white television set would still receive the signal. The public concerns were clear. If the FCC selected the CBS color system as the industry standard, which seemed possible since it was the obvious frontrunner regarding advanced development and actual demonstrations, then there wasn't a single home television set that would receive the broadcast. Conversely, although the RCA system was *theoretically* compatible, the company would provide no guarantees that the system would, ultimately, work or even when it would be ready. Faced with the dilemma of trying to select between the lesser of two evils, Hennock tried to find ways of coping with the problem of compatibility that would satisfy public interests.

One such strategy concentrated on whether the incompatibility problem might eventually be resolved through further research and development. In questioning Peter Goldmark of CBS, Hennock asked whether, given the improvements already made in the CBS system, it will "not be possible to continue to improve your system to eradicate and eliminate the incompatibility of it? In other words, will it not be possible to increase your 405-line black-and-white picture?"[42] Although considered by some to be an electronics genius, Goldmark doubted this could happen. She even asked Elmer Engstrom of RCA, CBS' primary competitor, whether there was "no way of overcoming the issue of [CBS] incompatibility?"[43] Approaching the problem from the opposite perspective, a second plan for coping with the incompatibility problem focused on ceasing production of television sets. As Hennock saw it, the thousands of sets rolling off of production lines only exacerbated the problem since all of them were incompatible with the CBS color system. As she put it to David Sarnoff of RCA, "Do you think the industry is messing things up by producing that many black-and-white [potentially incompatible] sets?"[44] From her perspective, the problem could be solved if RCA, and every other manufacturer who used RCA's patents, simply stopped producing its television sets and started producing sets with CBS color technology. While it may have been an idealistic position to take, one can easily imagine a consumer grumbling about giant corporations more interested in "making a buck" than making a decision in the public's interest.

Her desire to find a solution to the compatibility problem is nowhere better demonstrated than in the zeal with which she promoted multiple standards or, as they were called in the final FCC report, bracket standards. During the hearings she asked Elmer Engstrom of RCA whether he could "visualize a set of standards that could be drafted that would be broad enough to include both a compatible and incompatible system?"[45] In other words, Hennock supported developing a television set that would be able to receive both the CBS and RCA color television signal, the so-called "bracket" or multiple standards. It was an interesting idea, likely motivated by a New Deal ideal of communal responsibility and obligation, and represented a theoretical solution to the problem. Realistically, however, there was little chance that television manufacturers, lined up into RCA and CBS camps (most of whom were in the RCA camp), would ever agree to such a proposal.

Nonetheless, Hennock hammered away at witnesses, first establishing exactly *who* was working on color, and then wondering *why* they couldn't all combine their technological expertise and work together. She asked Thomas Goldsmith of DuMont whether there was "any way of getting the component parts of this industry to talk to each other about color and work for that workable system, try to achieve it? How do we do that?"[46] Likewise she asked Adrian Murphy of CBS whether he didn't "think that these systems are sufficiently flexible to be combined into one system, or perhaps a set of standards could be inclusive of both systems, the compatible and the incompatible? Don't you think they can be combined in some way?"[47] Exasperated with consistent refusals to consider bracket standards, she asked Frank Stanton of CBS whether the industry "couldn't . . . sit across the table and just try to come to some areas of agreement and submit them to the commission?"[48] Further piqued by industry non-cooperation, Hennock questioned whether an "engineer has a duty to his company and not to the public, and . . . must stick to that duty to his company, and must not confuse it with his duty to the public to give a good system. But when all these hearings are over, . . . then they can look around and see that there is public that has got to pay for [their decisions]."[49] Although promoting a plan that would clearly serve public interests, it was apparent from the responses she received that the plan did not serve corporate interests. Despite the fact that she received very little industry encouragement to support bracket standards, she remained devoted to the idea as a way to serve the public interest. In her separate opinion she emphasized the importance of bracket standards and urged industry members to cooperate with each other.[50]

Inquiries such as these, and many others, reveal that Frieda Hennock devoted much of her attention during the color television hearings to asking questions designed to serve public interests. Considerably less interested than fellow commissioners in the technical novelty of color television, and unimpressed with the corporate and engineering might represented at the hearings, she was more concerned with protecting the average consumer's interests. Understanding that the television set population was rapidly expanding, she wanted to know how quickly manufacturers would make color TVs available to the public, thereby preventing the majority of the population from being "taken for a second ride."[51] Also recognizing the great rush to color television would necessitate purchasing converters and/or adaptors, depending on which system was selected, Hennock demanded to know the costs involved for the average consumer, then doubted whether she or he would be very interested in making those technical alterations. She was particularly interested in the problems of incompatibility, especially since 7 million-plus television sets would potentially become useless (without adaptors). Incompatibility continued to trouble her long after the hearings. As she revealed in her separate opinion, the difficulties caused for the public by selecting an incompatible system included "immediate or eventual diminution of television service" and "the necessity of making an additional expenditure to maintain usefulness" of present television sets.[52] Her efforts to resolve the incompatibility problem, by encouraging the industry to work together to develop bracket standards, were met with a stone wall of uncooperation. Indeed, in an attempt to persuade the RCA group to cooperate with the CBS group to create bracket standards, she threatened to support the CBS system *unless* bracket standards were adopted.[53] Despite this, bracket standards never materialized.

Personal Interests and Color Television

While Hennock's questions were largely inspired by public interests, there is no doubt there were other motivations as well. By the time the color hearings commenced in September 1949, Hennock devoted herself to championing channel reservations for educational television (ETV), a position that played a significant role in the opinions she developed on many of the issues facing the commission. ETV was central to Hennock's personal political goals, since she hoped it would be the issue with which she would establish and cement a national political reputation. When the color television hearings began, she was already fully involved in organizing the educational television hearings (which started in November 1950). Throughout the period from 27 September 1949 to 25 May 1950, the duration of the color hearings, her views on educational television crystallized while she simultaneously became more active in her campaign for the channel reservations. During the second phase of the color hearings (27 February 1950 to 25 May 1950), Hennock made two speeches, during which she promoted educational television. [54] While she may have been annoyed with the distractions from more important issues caused by the color hearings, their length provided her with more time to develop a firmer understanding of the issues inherent to educational television, as well as marshal witnesses and evidence for the ETV hearings.

The color hearings also provided the opportunity to learn what obstacles any of the systems posed for ETV which, of course, would play a role in her final opinion. Once again the problem of CBS incompatibility loomed large. The difficulty began to reveal itself during the questioning of Frank Cowan of AT&T, who testified regarding the ability of either CBS or RCA to transmit their color signals via his company's coaxial cables.[55] Cowan revealed that CBS would have no difficulty transmitting a signal over their cables, but RCA would be unable to do so. This line of questioning stimulated Hennock's ETV nerve, however, for instead of focusing on whether CBS or RCA would be able to transmit their signal, she began to wonder how independent broadcasters, those not affiliated with either CBS or RCA's subsidiary NBC, would get a color television signal. Hennock had potential educational television broadcasters in mind when she asked Frank Stanton of CBS, "What would happen to stations that are independent broadcasters and are not connected with the cable for color?"[56] Despite Stanton's attempts to sidestep the question, Hennock persisted. "Then those stations which would represent the smaller cities, the smaller stations that cannot afford to be connected with cable or relay would have to spend a considerable amount of money for equipment to put color on their broadcasts, is that correct?"[57]

This revelation played a significant role in her ultimate decision not to support the CBS system, a technology that would have been disastrous for educational television broadcasters. Already facing considerable difficulty getting financing from university administrators and/or state legislators to start educational television stations, the costs would have been entirely prohibitive to start a station with CBS color since the equipment would not have been provided through a network affiliation. Moreover, the difficulties would have been exacerbated by the fact that no existing television sets would be able to receive the transmissions. In her separate opinion she detailed her concerns regarding the viewers broadcasters would lose should the CBS system become the industry standard.[58] "To the extent that there are receivers in the hands of the public which are unable to receive field sequential color broadcasts," she wrote, "every program broadcast under those standards entails a loss of audience for the broadcaster."[59] She continued, "With compatibility any program could be produced in color without loss of audience."[60] Already facing an uphill battle in trying to reserve 500 channels for noncommercial purposes, and facing a profit-oriented industry that wanted as many channels as possible, it was inconceivable to Hennock to intentionally create a situation in which it would be impossible for educational television stations to attract viewers. Devotedly believing that educational television was in the public interest, this issue played a significant role in Hennock's final opinion against CBS color.

Concerns regarding educational television were motivated by personal political interests, as well. Hennock's political "white horse" was educational television, the issue with which she would increase her political currency. Like any politician, she kept vigil for threats to her political livelihood, and the CBS color system represented such a menace. If the CBS color system became the standard for the industry, educational broadcasters would face a significant disadvantage even before the ETV hearings were held. In very personal terms, a threat to ETV was a threat to Hennock herself.

Dissent: The Color Television Decision

On 25 May 1950 the color television hearings closed. After fifty-four witnesses, nearly 12,000 pages of testimony, and hundreds of pieces of evidence, the commission was ready to begin a summer of executive sessions to choose the color system that would become the industry standard. Internal documents suggest that, although the commission considered a variety of solutions to the color dilemma, CBS was the clear favorite as early as 7 July 1950.[61] The commission released its decision under the *First Report of the Commission* on 1 September 1950.[62] The majority of the commissioners postponed a final decision until 29 September 1950, proposing to give the industry until that date to decide whether it would adopt bracket standards. Failure to adopt bracket standards, warned the commission, would result in a favorable nod to the CBS system.[63]

Frieda Hennock dissented from the majority FCC position regarding color television.[64] In a seven paragraph opinion she outlined her reasons for generally dismissing the CBS incompatible system and postponing a final FCC decision for a longer period of time to enable RCA to continue development of compatible color television. Not surprisingly, her primary concern was that the problem of "the great number" of potentially incompatible black-and-white sets "be contained at its present level."[65] However, unlike her colleagues, she could not fully endorse the CBS incompatible system and, indeed, believed that "the effect on our present VHF television service caused by the adoption of any system which is not compatible . . . would be very serious. The problems which it would pose for the present set owner and the broadcaster should loom large in our thinking, and we should do our best to avoid them if possible."[66]

Hennock then outlined "the problems" of selecting an incompatible color system as the industry standard. The most significant complication would be "an immediate or eventual diminution of television service."[67] Selection of the CBS color system, she argued, would result in rendering millions of TV sets useless at worst, or requiring those set owners to spend between $32 and $50 to adapt their set. While the majority opinion simply dismissed the problem of 7 million set-owners as "merely a temporary problem" which "would be diluted,"[68] Hennock asserted that "the magnitude of these problems is tremendous when it is realized that . . . there will be 10 million [television sets] in the hands of the public by the end of [1950]."[69] Consequently, she rightly recognized that the production of black-and-white television sets would continue, regardless of the FCC decision, thus exacerbating the incompatibility problem.

A second significant problem caused by an incompatible standard would be the considerable impact on broadcasters. Fewer than 100 television stations were on the air in 1950. Assuming that all of them would immediately begin broadcasting a limited number of "fringe" hours in color,[70] it was guaranteed that those hours would have no viewers, since unadapted TV sets could not receive the signal. Not surprisingly, broadcasters would face considerable difficulty selling advertising time during programs that *could not* be viewed. Indeed, this became the case.[71] While she does not mention the impact on noncommercial broadcasters specifically, the implications are clear. First, it isn't surprising that she didn't mention them. The educational hearings had not yet occurred and the commission hadn't yet made a decision regarding noncommercial reservations. To discuss the implication of the color decision on an issue that had not yet come before the commission would have been premature from a variety of perspectives, not the least of which would have been tipping her hand to the as-yet generally unsuspecting and/or uncaring commercial interests. In any case, if the CBS color system posed considerable operational risks to commercial stations who had either a network and/or local advertisers to help pay for the technology, then the threat to noncommercial broadcasters was compounded. Already begging administrators and legislators for start-up money, the costs would have skyrocketed if educational broadcasters were forced to purchase CBS incompatible color equipment. And for that extra cost, their audience size would have been exactly zero; not a compelling argument to make when pleading for money. Yet, while Hennock didn't specifically develop the problems CBS color would pose for ETV, she did explain that color television provided "untold potentialities for the improvement of television for education."[72] In her view, however, this meant compatible color was the only choice she could support.

As Hennock concluded in her dissent, the best resolution to the color television dilemma was to strongly encourage bracket standards so that all television sets would remain useful regardless of which color system was operating. She also urged the commission to defer making a final decision until 30 June 1950, rather than imposing the "improvident" deadline of 29 September 1950.[73] The additional nine months, she believed, could be critical for further compatible color development. If, at the end of that nine months, compatible color failed to develop further, she would support the CBS color system.

The television industry failed to support bracket standards, however, thereby forcing the Commission to adopt the CBS color system in its *Second Report of the Commission* on 10 October 1950.[74] In a second dissent, briefer and more strongly worded than the first, Hennock asserted that "many grave problems will be posed by the adoption of the incompatible field sequential color television system."[75] She reiterated her belief that the FCC should "make every effort to gain the time necessary for further experimentation leading to the perfection of a compatible color television system."[76] In the strongest wording possible, Hennock asserted that the FCC had "a moral obligation . . . to insure that a reasonable amount of valuable programming service will continue to be rendered to present set owners, both day and night, for a transitional period, e.g., three to five years, without the necessity for making an expenditure to change their sets."[77] By no coincidence, this same 3 to 5 year time period would also provide educational television sufficient time to develop.

In the six weeks between the *First Report* and the *Second Report*, Hennock's grudging support for the CBS color system virtually evaporated. By the time the *Second Report* was issued, she all but abandoned the incompatible system in favor of continued development of the RCA system. The second dissent provides clearer evidence of Hennock's public and personal motivations for supporting compatible color television. As she outlined in the *First Report*, the CBS system did not serve the public's interest. Incapacitating the millions of sets in use—the *only* sets in use—or requiring additional equipment to maintain their usefulness was not in the *public's* best interest, according to Hennock. Certainly the cost-ly equipment and loss of audience and revenue was not in the broadcast-er's best interest. In the time between the close of the color hearings (25 May 1950) and the release of the *Second Report* (10 October 1950), Hennock exerted considerable energy organizing the ETV hearings. The more deeply involved she became with ETV, the more firmly she sup-ported compatible color.

Selection of the CBS system as the industry standard was roundly crit-icized. Major manufacturers of TV sets, most of whom aligned with RCA during the hearings, flatly refused to manufacture any sets using CBS technology and, further, continued to manufacture black-and-white sets.[78] In an editorial the *New York Times* received the FCC's decision with "con-sternation and dismay" and noted that "few voices have been raised in the commission's defense." *Business Week* outlined the reasons why the CBS system might have considerable difficulty launching, despite FCC sup-port. Jack Gould, radio and television columnist for the *New York Times*, believed the color decision left the industry in "a state of unprecedented turmoil and confusion," and *Time* declared that "it was the most confused day since Orson Welles . . . launched his invasion-from-Mars [sic]."[79]

Hennock's dissent was frequently noted in press reports. Soon after the *Second Report* was issued, *U.S. News and World Report* identified her as one of two dissenters to the color decision,[80] and the *Washington Post* quot-ed her belief that the FCC had a "moral obligation" to the public.[81] But Hennock also used several opportunities to more publicly voice her dissent. On 15 September 1950, only ten days after the *First Report* was issued, she addressed the National Association of Women Lawyers, who were meeting in Washington, D.C. She described the "pictorial splendor" of color televi-sion, then asserted that the FCC must make a decision "to authorize the sys-tem which will give to the television viewer, present and future, the most satisfactory service technically, and at the cheapest total cost."[82] As a guest on "Meet the Press" on 10 June 1951, one of the issues she discussed with the panelists was color television.[83] After explaining the commission's decision, she concluded by asserting that "Now, I disagreed with that opin-ion, of course." Later she claimed that "it would be in the public interest to see any improvement in color and I do think the compatible system is the answer to a color question, to the final answer." Even eight years later, in 1958, Hennock continued to remind people that she voted against CBS color. Called before a congressional subcommittee investigating regulatory agencies, Hennock declared her opposition to CBS color. A legislator stat-ed, "You mentioned about CBS and you were bragging about the incident." "Yes," she responded, "bragging on it." "So it is the responsibility of the commission and they are the ones who made the mistake, not the Congress" the legislator asserted. "Right," answered Hennock.[84]

EPILOGUE

By 1958 Frieda Hennock was justifiably proud of her position on the color television decision, but the road to that victory was indirect and arduous. Immediately following the *Second Report*, RCA filed a lawsuit in the Chicago federal district court challenging the commission's decision.[85] The United States Supreme Court eventually agreed to hear the case and, on 28 May 1951, ruled that the FCC had sufficient evidence to warrant selecting the CBS system as the color standard.[86] Less than two weeks later television manufacturers, led by RCA, refused to produce television sets using CBS color technology.[87] Since its main business was broadcasting, CBS faced considerable difficulty finding enough manufacturers to produce color television sets. Therefore, when Defense Mobilizer Charles Wilson asked CBS to cease production of color TV sets to support Korean mobilization efforts, the network complied immediately.[88] Many television manufacturers suspiciously viewed the speed with which CBS complied, believing that the network used this request to escape the burdens of color television.[89] Thereafter, color television virtually disappeared from the broadcast landscape until March 1953 when the House Committee on Interstate and Foreign Commerce held hearings to find out when color television would be available to the public, at which FCC Chair Paul Walker testified that the commission would review their decision.[90]

On 7 August 1953 the FCC began to change its position regarding color television standards. On that date the commission initiated rule-making proceedings "toward adoption of new rules for color TV transmissions on the basis of 'compatible' signal specifications proposed by the National Television System Committee."[91] Finally, on 17 December 1953 the Federal Communications Commission established compatible color as the national television standard.[92] Although present at the meeting to adopt RCA technology, the official record reads "Commissioner Hennock present but not voting."[93] It is unclear why she refused to participate in a vote that vindicated her original position, although *Broadcasting* magazine provides a tantalizing clue. It is possible that her relationship with her fellow commissioners, already difficult,[94] had strained to the point of excluding her from participating in decisions. *Broadcasting* reported that when the commissioners met in December

1953 to vote on the color issue, Hennock protested that Chairman Hyde demanded a final decision that day and punctuated her objection by walking out of the meeting. There is no reason to necessarily doubt that this occurred; Hennock often left commission meetings either to dramatize a point or to check on procedural matters with the General Counsel.[95] During her absence the remaining six commissioners voted on the color decision. Hennock returned to the meeting and insisted that she wanted to participate. Indeed, her personal records indicate that she had every intention of voting on the decision, as evidenced by comments and edits she wrote on her copy of the FCC inter-office memorandum that was circulated prior to the meeting.[96] Her colleagues refused to take another vote and, instead, agreed to note that "Commissioner Hennock [was] present but not voting."[97] These kinds of procedural shenanigans were questioned by a House subcommittee.[98] Unfortunately, there is little documentation to either support or defy *Broadcasting*'s report. Neither the magazine nor its editor, Sol Taishoff, were Hennock supporters, thereby raising credibility issues regarding the report. Consequently, there may be other reasons to explain Hennock's nonparticipation in the final color vote. It is possible that, believing the FCC had more important issues to consider, she simply didn't involve herself in the color decision after 1950. As she revealed in 1950, she held "no special brief for either system."[99] It is also possible that taking a stand on the issue wasn't necessary once the educational reservations were made. It is equally likely that the behavior of television manufacturers simply aggravated her to the point of refusing to participate in the final decision. By December 1953 major television interests, particularly RCA, had flouted FCC authority and continued to manufacture millions of TV sets, thereby aggravating the problem of incompatible television sets. In Hennock's eyes, however, their more egregious offense was the opposition they mounted against educational television. By late 1953 it was inconceivable that she would literally vote for RCA on any issue, largely due to Sarnoff's vocal opposition to reserving television channels for educational television. Whatever the specific circumstances were, when the color ordeal finally ended, Hennock's final official position on the issue was never recorded.

CONCLUSION

The color television decision was the first significant rule-making procedure in which Hennock participated from beginning to end. However, she was neither politically nor personally invested in the issue except as it related to serving the public and protecting educational television.[100] She recognized the significance of the color decision to the lives of average Americans, consumers who would literally pay for the judgments made by the Federal Communications Commission. Given her interest in serving the public, she focused her cross-examination questions on the practical issues at hand. The most aggravating aspect of the color television hearings, especially for someone like Hennock who was interested in serving the public, was corporate refusal to cooperate in the development of color television. In her view, the FCC and all of the corporate interests should have been working together for the public's benefit. She found herself embroiled in a three-way conflict involving the FCC, CBS, and RCA. As one historian described Hennock, she was a "dissident voice" on the FCC,[101] and her experiences and motivations during the color television decision are significant indicators of the issues future "dissidents" might face, such as Newton Minow, in which public and corporate interests collided.

Committed as she was to serving public interests, she was equally devoted to furthering her own political goals. When Hennock walked into the Commerce Department auditorium on 26 September 1949 to participate in the first color television hearing, she entered the room already committed to developing educational television. ETV was the perfect issue with which to make a national political name for herself. Educating the masses through televisual means served public interests while simultaneously serving her personal, political agenda by acting as its champion. With little real interest in the color television hearings themselves, she used them to detect any threats to educational television.

From a wider historical perspective, Hennock and her position at the FCC are a rich case study. First, the dissent recorded in the *First Report* and *Second Report* registered her belief that the CBS incompatible color television technology was the wrong choice as the standard for the industry. In hindsight, her opinion appears to be prophetic. In just three years the commission, spurred on by congressional investigation, reconsidered its position and established compatible color television as the industry standard. Hennock had no clear glimpse of the future, however, and certainly did not know that the industry would simply ignore the FCC's original decision. What she had, that the other commissioners seem to have lacked, was a non-bureaucratic understanding of the public and its concerns, accompanied by a deep suspicion of corporate interests. Current communications regulators could learn a lesson or two from Hennock.

Second, Hennock's dissents in the color television decision, like her minority opinions in other significant cases such as the Fairness Doctrine and the UHF debacle, are evidence of her active role as an FCC commissioner. She did not simply capitulate to her male colleagues, as might have been expected of a female commissioner (especially the *first* female commissioner), but instead consistently took independent positions on a variety of issues. Hennock may be indicative of a large number of women who played pivotal, active roles in broadcasting history, but whose contributions have yet to be identified or illuminated.

Finally, her dissenting opinions (as well as her cross-examinations) provide a fuller picture of the broad range of issues inherent to the color television decision. In particular, one gets a deeper sense of the effects of the decision on the general public through Hennock's dissent than through the extensive justifications provided in the majority opinion. Moreover, the deep suspicions she communicated about corporate interests in her opinions represent counterpoints to the public relations-oriented stories often found in trade magazines such as *Broadcasting*, in whose eyes the major broadcasting companies could do no wrong.

Ultimately, however, Hennock's appeal lies in her refusal to "play the game" at the FCC. She didn't acquiesce to corporate pressures, as previous commissioners had done. She followed her own course at the commission, guided by a deep commitment to the intertwined interests of educational television and personal political goals. Personal and public interests were the motivations behind the color television dissent.

NOTES

1. Mark Hatch, "FCC Lady Member Gives Her Views on Color TV Muddle," *Boston Sunday Post*, 22 October 1950, p. A4.

2. Personal interview with Mr. Stanley Neustadt, 12 February 1998 (hereafter cited as Neustadt interview).

3. U.S. Congress, House, Interstate and Foreign Commerce Committee, Hearings for the Investigation of Regulatory Commissions and Agencies, 85th Cong., 2nd sess., p. 2368 (hereafter cited as House, Hearings for the Investigation).

4. *First Report and Order*, 41 FCC 5 (1 September 1950); "Television: Green Light to Black and White," Time, 31 March 1947, p. 70.

5. *First Report and Order*, p. 5.

6. *First Report and Order*, p. 5; "Television: Green Light," p. 70.

7. *First Report and Order*, p. 7.

8. In 1948 the FCC issued the infamous "freeze," a period during which the agency refused to license any television stations until a variety of technical problems could be resolved. The most significant problems revolved around an insufficient number of frequencies allocated for television broadcasts, combined with co-channel and adjacent-channel interference difficulties.

9. Kenneth Bilby, *The General: David Sarnoff and the Rise of the*

Communications Industry (New York: Harper and Row Publishers, 1986), p. 183.

    10. Ibid.

    11. Neustadt interview; "TV Color's Future: 7 Who Rule," *U.S. News and World Report*, 27 October 1950, p. 34.

    12. Jack Gould, "Time for Action," *New York Times*, 29 January 1950, sec. 2, p. 11; "New Company Shows Video Color to FCC," *New York Times*, 21 February 1950, p. 46; Herbert Murphy, "FCC Still Holding Off on Color Decision," *Barron's*, 10 April 1950, p. 11; "Johnson Lauds FCC," *Broadcasting*, 15 May 1950, p. 62; "The Big Fight," *Newsweek*, 30 October 1950, p. 54; Rosel Hyde to Jim Robertson, Series 1, Box 2, Folder 10, Jim Robertson Collection, Public Broadcasting Oral History Project, National Public Broadcasting Archive, University of Maryland-College Park, MD, (hereafter cited as Robertson Collection).

    13. U.S. Congress, Senate, Interstate Foreign Commerce Committee, Report of the Advisory Committee on Color Television, 81st Cong., 2nd sess., p. III.

    14. Fears that color television might interfere with the sales of black-and-white television sets were widely reported in the press. See for example, "Color Television Again Under Study," *New York Times*, 19 February 1950, Sec. 3, p. 9; "Is CBS Stuck with Color?" *Business Week* (21 October 1950): p. 49; Leonard Engel, "Should You Buy Color Television?" *The Nation*, 11 November 1950, p. 430; Saul Carson, "On the Air: Color Controversy," *New Republic*, 13 November 1950, p. 22.

    15. "Re:Petition of Columbia Broadcasting System for Color Television Transmission Standards," undated, Box 2/Folder: Color TV, Broadcast Bureau-History of Color Television (149H), FCC Archives, National Archives and Records Administration, College Park, MD (hereafter cited as NARA).

    16. See Kristin Thompson and David Bordwell, *Film History: An Introduction* (New York: McGraw-Hill, 1994).

    17. House, Hearings for the Investigation, p. 2368.

    18. "Twinkle, Flash & Crawl," *Time*, 28 November 1949, p. 49.

    19. Ibid; *First Report and Order*, p. 17.

    20. "Twinkle, Flash & Crawl," p. 49; *First Report and Order*, p. 17.

    21. *First Report and Order*, p. 17.

    22. J. Frank Beatty, "The Color Triangle," *Broadcasting* 27 February 1950, p. 53; "Twinkle, Flash & Crawl," p. 49.

    23. *Notice of Further Proposed Rulemaking*, 41 FCC 948, 11 July 1949.

    24. Interview with Mr. Arthur Stambler, 16 May 1996, (hereafter cited as Stambler interview).

    25. Tex McCrary and Jinx Falkenburg, "New York Close-Up," *New York Herald-Tribune*, 15 June 1950.

    26. U.S. Congress, Senate, Official Report of Proceedings Before the Federal Communications Commission, 82nd Cong., 1st sess., 23 March 1950, Vol. 38, p. 7339, (hereafter cited as Official Report).

27. Morris Novik to Jim Robertson, Series 1, Box 3, Folder 1, Robertson Collection.

28. Official Report, 10 April 1950, Vol. 44, p. 8396.

29. Official Report, 10 April 1950, Vol. 44, p. 8400.

30. Gross testimony, Official Report, 11 October 1949, Vol. 11, p. 3519; Baker testimony, Official Report, 1 May 1950, Vol. 52, p. 9703; Engstrom testimony, Official Report, 11 April 1950, Vol. 45, p. 8594; Sarnoff testimony, Official Report, 3 May 1950, Vol. 54, p. 10215.

31. Official Report, 23 March 1950, Vol. 38, p. 7339.

32. *First Report and Order*, p. 51.

33. House, Hearings for the Investigation, p. 2368.

34. House, Hearings for the Investigation, p. 2367.

35. Official Report, 11 October 1949, Vol. 11, p. 3564.

36. Official Report, 1 November 1949, Vol. 21, p. 5315.

37. Official Report, 22 March 1950, Vol. 37, p. 7293. The analogy to FM radio is an interesting one. From a naive perspective, it's an appropriate example to use when questioning whether the industry really has the public's interest in mind, since the public did not express interest in FM radio until the 1960s. It is quite possible that Hennock didn't know that Sarnoff/RCA were instrumental in preventing the development of FM radio, thereby limiting its growth to Edwin Armstrong's Yankee Network for many years.

38. Official Report, 12 October 1949, Vol. 12, p. 3704.

39. Official Report, 19 October 1949, Vol. 16, p. 4369.

40. Official Report, 12 October 1949, Vol. 12, p. 3654.

41. Official Report, 27 September 1949, Vol. 2, p. 2228.

42. Official Report, 17 October 1949, Vol. 14, p. 3997.

43. Official Report, 11 April 1950, Vol. 31, p. 6133.

44. Official Report, 3 May 1950, Vol. 54, p. 10200.

45. Official Report, 27 February 1950, Vol. 31, p. 6167.

46. Official Report, 1 November 1949, Vol. 21, p. 5306.

47. Official Report, 27 February 1950, Vol. 32, pp. 6247-6248.

48. Official Report, 22 March 1950, Vol. 37, p. 7156.

49. Official Report, 2 May 1950, Vol. 53, p. 9902.

50. *First Report and Order*, p. 51.

51. House, Hearings for the Investigation, p. 2392.

52. *First Report and Order*, p. 52.

53. *First Report and Order*, p. 51.

54. Frieda Hennock, "The Place of Radio and Television in the Future," speech presented to the University of Pennsylvania, 20 April 1950, Box 8, Folder 104, Frieda Hennock Simons collection, Schlesinger Library, Radcliffe College, Cambridge, MA, (hereafter cited as FHS); Frieda Hennock to Symposium on the Regulation of Radio and Communication, 17 May 1950, Mount Holyoke College, Box 8, Folder 104, FHS.

55. Official Report, 17 March 1950, Vol. 36.

56. Official Report, 22 March 1950, Vol. 37, p. 7148.

57. Ibid.

58. *First Report of Commission*, 41 FCC 53.

59. *First Report of Commission*, p. 53. Hennock specifically addresses the advertising losses broadcasters will face if the CBS color system is selected.

60. Ibid.

61. Memo to Chief Engineer, 7 July 1950, Box 1/Folder:Color TV-1950–1957, Broadcast Bureau-Color Television (149–H), FCC Collection, NARA; Memo to Chief Engineer, 20 July 1950, Box 1/Folder:Color TV-1950–1957, Broadcast Bureau-Color Television (149–H), FCC Collection, NARA.

62. *First Report of Commission*, p. 1; "CBS Color Video Favored by Board," *New York Times*, 2 September 1950, p. 17; "FCC Favors CBS Color," *Broadcasting*, 4 September 1950, p. 4; "CBS Color Gets the Nod," *Newsweek*, 11 September 1950, p. 65; "Color Enigma," *Time*, 11 September 1950, p. 73.

63. *First Report of Commission*, p. 48.

64. *First Report of Commission*, pp. 51–53.

65. *First Report of Commission*, p. 51.

66. *First Report of Commission*, p. 52.

67. *First Report of Commission*, p. 52.

68. *First Report of Commission*, p.53.

69. Ibid.

70. *First Report of Commission*, p. 52.

71. "CBS Color Video Starts Nov. 20; Adaptors Needed by Present Sets," *New York Times*, 12 October 1950, p. 6; William Freeman, "Video Set Sales Decline at Stores," *New York Times*, 22 October 1950, Sec. 3, p. 3; "Is CBS Stuck with Color?" p. 49; "Video Set Owners Get Reassurance," *New York Times*, 23 October 1950, p. 25.

72. *First Report of Commission*, p. 53.

73. Ibid.

74. *Second Report of the Commission*, 41 FCC 111, (10 October 1950).

75. *Second Report of the Commission*, p. 122.

76. Ibid, p. 123.

77. Ibid.

78. Jack Gould, "Public, TV Industry Stirred by FCC Ruling on Color," *New York Times*, 13 October 1950, p. 1; "Television Chaos," *New York Times*, 18 October 1950, p. 32; "Is CBS Stuck with Color?" p. 49; Jack Gould, "Television in Color," *New York Times*, 22 October 1950, Sec. II, p. 11; "Color Climax," *Time*, 23 October 1950, p. 66; Engel, "Should You Buy Color Television?" p. 430; Carson, "On the Air," p. 22.

79. Gould, "Television in Color," p. 11; "Color Climax," p. 66. Only *The Nation* and *New Republic* supported the FCC.

80. Commissioner George Sterling also registered a dissenting opinion in the *Second Report*, primarily basing his opinion on the commission's failure to

provide manufacturers adequate time to respond to the concept of bracket standards, as well as the agency's refusal to allow further compatible color development except on an experimental basis. See *Second Report of the Commission*, 41 FCC 116.

81. "TV Color's Future: 7 Who Rule," *U.S. News and World Report*, 27 October 1950, p. 34; Sonia Stein, "FCC Approves CBS System for Color TV," *Washington Post*, 12 October 1950, p. 1. *U.S. News and World Report* identified Commissioner George Sterling as a dissenter in the *Second Report*. Sterling supported the majority position in the *First Report* then dissented in the *Second Report*.

82. Frieda Hennock, "The Free Air Waves, An Administrative Dilemma," *Women Lawyers Journal* 36 (Fall 1950): p. 7; "FCC Let-Up Period," *Broadcasting*, 25 October 1950, p. 38.

83. Frieda Hennock, NBC broadcast, "Meet the Press," 10 June 1951. Manuscript provided by the Manuscript Division of the Library of Congress. Preparatory material for the appearance may be found in FHS 7/97.

84. House, Hearings for the Investigation, p. 2392.

85. "2 Television Manufacturers Sue to Halt CBS Color Broadcasts," *New York Times*, 18 October 1950, p. 1; "The Big Fight," *Newsweek*, 30 October 1950, p. 54; "Death of Color TV," *Business Week*, 30 December 1950, p. 24; Radio Corporation of America et al. v. United States et al., 95 F. Supp. 660; Jack Gould, "High Court Backs CBS Color Video," *New York Times*, 29 May 1951, p. 1

86. RCA et al. v. U.S. et al., 341 U.S. 412, 71 S.Ct. 806.

87. Carson, "On the Air," pp. 22–23.

88. "Color TV Shelved as a Defense Step," *New York Times*, 20 October 1951, p. 1.

89. "DuMont Challenges Wilson on Color TV," *New York Times*, 21 October 1951, p. 47; "Color TV is Stopped Cold," *Business Week*, 27 October 1951, p. 21.

90. "Color TV Inquiry Set," *New York Times*, 16 March 1953, p. 22; U.S. Congress, House, Interstate and Foreign Commerce Committee, Color Television, 83rd Cong., 1st sess., March 1953.

91. Federal Communications Commission, *Nineteenth Annual Report of the Federal Communications Commission* (Washington, D.C.: Government Printing Office, 1954), p. 9.

92. In the Matter of the Commission's Rules Governing Color Television Transmissions, 41 FCC 658, 17 December 1953.

93. In the Matter of the Commission's Rules Governing Color Television Transmissions, 41 FCC 658, 17 December 1953.

94. In April 1951 India Edwards, Director of the Women's Division of the Democratic National Committee, wrote to President Harry Truman that Hennock "has worked under great difficulties and in the face of opposition and prejudice." Edwards to Truman, 10 April 1951, Truman's Secretary's files, HST.

95. House, Hearings for the Investigation, p. 2385.

96. "Inter-Office Memorandum Re: Color Decision," 9/130, FHS.

97. "Closed Circuit," *Broadcasting*, 21 December 1953, p. 5.

98. House, Hearings for the Investigation, pp. 2382–2387.

99. Hatch, "FCC Lady Member," p. A4.

100. Hennock's lack of interest in color television is clearly evidenced in the paucity of material regarding the issue in either her personal papers at the Schlesinger Library, or her FCC papers at the Truman Library. Both locations contain considerable documentation regarding her role in both educational television and UHF.

101. Robert W. McChesney, *Telecommunications, Mass Media, and Democracy: The Battle for the Control of U.S. Broadcasting, 1928–1935* (New York: Oxford University Press, 1993), p. 250.

CHAPTER 4

Missed Opportunities:
The UHF Debacle

While color television has flourished in the United States since the FCC made its final decision in December 1953, the fate of another issue considered during the "freeze" has been considerably more problematic: UHF. Television stations assigned to broadcast on the ultra high frequencies have historically faced the twin problems of technical deficiencies (compared to VHF stations) and the dearth of broadcast network affiliations, resulting in an industry perception that UHF television was a "second-class" citizen to VHF stations. Since 1987 the fortunes of UHF owners have gradually improved. Poor transmission range and picture quality have been corrected through coaxial cable transmission, digital television (DTV), and advanced television (ATV), while simultaneously many UHF stations finally found themselves in the happy position of affiliating with a national broadcast network, whether Fox, ABC, CBS, NBC, WB, UPN, or the newly created PaxNet. But the road to this end was exceedingly difficult and unnecessary. The technical weaknesses faced by UHF broadcasters may have been overcome if the Federal Communications Commission had not made several critical errors in judgment regarding policy decisions.

Frieda Hennock was in a unique position to analyze, and possibly foresee, the problematic development of UHF. Her devotion to the development of educational television guided the positions she took on key broadcast regulatory decisions. It was central to her decision to support the RCA "compatible color" television standard in 1950.[1] But while her ETV interests resulted in a color television opinion that appears prescient, those same interests left her blinded to the deficiencies of both UHF's physical characteristics and the FCC policies governing their use. Had Hennock paid closer attention to the testimony provided during the allocation hearings and been somewhat less distracted by her single-minded devotion to promoting educational television, she might have recognized those deficiencies and fought against them before they became administratively entrenched. Certainly a lone commissioner could not necessarily have prevented the eventual UHF debacle. But the zeal with which she approached educational television was successful in reserving television channels for exclusive noncommercial use. Similar attention and enthusiasm directed at the development of UHF, which was critically important to the progression of ETV, may have prevented future woes to both UHF broadcasters and her own educational television interests.[2]

The "UHF mess," as it has been called,[3] represents an interesting case study in Hennock's tenure at the FCC. So committed was she to promoting educational television, to viewing everything through a lens colored by ETV, that she was blinded to the testimony that signaled threats to UHF's survival and, consequently, the development of ETV. She failed to appreciate the basic threat inherent to the intermixture of UHF and VHF channels, just as she did not fully understand the extent to which television manufacturers and networks dictated the reality of that medium's development. These miscalculations eventually required her to go on the defensive, seeking the help from the only group of people—legislators—who could realistically resolve the UHF dilemma. Unlike the ETV campaign, in which she successfully appealed to educators, citizens, and legislators *prior* to the hearings and final FCC decision, Hennock was unable to demonstrate similar success with the UHF debacle. In no small measure, UHF was as important to fulfilling Hennock's personal and political interests as was ETV. Unlike educational television, her efforts to salvage UHF failed completely. This is not to say that Frieda Hennock could have prevented the "UHF mess;" the problems were too complex, too well established for one person to have prevented them. Rather, the point is that her vision of noncommercial television was so focused, she expended so much effort demonstrating that educators were worthy of using the valuable and scarce television resources, that she missed seeing two of the greatest threats to its existence: intermixture of UHF and VHF channels, and the power of the commercial broadcasting industry. Concomitantly, the personal political stakes entailed with establishing ETV, the hubris involved with promoting a cause with which *she* would be identified, blinded her to the weaknesses of her schemes. Like politicians before and since, Hennock didn't see all of the underlying threats to her master plans.

THE ALLOCATION HEARINGS

On 16 October 1950 the Federal Communications commissioners once again assembled to hear testimony regarding the development of television in the United States. Hennock was poised for action. She recognized that a large portion of the reservations she sought would occur in the UHF frequency band. Understanding the significance to educational television of reserving considerably more spectrum space for television broadcasts,[4] she became a student of UHF, analyzing its technical and economic implications. As a result, throughout the hearings,[5] four dominant themes pervaded Hennock's cross-examination of witnesses: the status of research on UHF transmitters and receivers, the quality and cost of producing UHF signals, intermixture of UHF and VHF signals, and educational television's place in channel allocations. In each area Hennock's interests in serving both the public and her own personal goals, particularly through ETV, are apparent.

UHF Transmitters and Receivers

One of the lessons Hennock learned during the color television hearings was the importance of the timely development of equipment. Clearly the development of UHF stations depended upon technical improvements in transmitters, necessary to relay television signals from the station to home antennas, and receivers or television sets. Without this basic technology, UHF stations were worthless. Since it was apparent that the public's thirst for television could most effectively be accomplished through a nationwide system dependent on UHF stations, and since it was likely that many of the educational reservations would occur in the UHF band, it was vital for her to determine the state of transmitter and receiver development.

The news was not encouraging. Witness after witness explained that it was "nearly impossible to get UHF transmitters."[6] Albert Murray of Philco, Thomas Goldsmith of DuMont, Raymond Guy of RCA, and Frank Kear of ABC all were forced to admit that UHF transmitters were in the earliest stages of research and development; Kear confessed that it was "unfortunate that we don't know more."[7] Hennock was incredulous. "Are you as surprised by this condition as I am?" she asked Albert Murray.[8] Having learned that UHF transmitters were virtually non-existent except as experiments, she tried to determine who was responsible for the failure of its development. Her immediate suspicions fell upon the manufacturing industry whom, she learned during the color hearings, could be quite adept at stalling technological growth. She wondered aloud to Albert Murray whether "the industry hasn't gotten into it and hasn't been sufficiently interested in really doing research in it and looking into it—[because it is] too busy with other things."[9] Her intuition was astute. Broadcasting historians have since argued that the major television manufacturers—particularly RCA—intentionally slowed research and development of UHF because of their ownership of VHF stations and financial interests in VHF network affiliations.[10]

Equally as distressing was the news that receivers (television sets) capable of UHF reception were only in the early stages of research and development. The problems were twofold. First, as one witness testified, it was expected that television sets would receive clearer pictures on the lower UHF band, thereby suggesting that channels in the upper UHF band would not be desirable.[11] This problem was inconsequential, however, since manufacturers were devoting little effort to developing television sets that could receive UHF signals at all (assuming a transmitter could be created to deliver the signal), and were more interested in marketing receivers that were VHF capable only. By the seventh day of the hearings, the problems regarding UHF receivers were clear to Hennock. "What you are worried about," she put to a witness, "is not being able to get receivers for your ultra-high area because the manufacturers will continue to build [only] the VHF." "That is my main worry, yes," the witness replied.[12]

Given that the UHF research and development was clearly lagging, Hennock questioned when transmitters and receivers would be ready for mass manufacture. "How many years will it take to build some equipment?" she demanded of Albert Murray.[13] The answers were again disappointing, as engineers refused to predict when UHF equipment would reach the stage at which broadcasting would be feasible. Only one witness was willing to express that "it will still be several years before you have commercial transmitters or any substantial production of commercial receivers in the UHF band."[14] Hennock was nonplussed by what she learned about the preliminary research in UHF transmitters and receivers. "It is a little baffling to me that everyone wants these channels so badly," she admitted, "and they are so badly needed for this great art and development and not more has been done with it."[15] Still somewhat naive, Hennock assumed everyone in the industry wanted television to develop as she did, and she accepted their word that they were working as quickly as possible on the problems. Indeed, her bafflement aside, she did not consider the lack of development a serious threat to UHF; she made no mention of the fact in her *Sixth Report and Order* dissent.[16] At the time of the allocation hearings, she simply knew that the UHF channels were vital to both the creation of a nationwide system of broadcasting as well as to noncommercial television and she assumed that the receivers and transmitters would be ready when needed. She ultimately recognized that not *everyone* wanted those channels so badly, an understanding she developed too late.

Quality and Cost of UHF Signals

Lack of research in the transmission and reception of UHF signals was a fundamental problem for potential broadcasters, but equally significant were the parallel problems of the quality and cost of those transmissions. In other words, how much would it cost a broadcaster to transmit a clear picture to a large viewing audience? Again, the answers were complex and disheartening. Research conducted by both FCC and industry engineers revealed that UHF signals neither traveled as far as VHF signals (being more prone to interference from geography and buildings) nor delivered as clear a picture. Further, the problems intensified as one progressed further into the UHF band. Raymond Guy of RCA testified that their experimental station in Bridgeport, Connecticut transmitted an excellent picture to only 59% of the viewers within a 5-mile radius of the transmitter, a figure that dropped precipitously to only 5% receiving an excellent picture within a radius of 10 to 15 miles.[17] The only way to alleviate the coverage problems inherent to UHF was to transmit with considerably more power than that which VHF stations transmitted. Again, assuming that such a transmitter could be developed, UHF broadcasters would spend considerably more on electricity than would VHF broadcasters.

Judging by the testimony provided by some witnesses, the immediate future of UHF looked grim. Transmitters and receivers were virtually nonexistent. UHF signals did not travel as far, were easily interrupted by physical blockades, and did not transmit images as clearly as did VHF. Ameliorating the problems would require tremendous financial outlays by UHF broadcasters to pay for both research and development of transmitters as well as increased electric bills, with no guarantee that anyone was watching their programming because most television sets didn't receive UHF signals and the networks generally refused to affiliate with UHF stations. It is no surprise that Hennock questioned how long it would take a UHF operator to make a profit. "What will he do by way of losses? Will it be five years after he gets on the air, three years? Is there any hope we can induce him—I want to give him something to induce him to get in [to UHF]."[18] She later wondered aloud, "what is the good of ultrahigh?"[19] Nonetheless, she pinned many of her ETV hopes on UHF.

Manufacturers would deliver transmitters and receivers, as they assured her they would, which, coupled with enough transmitting power, would alleviate the problems of picture quality. Enough UHF stations on the air, especially educational channels, would naturally provide the competition the networks needed to loosen their stranglehold on the industry. The hopes Hennock placed on ETV, both in terms of serving the public interest by providing expanded programming options and serving to strengthen her own personal political currency, blinded her to the significant impediments to UHF, as were becoming clearer during the allocation hearings.

Intermixture

One of the fundamental questions the commission had to answer revolved around the relationship between UHF and VHF signals. While some argued that television ought to be confined to the UHF band alone,[20] the FCC was predisposed to intermixing channels, such that some communities would be assigned channels from both the VHF and UHF bands. It was an issue with which Hennock was deeply concerned, given the likelihood that educational television would receive many UHF assignments and, further, that communities assigned intermixed channels would almost certainly be disadvantaged in terms of programming options. She frequently asked witnesses to explain their positions on intermixture (which she often called "admixture"). She clarified Thomas Goldsmith's testimony by asking whether DuMont's allocation plan, which opposed intermixture, contended "that because the cities will not mix UHF and VHF, there won't be a squeeze on the UHF broadcaster by the VHF broadcaster and that, therefore, UHF would get a better chance?"[21] He assured her that UHF stations would fare much better if they were not required to compete directly with VHF stations. She similarly summarized other testimony that argued second-class citizenship for UHF stations prohibited from direct competition with VHF: "You want UHF stations to get an equal break with the VHF stations for the sets and the population in the populated areas, as distinguished from the DuMont plan, which says, no admixture, is that correct? . . . And you feel that by not putting as many of them, as many UHF stations, into the large cities as possible we are not giving you a just and even break?"[22] Throughout the hearings, her questions did not reveal a particular position regarding intermixture. Rather, she was more likely to frame her questions as genuine inquiries: "How do you feel about the FCC allocation plan with regard to admixture of UHF and VHF?"; "Would you be against the separation of UHF and VHF in separate cities?"; "Do you think a UHF station in New York . . . would have a chance of existing [in the same market as seven VHF stations]?"[23] One witness described intermixture as "suicidal" but nonetheless supported it, believing that it would encourage manufacturers to develop television sets capable of receiving UHF signals.[24] Unfortunately, Hennock failed to follow up on the "suicidal" aspects of intermixture.

Educational Television

Intermixture, transmitters, and receivers were certainly important aspects of the allocation hearings, but Hennock's overriding concern was educational television. For months she had been traveling the country crusading in favor of channel reservations for noncommercial television stations and cajoling educators to participate in the upcoming educational hearings.[25] The current allocation hearings were crucial ground to cover. Not only could Hennock get a feel for the potential problems that would face educational broadcasters assigned to a UHF station, obstacles she might be able to alleviate, but testimony provided during the hearings might also serve as a barometer for the arguments opponents might offer against noncommercial reservations.

Assuming that commercial interests would oppose noncommercial channel reservations, Hennock was particularly interested in the positions taken by companies such as DuMont, ABC, CBS, and RCA regarding set-asides. She must have been somewhat relieved to learn that none of the major companies opposed the philosophical question of reserving channels for educational use. Further questioning revealed hidden obstacles, though. The DuMont allocation plan confined educational channels to the very highest regions of UHF.[26] When Hennock pressed Goldsmith, he agreed that the noncommercial channels could easily be moved. Similarly, although Frank Kear of ABC professed support for educational channels, Hennock's continued questioning revealed his belief that such reservations should not be held "indefinitely." Indeed, he asserted that "if there is nobody asking for them in the educational groups, they should be made available to the general public."[27] This knowledge proved useful during the ETV hearings as Hennock was able to prepare counter arguments against this potential ETV threat.

Given the considerable amount of testimony regarding the quality and range of UHF signals, Hennock also queried witnesses about the effect this might have on educational broadcasters. This was a particularly relevant line of questioning, given the fact that nearly all of the witnesses assumed that noncommercial broadcasters would be confined to UHF channels. With this in mind, Hennock asserted that "there are certain educational institutions that are coming in here, and they might be given some very bad channels. I want to know which are the bad ones and which are the good ones."[28] While questioning Thomas Goldsmith regarding DuMont's allocation plan, she wondered aloud: "Eight hundred thirty-six to eight hundred ninety [megacycles], that you wanted for the educators. . . . I thought that as they got higher they covered less area, needed more power, and so forth,"[29] as if to say "are you intentionally trying to short-change educators?" Later in the proceedings she bluntly told one witness that she was "particularly interested [in the problems inherent to UHF] because there are certain applicants here who should be protected—they are not around—I am speaking of educators particularly. I want to know what awaits them in UHF and what part of that band is not good for them."[30]

As troubled as she was about UHF channel assignments, Hennock made it clear that *she* didn't assume that all noncommercial stations would be confined to those frequencies. Hennock believed that educational broadcasting had as much right to the highly favored VHF channels as did the commercial licensees, a point she repeatedly stressed. The following exchange is an indication of the manner in which Hennock challenged assumptions regarding commercial and noncommercial broadcasting:

Witness: Well, I believe in the VHF there are not enough frequencies to take care of the educational requirements without putting a hardship on the general public.

Hennock: It is a terrible hardship on the public to have educators on VHF?

Witness: No, I did not say that.

Hennock: Yes, you did, I beg your pardon.

Witness: I was saying this, that the public needs television service.

Hennock: From whom?

Witness: From anyone who can provide them good programming.

Hennock: Why do they have to come in and show that they can use the channels like commercial stations can? Why does the public need the commercial stations, first? Are you going to put the educators on the defensive in VHF?[31]

Hennock concluded this line of questioning by asserting that "I do not want educators put on the defensive with regard to VHF or any other part of that band. These channels belong to the public."[32]

She proved tenacious in her belief that educators had equal claims to VHF channels. She was particularly relentless with Thomas Goldsmith, who testified regarding the DuMont allocation plan which set aside the highest UHF channels for educational use. "Every time you say UHF for education, I am going to say VHF" she told Goldsmith.[33] Three days later she asked Goldsmith whether he didn't "have any objection to the educators getting different channels" than those allocated in DuMont's plan.[34] Indeed, "getting different channels" might prove beneficial to UHF in a plan she apparently devised while listening to testimony. Since commercial VHF stations allegedly represented unfair competition for commercial UHF stations, then "giving some of these VHF channels to educators might be a good leveling off process to give UHF impetus to get it started."[35] Finally, in an exchange with another witness, Hennock's point was clear:

Witness: There seems to be a great demand for the VHF channels from commercial interests.

Hennock: You think these channels belong to them?

Witness: I think they will probably be much more energetic in their presentation of their needs for them than the educational interests are likely to be.

Hennock: Do you think that this Commission should only consider the energetic presentation of commercial interests or the amount of energy that goes into an application in determining this important issue?

Witness: I think they should consider the public need and the public welfare in the situation, and it is perhaps—

Hennock: You don't think, then, that educators can serve the public well with television channels?[36]

Devoting so much effort to assessing the quality of UHF transmissions and promoting educators' right to VHF channels was a significant miscalculation on Hennock's part. The record was clear regarding UHF signals; engineering tests convincingly demonstrated their weaknesses compared to VHF signals. Moreover, utilizing the allocation hearings to promote ETV so extensively was a waste of time. She was already regarded as the leading proponent of ETV, so she didn't need to establish her preeminence as its champion. The opportunity to prove educators were worthy of receiving television channels was also the focus of the upcoming educational hearings, set to begin in late November 1950.

For all of her interest in investigating the impact of transmitters and receivers and demonstrating educational television's rightful place in VHF, Hennock failed to appreciate the significance of intermixture to the future of UHF television and, hence, ETV. This despite the fact that one witness referred to intermixture as "suicidal" and another called it "wishful thinking."[37] Only once during the nine days she attended hearings did she broach the subject of intermixture's impact on educational television. While cross-examining Thomas Goldsmith regarding his belief that television channels should not be intermixed, she questioned what he would do in the case of New York City, which already had seven VHF channels on the air and the likelihood that they would not receive any more VHF assignments. "What are you going to do with the educators?" she asked, "Are you going to give them that part of the UHF band? Then you will have to go against your own theory."[38] Rather than following the intermixture line of questioning, however, Hennock was more interested in proving the point that noncommercial channels should have equal access to VHF. Throughout the hearings, she missed the more fundamental point that several witnesses made: intermixture would be devastating to UHF station owners. Her absolute devotion to proving the worthiness of educational television reservations blinded her to the effects of intermixture. She did not heed the warnings of witnesses who asserted that intermixture was a bad idea.

On 1 November 1950, Hennock attended the allocation hearings for the last time, although the hearings continued for eight more days. Indeed, her decision not to attend nine of the last eleven days of allocation hearings undermined any opportunities she may have had to get a clearer picture of intermixture. Again, her devotion to educational television clouded her judgment. The final eleven days of the allocation proceedings immediately preceded the ETV hearings. Rather than attend the allocation hearings, she used that time to prepare for ETV. As she told a friend on 21 November 1950 (a date on which she missed the final allocation hearing), "My educational hearings start next Monday. I am working fourteen hours a day under terrific pressure."[39] Her failure to appreciate the problems inherent to intermixture should not be dismissed. In the following years, intermixture proved to be one of the major factors contributing to the underdevelopment of both UHF television and ETV. Hennock's oversight was a significant miscalculation that weakened her plans for serving both public and personal interests. The failure of both UHF and ETV to grow and prosper resulted in a greatly diminished television service from what was theoretically possible and administratively intended. The weakness of UHF also became a fundamental reason explaining ETV's lack of growth which, ultimately, devalued Hennock's potential political currency.

SIXTH REPORT AND ORDER

On 11 April 1952 the FCC released its *Sixth Report and Order*, ending the "freeze" on television licensing and outlining its decisions regarding channel allocations.[40] With this report, the commission established four fundamental policies that are relevant to this chapter. First, virtually the entire UHF bandwidth was reserved for television broadcasting, from 470 to 890 mc. Second, the FCC reserved more than two hundred channels for noncommercial broadcasting.[41] Third, the commission adopted the policy of intermixture, arguing that "UHF stations will eventually compete on a favorable basis with stations in the VHF."[42] As Sterling and Kittross explain, "the FCC's hope—or, in light of the commission's penchant for ignoring engineering advice, fantasy—[was] that UHF and VHF were equal."[43] Turning a blind eye to considerable testimony that revealed the lack of transmitters and receivers, the commission asserted that there was "no reason to believe that American science will not produce the equipment necessary for the fullest development of the UHF."[44] The majority of the commissioners continued by asserting that "present equipment and economic problems may temporarily handicap operations in the new UHF band and place certain communities at a disadvantage. Such immediate considerations, however, cannot be allowed to obscure the long-range goal of a nationwide competitive television service, in which stations in both the UHF and VHF bands will constitute integral parts."[45] Fourth, the majority decided to allow VHF stations to increase their power levels and antenna heights, thereby increasing their broadcast coverage areas.[46] Frieda Hennock joined the majority in most of these decisions. She later testified that she and the other commissioners "thought we were opening up over 2,000 channels for television. We were delighted, because it was a lot of hard work, we wanted to get television to the people as quickly as possible."[47]

Hennock did not entirely support all of the policies contained in the *Sixth Report and Order*. She strenuously dissented against increasing VHF power levels and antenna heights, however, which she believed "unduly and unnecessarily enhanced the VHF at the expense of the UHF."[48] Hennock had reason for concern. The weaknesses inherent to UHF transmissions already disadvantaged them to VHF stations, and threatened the effectiveness of a nationwide television service. Moreover, fully two-thirds of the educational reservations were in the UHF band. She was particularly distressed that "the commission apparently [had] minimized or disregarded" the "serious economic problems facing the development of the UHF against presently existing or future VHF" stations that would be exacerbated by increasing power and antennas.[49] Already lagging far behind VHF station development, UHF operators faced enormous equipment and economic problems; transmitters and receivers were nowhere near the assembly line, networks were not interested in affiliating with UHF stations, consequently advertisers weren't interested in buying air time on UHF stations to promote their products. As far as Hennock was concerned, "to increase power and height now is irrevocably to cast the die in favor of VHF and to take an unnecessary gamble with the future of our entire television system."[50] She was absolutely right; she correctly predicted the difficulties UHF operators would face as a result of competing with VHF stations, but was unable to see the real problem with intermixture.

Here again, though, she failed to see the more basic deficiencies in the FCC plan. She continued to assume, as did the rest of the commission, that UHF and VHF were essentially equal. As such, intermixture was not a concern. She likewise maintained her faith that manufacturers and networks would eventually live up to their responsibilities of producing transmitters and receivers, and affiliating with UHF stations. From Hennock's perspective, UHF and VHF stations were fundamentally equal; the majority decision to allow VHF stations to boost power levels and increase antenna heights created the imbalance that would result in continued network preference for VHF stations. This was only a minor part of the overall picture, however. Intermixture, in fact, was the fundamental problem, because the VHF and UHF signals were *not* equal. From a purely technical point of view, VHF signals transmitted clearer pictures over greater distances. While engineers assured the commission that UHF signals could be strengthened to the point of equality with VHF, many of those same engineers worked for companies (especially RCA) whose interests laid in maintaining that inequality. These were oversights she later regretted. Ultimately recognizing the roles both intermixture and the industry played in impeding the growth of UHF, she was forced into a defensive position trying to undo the damage done by combining UHF and VHF in the same markets. By 1958 her opinion of the *Sixth Report and Order* had changed considerably. "To me," she testified, "that sixth report and order was the worst thing that came out of that Commission."[51] As Erwin Krasnow later revealed, "throughout the 1950's the FCC spent much time dealing with the consequences of this 1952 decision."[52]

INTERIM PERIOD, 1952–1954

In April 1952, though, the FCC was "delighted" with their decision, and they turned to the enormous task of reviewing the hundreds of television license applications that had accumulated during the "freeze," and licensing those they believed most qualified. The more television stations went on the air, the more it appeared as if the television crisis was over. The popular press looked at the UHF allocations and pronounced "a promising new era" for television; *Business Week* pondered whether it might be "the promised land" of television broadcasting.[53] *Broadcasting* magazine heralded the initial broadcasts of UHF stations, explained network affiliation plans for UHF, and downplayed equipment costs for consumers who wanted to receive UHF signals. Even *Popular Mechanics* claimed that consumers would "have very little difficulty in tuning [UHF signals] in with [their] present TV receivers." The jubilance of nationwide television could hardly be contained by the press. "Here comes TV for the whole country," *Popular Science* proclaimed, "and not just a few metropolitan centers will enjoy television when new ultra-high frequency stations go on the air."[54] Indeed, UHF television appeared to be the savior for all of those Americans who wanted to watch Milton Berle and Howdy-Doody, but were unable to do so. Only a few contradictory opinions were expressed amid the din of praise for UHF. *Newsweek* asserted that "UHF is full of problems. Transmitters, antennas, and sets all cost more; and the 'upstairs' signal often does not travel as far or as well." *Consumer Reports* told its readers that there was "a great deal of misinformation about UHF, and many erroneous ideas about it are going the rounds."[55] Judging by most press accounts, however, UHF was the answer to television's problems.

FCC statistics seemed to validate the rosy picture painted by press reports. By the end of the fiscal year 1953 (June 1954), the FCC had licensed 256 UHF stations, representing 64% of all of the post-freeze grants.[56] The commission was so pleased with UHF's apparent progress that, in July 1953, it revised its licensing review policy that prioritized UHF applicants, which was intended to help UHF stations get a "head start" on VHF competition in intermixed communities. As of that date UHF stations would no longer get priority attention from the FCC. It was an ill-advised decision, but represented only a portion of the problems UHF operators faced, dilemmas that were not clearly reported in FCC records. By 1954, manufacturers were still not producing the transmitters that UHF operators needed to deliver their signals, nor were they manufacturing adequate numbers of television sets that could pick up UHF transmissions. The networks preferred to affiliate with VHF stations, whose signals could travel farther to larger audiences (especially since the FCC allowed them to boost their power levels and antenna heights), and advertisers preferred to promote their products on the stations reaching the largest number of people. UHF operators were in a no-win situation.

Like her fellow commissioners, Hennock's attentions were devoted elsewhere during this interim period. She was committed to persuading educators and administrators to take advantage of the channel reservations for educational broadcasting. Consequently, she paid little attention to the growing UHF problems. Although she vigorously dissented from the July 1953 policy revision, arguing that "a priority for UHF applications is necessary for the assured establishment of an integrated VHF-UHF nationwide television service,"[57] this minority opinion does not reveal any particular insight regarding the worsening disadvantages faced by UHF operators. Her apparent lack of interest in UHF is further evidenced by the fact that she didn't attend a preliminary meeting between the Senate Communications subcommittee and the Federal Communications commissioners in March 1954.[58]

UHF problems did not escape the notice of others, however. In March 1954 the Senate Interstate and Foreign Commerce Subcommittee on Communications, chaired by Senator Charles E. Potter, decided to investigate the failure of UHF television development.[59] Sol Taishoff, editor of *Broadcasting*, described the UHF situation as "one of confusion and contradiction."[60] Jack Gould, radio and television columnist for the *New York Times,* claimed that "a growing crisis is affecting television across the country and it can be summed up in one phrase: 'ultra-high frequency.' "[61] The Potter Subcommittee decided to investigate the issue.

Just when Hennock finally realized the true significance of the UHF problem is unknown. Perhaps it was the need to understand why educational television was growing so slowly that caused her to take note of UHF. The first educational television station didn't go on the air until May 1953,[62] and by May 1954 only six were operating, half of which were UHF.[63] When casting about for explanations for ETV's slow growth, she must have realized that UHF assignments contributed to educational television's problems. Nonetheless, as late as 5 April 1954 *Broadcasting* reported that only FCC Chair Rosel Hyde was expected to testify before the Potter Subcommittee regarding UHF, "although other commissioners may be invited to give their views."[64] There is little evidence to suggest she gave the issue much weight at all until she testified before the Potter Subcommittee in May 1954.

THE POTTER SUBCOMMITTEE

Hennock compensated for her inattention by becoming the leading proponent of decisive measures to alleviate the UHF problem. As she indicated in her dissenting opinion in the *Sixth Report and Order*, the die was cast in 1952 regarding the future of UHF. Since the policy had now been in place for over two years, Hennock was forced to take a defensive position against a well-entrenched policy to try to get it repealed, especially since it was so intimately connected to the success of ETV. The only group who realistically had the ability to reverse the FCC's scheme was legislators; specifically, the Potter Subcommittee. It was to this group of Senators she directed her most forceful comments. She appeared before the subcommittee on 19 May 1954.[65] She did not equivocate. "The success of the nationwide competitive television system *is completely and inextricably* bound to the fate of UHF," she informed the senators.[66] She continued to elucidate the benefits to be achieved from a nationwide television system if bold steps were taken to alleviate the impediments to UHF's progress, the most important of which was intermixture. "I am now convinced," she told the subcommittee, "that the approval of intermixture was a basic mistake. It has enabled VHF to smother UHF. I take my due share of the blame for creating this problem. But that is not enough. Something must be done now to enable UHF to survive."[67] She then described the five steps that she believed must be taken to protect UHF.

Her five proposals were nothing short of extraordinary. The first step, she argued, was "to impose an immediate freeze on all grants of new construction permits for VHF stations and new allocations of VHF channels."[68] Although originally the idea of the UHF Industry Coordinating Committee,[69] they found a vocal spokesperson in Frieda Hennock, who delivered the idea to the Potter Subcommittee. The second proposal hearkened back to her dissenting opinion in the *Sixth Report and Order*, in which she decried the majority's decision to allow increased power levels and antenna heights for VHF stations. She explained that "one of the major difficulties facing UHF is the overlapping service areas of large VHF stations, causing blanketing of UHF stations. The most obvious and forthright remedy is to cut down these service areas."[70] In response to a senator's question, Hennock later explained that UHF stations "had a right to assume that a city without UHF in the plan would remain so. . . . But, suddenly, stations from the larger cities blew in and covered that city" with their VHF signal, because the FCC gave them permission to do so.[71] Her third proposal required that VHF transmitters be located in close proximity to the actual community the VHF station was licensed to serve. Current FCC regulations allowed licensees to place their transmitter virtually anywhere they chose, thereby frequently forcing UHF operators to compete with them when, according to FCC allocation plans, they should not be competing for the same audience.[72] Fourth, Hennock supported Senator Edwin Johnson's bill to "remove excise tax from UHF-equipped receivers."[73] Lack of television sets to receive UHF signals continued to be a significant and fundamental problem for UHF operators, according to the UHF Industry Coordinating Committee.[74] Perhaps manufacturers could be induced to produce UHF-capable receivers if they were given a tax break for doing so, Hennock reasoned. Finally, revealing limited recognition of the networks' influence over the development of UHF (or at least an unwillingness to single them out) and attempting to encourage the broadcast networks to affiliate with UHF stations, Hennock supported Senator John Bricker's bill that would create network regulation.[75]

One month later, on 22 June 1954, Hennock returned to provide rebuttal testimony to the Potter Subcommittee.[76] The intervening month since her previous appearance sharpened her insights and weakened her inclination not to lay blame at any specific doorstep. Hennock began her testimony by drawing sharp comparisons between the development of FM radio and UHF television. "In both cases," she argued, "two new services were awaiting a chance to get going in a new spectrum space, whose virtues were proclaimed far and wide."[77] Then, just as with FM radio and its efforts to compete with AM radio, UHF faced FCC policies that favored VHF channels, receivers were not manufactured to tune into UHF signals, and networks would not affiliate with UHF stations. Despite the apparent benefits of UHF television, it, like FM before it, was the victim of concerted efforts to prevent its development. Progressing from analogy to specific examples, Hennock continued her testimony by refuting many of the arguments made against UHF television stations: they were not simply experiencing the same kinds of "growing pains" that early VHF stations had,[78] and "de-intermixture" was the only solution to the problem.[79] She reserved particularly harsh criticism for the networks, revealing a fuller understanding of their ability to stall UHF growth and a willingness to single them out. Network assurances that they were interested in affiliating with UHF stations were "a sham and a farce" according to Hennock.[80] Moreover, she argued, the networks were guilty of ignoring business practices based on fair competition and were, in fact, engaging in "artificial restriction" of the broadcast industry. She went on to paint a hypothetical picture for the senators:

Suppose two networks should constitute virtually the sole source of popular programs, so that the life or death of a television station would depend on the nod of one or the other of these two networks, and, in fact, they and not the commission would determine the number and location of television stations, would this be evidence of free competition or monopoly? . . . I ask whether, in the public domain of television communication, the control of 85 percent of all TV network advertising revenue by two networks is evidence of [a] healthy economic base for the industry.[81]

"Action is needed now," she urged the senators. "A few deft strokes by this committee are all that is needed."[82]

The final weapon in her arsenal to protect UHF was educational television, the true motivation for her sudden interest in their troubles. She reminded the committee members that "there is testimony in the record which shows that if UHF dies, 15 States [sic] some of them the most populous, will be without educational reservations."[83] Not only was this unthinkable to Hennock, but she understood that educational television was held sacred by current and previous governmental leaders, including Senators Bricker, Johnson, Tobey, and President Truman. It was a trump card she hoped would sway the subcommittee.

Indeed, the Potter Subcommittee held sufficient power to force the FCC to reconsider its UHF policies; pleading with them for the future of UHF television was a wise move on Hennock's part. She also recognized, however, the influence members of the broadcasting industry had over the destiny of UHF. She joined other FCC commissioners on a panel before the National Association of Radio and Television Broadcasters (NARTB) on 27 May 1954 and beseeched its members to support both a freeze on VHF licenses and, more drastically, the complete move of all television broadcasting to UHF. Intermixture was accountable for all of UHF's problems. She explained to them that, having heard the testimony of the UHF Industry Coordinating Committee (who testified before the Potter Subcommittee immediately following Hennock),[84] she was "now firmly convinced that only the eventual move of the TV service into the UHF band can save the patient."[85] She went on to explain to the NARTB that it was long recognized that the twelve channels on VHF were insufficient for a nationwide television service. Yet, as a result of the many obstacles thrown in the path of UHF development, the industry was drifting in the direction of just such a limited system of broadcasting. Gradual elimination of all VHF channels accompanied by a complete shift into UHF, Hennock argued, was the only way a truly nationwide television system could develop. As she explained, "that this action must be taken is the conclusion which I have drawn from the gloomy picture that was so vividly and forcefully presented last week to the Senate Committee, the Commission, the broadcasting industry, and the people of the United States."[86]

Hennock's public comments regarding the status of UHF television drew stinging criticism from fellow commissioners also participating on the NARTB panel.[87] Commissioner Sterling called Hennock's statements "rash," and asserted that "no one can generalize about placing television in UHF channels." Commissioner Bartley asserted his belief that no one on the commission should "advocate any side while the matter was under consideration in Congress," to which Commission Chair McConnaughey added that commissioners "should not take an attitude 'until all sides have been heard.' "[88] Hennock responded to the public rebukes by asserting that "she felt it would have been inappropriate for her to appear before the NARTB convention and fail to discuss her views frankly."[89] As she wrote to Benjamin Abrams regarding her efforts to salvage UHF, "as you know, the main thing in the fight is to keep punching until the last minute and that is all I can do."[90] In a telling remark, however, she reported that she had "not been able to do much on educational television during this ultra high squabble. These balls fly so fast it seems I can only catch one at a time."[91]

THE UHF DISSENT

Responding to congressional pressure to take action to alleviate the UHF situation, the FCC re-evaluated its policies and, in August 1954, the majority decided to consider granting UHF licenses for stations that would not broadcast local live programming.[92] In other words, the UHF station would be used to extend the reach of VHF stations by duplicating their programming. Hennock was furious with this decision and amended the one-page notice with a 12-page dissent. In no uncertain terms she declared that "the Commission's ruling kills UHF television."[93] She explained in detail how the commission's decision would deliver "the final mortal blow" to UHF by making it simply a satellite extension of VHF and, concurrently, powerful network interests. It would extinguish all hopes for a truly nationwide system of broadcasting, she argued, and financially debilitate the many UHF broadcasters already on the air. She reiterated the FM analogy drawn for the Potter Subcommittee, as this step mirrored earlier FCC decisions to allow FM stations to duplicate AM programming. She concluded her dissent by urging six "emergency measures" and four "additional measures," all of which she'd explained before the Potter Subcommittee. The "ultimate measure," she argued, was the "transfer of all television broadcasting to the UHF band. So long as television continues to operate as an intermixed system of both VHF and UHF, the fact that it has become possible to blanket the country with very few stations operating in the twelve VHF channels will continue to exert over-powering [sic] allure to those whose interests are served by an economy of scarcity. The continued existence of an intermixed TV system by its very nature perpetuates the threat to effective competition in the industry."[94]

Not satisfied with simply writing a strongly worded dissent, Hennock informed powerful people of both the FCC decision and her dissent. She mailed copies of it to many members of Congress, UHF broadcasters, and other influential people associated with the industry. Many responded to her dissent.[95] Many UHF operators also responded to her dissent, praising her "outstanding analysis of the situation."[96] Seymour Krieger, director of the New York City Municipal Broadcasting System declared that no "single individual has done as much as you in crystallizing for the public the difficulties of UHF operation."[97]

EPILOGUE

Hennock's efforts were too little, too late, however. Despite her strongly worded arguments against intermixture and monopolistic networks, despite the support she received from UHF operators and sympathetic legislators, the problems of UHF were too entrenched to be easily resolved. She continued to work on the problem throughout the last months of her tenure as a Commissioner, writing reports to the Senate Interstate and Foreign Commerce Committee,[98] dissenting on commission decisions that affected UHF,[99] and encouraging UHF operators. As late as 1958, former commissioner Hennock continued to detail the variety of obstacles that resulted in UHF being "as dead as it is."[100] She laid particularly harsh blame on industry lobbyists, who were able to "honeycomb [FCC] offices" and participate in decisions in ways that "were not in writing . . . not in the notice, and not in the written comments."[101] The ability of industry lobbyists to influence decisions was "one of the worst practices," Hennock asserted.[102]

Network lobbying aside, the FCC failed to actively respond to the UHF dilemma. The same two fundamental and related problems continued to plague UHF from the 1950s into the late 1980s: inability to overcome the technical difficulties of range and picture quality, and failure of broadcast networks to affiliate with UHF stations. As late as 1994 the technical problems of UHF transmissions remained problematic. As one engineer put it, "There's no way you can get around the physics."[103] Moreover, transmitters provided few options for improving range or picture clarity, although digital technology promised to ameliorate the problem. Throughout the same time period the broadcast networks consistently refused, as often as possible, to affiliate with UHF stations, largely due to the range and picture quality problems.

The 1990s have been rosier times for UHF, however. In 1987 the Fox television network began developing. Forced to affiliate with the only stations available, usually independents assigned a UHF channel, Fox finally began providing UHF stations the access to programs and national advertisers they always needed, especially after the network won the rights to broadcast NFL football games in 1994.[104] One of the most significant boosts to UHF stations came in 1994, when Fox and New World Communications joined forces.[105] The resulting deal required many major-market stations, with VHF assignments and historically affiliated with either ABC, CBS, or NBC, to become Fox affiliates. The "big three" networks were then forced to affiliate with the former Fox station, thereby necessitating affiliation with a UHF station. As a result, the "big three" were obliged to move into the UHF range.

Network shifts into the UHF range were made a bit less painful, perhaps, by certain technological improvements as well. One such refinement is cable television technology. The technical difficulties of UHF transmissions are all but eliminated when transmitted by coaxial cable; the range may be vastly increased and picture quality may be improved significantly when audiences receive their pictures through cable rather than broadcast transmissions. Increased range and picture quality, of course, may result in higher quality programming and advertiser willingness to buy air time. The future of digital television (DTV) and advanced television (ATV) also provide hope for improved UHF transmissions.[106]

While UHF may finally be coming into its own, the road to this end was economically risky, technologically difficult, and administratively unnecessary. The blame for failing to foresee the problems that UHF development faced cannot be laid entirely at Frieda Hennock's doorstep. As someone who consistently devoted her attentions to serving public interests and as the leading proponent of the development of educational television, however, she was the commissioner in the best position to analyze the deficiencies of the proposed intermixture of VHF and UHF, the technical development of transmitters and receivers, and the influence of the networks and major television manufacturers. Simultaneously vigilant of most threats to her pet project and devoted to serving public interests rather than corporate ones, her single-minded allegiance to ETV left her blind to the dangers inherent to UHF which, ultimately, also lessened the eventual effectiveness of educational television. Had Hennock, or any of the other commissioners, approached the allocation plans with the same careful planning with which she approached ETV, the development of UHF may have followed a much different path.

NOTES

An earlier version of this chapter appeared in *Journal of Broadcasting and Electronic Media* 44(2) (Spring 2000).

1. *First Report of the Commission*, 41 FCC 51; *Second Report of the Commission*, 41 FCC 122.

2. In April 1952 the FCC issued its *Third Report and Order*, which reserved more than 240 television channels strictly for educational, noncommercial broadcasts. Many of those ETV channels were in the UHF band, making the success of both ETV and UHF closely related. Indeed, as of 1995, 82% of the channels reserved for noncommercial use were located in the UHF band (*1995 Broadcasting Yearbook*, p. C-185).

3. Christopher H. Sterling and John M. Kittross, *Stay Tuned: A Concise History of American Broadcasting* (Belmont, CA: Wadsworth Publishing Co., 1990), p. 356.

4. The FCC's original allocation plan, released in July 1949, called for the reservation of 42 channels on the UHF band. By the time the *Sixth Report and Order* was released in 1952, the FCC had been persuaded that seventy new channels were necessary to accomplish the goal of creating a nationwide television system.

5. It should be noted that Hennock's attendance record at the allocation hearings was poor. She attended nine out of twenty days.

6. U.S. Congress, Senate, Official Report of Proceedings Before the Federal Communications Commission, 82nd Cong.,1st sess., 19 October 1950, Vol. 71, p. 13144. Hereafter cited as Official Report.

7. Official Report, 26 October 1950, Vol. 75, p. 13953.

8. Official Report, 19 October 1950, Vol. 71, p. 13146.

9. Ibid, p. 13162.

10. See Erwin G. Krasnow, *The Politics of Broadcast Regulation* (New York: St. Martin's Press, 1973); J. Fred MacDonald, *One Nation Under Television: The Rise and Decline of Network TV* (New York: Pantheon Books, 1990); Sterling and Kittross, *Stay Tuned*.

11. Official Report, 26 October 1950, Vol. 75, p. 14004.

12. Official Report, 26 October 1950, Vol. 75, p. 14007.

13. Official Report, 19 October 1950, Vol. 71, p. 13146.

14. Official Report, 31 October 1950, Vol. 77, p. 14260.

15. Ibid, p. 13153.

16. *Sixth Report and Order*, 41 FCC 582 (11 April 1952)

17. One must interpret these figures with some suspicion, since it was a representative of RCA delivering the information.

18. Official Report, 26 October 1950, Vol. 75, p. 13956.

19. Ibid, p. 13871.

20. Some people believed that the 12-channel VHF band was insufficient to support a nationwide system of television broadcasting.

21. Official Report, 24 October 1950, Vol. 73, p. 13608.

22. Official Report, 25 October 1950, Vol. 74, p. 13687.

23. Official Report, 25 October 1950, Vol. 74, p. 13704; 26 October 1950, Vol. 75, p. 14006; 31 October 1950, Vol. 77, p. 14297.

24. Official Report, 26 October 1950, Vol. 75, p. 14006.

25. Susan L. Brinson, "Frieda Hennock: FCC Activist and the Campaign for Educational Television," *Historical Journal of Film, Radio, and Television* 18(3), pp. 411–429.

26. Official Report, 24 October 1950, Vol. 73, pp. 13513–13514.

27. Official Report, 26 October 1950, Vol. 75, p. 13948.

28. Official Report, 19 October 1950, Vol. 71, p. 13142.

29. Official Report, 24 October 1950, Vol. 73, pp. 13524–13525.

30. Official Report, 31 October 1950, Vol. 77, p. 14262.

31. Official Report, 20 October 1950, Vol. 72, pp. 13296–13297.

32. Ibid, p. 13298.

33. Ibid, p. 13360.

34. Official Report, 24 October 1950, Vol. 73, p. 13514.

35. Ibid, p. 13660.

36. Official Report, 31 October 1950, Vol. 77, p. 14290.

37. Official Report, 24 October 1950, Vol. 73, p. 13500.

38. Official Report, 24 October 1950, Vol. 73, p. 13614.

39. Hennock to Alicia D. Fraser, 21 November 1950, Box 1/Folder 18, Frieda Hennock Simons Collection, Schlesinger Library, Radcliffe College, Cambridge, MA, (hereafter cited as FHS)

40. *Sixth Report and Order*, 41 FCC 148.

41. Ibid, pp. 158–167.

42. Ibid, p. 208.

43. Sterling & Kittross, *Stay Tuned*, p. 357.

44. *Sixth Report and Order*, p. 208.

45. Ibid, pp. 208–209.

46. Ibid, pp. 189–197.

47. U.S. Congress, House, Interstate and Foreign Commerce Committee, Hearings for the Investigation of Regulatory Commissions and Agencies, 85th Cong., 2nd sess., p. 2393, (hereafter cited as House, Hearings for Investigation).

48. *Sixth Report and Order*, p. 582.

49. Ibid, p. 583.

50. Ibid, p. 585.

51. House, Hearings for the Investigation, p. 2399.

52. Krasnow, *The Politics of Broadcast Regulation*, p. 96.

53. "A Promising New Era Begins for Television," *Life*, 17 September 1951, p. 63; "Ultra High Frequency: The Promised Land of TV?" *Business Week*, 9 August 1952, p. 42.

54. "Upper UHF Operation Begins This Week, Target Dates Show," *Broadcasting*, 9 February 1953, p. 58; "UHF Outlets," *Broadcasting*, 9 March 1953, p. 5; "ABC of Radio and Television," *Broadcasting*, 30 March 1953, p. 89; Frank L. Brittin, "Ultra-High Frequency TV Stations Due in 1952," *Popular Mechanics*, October 1951, p. 228.

55. "'Upstairs' TV," *Newsweek*, 6 October 1952, p. 68; "TV: Answers to Some Questions on What UHF Means to TV Set Owners," *Consumer Reports*, June 1952, p. 305.

56. Federal Communications Commission, *Nineteenth Annual Report of the Federal Communications Commission* (Washington, D.C.: Government Printing Office, 1954), p. 4.

57. "Dissenting Views of Commissioner Hennock," 17 July 1953, Box 11, Folder-Dissenting Views #4, Frieda B. Hennock Collection, Harry S. Truman Presidential Library, (hereafter cited as FBH).

58. "Potter Subcommittee Meets, Sees Public Hearings on UHF Troubles," *Broadcasting*, 8 March 1954, p. 46.

59. "Senate Unit Launches Radio-TV Study," *Broadcasting*, 1 March 1954, p. 51; "Potter Subcommittee Meets," p. 46; "Hill Readies List of Witnesses on UHF," *Broadcasting*, 5 April 1954, p. 52; Jack Gould, "The Crisis in UHF," *New York Times*, 18 April 1954, Sec. II, p. 9; Alvin Shuster, "Video Expansion in U.S. Imperiled," *New York Times*, 19 April 1954, p. 41; "Senate UHF Hearing Again Postponed; New Date May 19," *Broadcasting*, 10 May 1954, p. 55.

60. "Getting the UHF Story," *Broadcasting*, 12 April 1954, p. 134.

61. Jack Gould, "The Crisis in UHF," *New York Times*, 18 April 1954, Sec. II, p. 9.

62. Station KUHT in Houston, Texas. FCC, *Nineteenth Annual Report*, p. 4.

63. Federal Communications Commission, *Twentieth Annual Report of the Federal Communications Commission* (Washington, D.C.: Government Printing Office, 1955), p. 6.

64. "Hill Readies List of Witnesses on UHF," *Broadcasting*, 5 April 1954, p. 52.

65. U.S. Congress, Senate, Senate Interstate and Foreign Commerce Committee, Status of UHF and Multiple Ownership of TV Stations, Hearings Before the Subcommittee on Communications of the Committee of Interstate and Foreign Commerce, 83rd Cong., 2nd sess., pp. 187-196, (hereafter cited as Status of UHF); "Testimony of Commissioner Frieda B. Hennock before the Potter Subcommittee," 19 May 1954, 11/Dissenting Views #1, FBH.

66. Status of UHF, p. 188.

67. Ibid.

68. Ibid, p. 189.

69. "FCC Asked to Suspend All TV Grants Until Hearings Are Held on Hill," *Broadcasting*, 19 April 1954, p. 48; "Why UHF Operators Want Another Freeze," *Broadcasting*, 3 May 1954, p. 52.

70. Status of UHF, p. 190.

71. Ibid, p. 193–194.

72. Ibid, pp. 190–191.

73. Ibid, p. 191.

74. "UHF Group Formed to Plan Senate Hearing Strategy," *Broadcasting*, 26 April 1954, p. 52; "Why UHF Operators," p. 52.

75. Status of UHF, p. 191; "Freeze of New VHF's Asked by UHF Stations," *Broadcasting*, 24 May 1954, p. 119.

76. Status of UHF, pp. 1060–1071; "Testimony of Commissioner Frieda B. Hennock before the Potter Subcommittee," 22 June 1954, 11/Dissenting Views #1, FBH.

77. Status of UHF, p. 1061.

78. Ibid, p. 1063.

79. Ibid, pp. 1065–1066.

80. Status of UHF, p. 1063.

81. Status of UHF, p. 1064.

82. Ibid, p. 1069.

83. Ibid, p. 1068.

84. Ibid, p. 196.

85. Statement of Commissioner Frieda B. Hennock on the FCC Panel at the NARTB Convention, 27 Mary 1954, 11/Dissenting Views #4, FBH. This statement was also included in the record of her testimony before the Potter Subcommittee, Status of UHF, pp. 1069–1071.

86. Ibid.

87. "Members of FCC Clash on UHF Issue," *New York Times*, 28 May 1954, p. 30; "Hennock Reiterates Plea for All-UHF; Sterling Challenges at NARTB Panel," *Broadcasting*, 31 May 1954, p. 63.

88. "Hennock Reiterates," p. 63.

89. "Hennock Reiterates," p. 63.

90. Hennock to Abrams, 13 July 1954, 1/Corresp Re:ETV-A, FBH.

91. Ibid.

92. "Commission to Consider Applications for UHF Television Stations Proposing No Local Programming," 54 FCC 991.

93. Ibid.

94. Ibid.

95. Many letters responding to Hennock's UHF dissent may be found in Boxes 10 & 11/UFH Corresp., FBH. Among those letters are replies from Lyndon Johnson, Edwin Johnson, John Bricker, Estes Kefauver, Eva Bowring, and many others.

96. Fred Weber to Hennock, 13 August 1954, 10/Corresp-UHF dissent, FBH.

97. Seymour Krieger to Hennock, 16 August 1954, 10/Corresp-UHF dissent, FBH.

98. Hennock to Magnuson, 25 May 1955, 3/31, FHS.

99. Dissent of Commissioner Hennock from the Commission's Decisions of September 8 not to Grant Requested Extension of Time for completion of construction of Stations KLYN-TV at Amarillo, Texas and KHTV at Hibbing, Minnesota. Found in 9/123, FHS.

100. House, Hearings for the Investigation, p. 2372.

101. Ibid, p. 2399.

102. Ibid.

103. Chris McConnell, "NFL on Fox Highlights UHF Shortcomings," *Broadcasting*, 17 October 1994, p. 60.

104. Ibid.

105. Richard Zoglin, "Murdoch's Biggest Score," *Broadcasting*, 6 June 1994, p. 54.

106. Chris McConnell, "UHF Spectrum: Telcom's New Hot Property," *Broadcasting*, 29 July 1996, p. 20.

CHAPTER 5

"The Mother Protector, and Fighter": The Campaign for Educational Television

Educational television was the perfect political vehicle for Frieda Hennock. In accomplishing the regulatory framework for developing ETV, Hennock could satisfy her twin desires of contributing both the public good and her own political interests. She was a strong believer in the power of education to transform individuals; her own life and education in America were testament to the gift of education. She wanted to share that gift with Americans who, for whatever reason, had not received complete curricular instruction. She wanted to give them alternatives to Milton Berle and Howdy-Doody. In Hennock's eyes there was no greater good she could accomplish, nothing more obviously in the public interest, than establishing educational television. Yet her devotion to public interests was matched with an equal commitment to personal goals. ETV was tailor-made for that purpose. All politicians know that they must have an issue, a platform, on which to acquire and maintain political clout, and Frieda Hennock was a politician. From the moment she became a commissioner, Hennock kept a watchful eye open for an issue she could make her own. Arthur Stambler, her confidential legal assistant during the educational television hearings, revealed that "she was looking for an issue. . . . This was an enormously ambitious woman. She needed an issue. She needed a white horse." Keith Tyler, with whom Hennock worked very closely during the educational television hearings, later described her as "a woman who wanted a cause."[1] "She was a smart politician," Tyler noted, "and she knew that to get prominence you had to have a cause that you stood for."[2] Equally as important, ETV was a safe political issue for a woman during a conservative period. Nobody would fault a woman for wanting to educate America's children; it seemed like a "natural" response for a woman.

Frieda Hennock did not join the FCC with an interest in educational television. Once discovered it became the guiding influence for the positions she took during the "freeze." Her staunch support of the RCA "compatible" color television system resulted from the inherent dangers the CBS "incompatible" system represented to ETV. While her devotion to ETV served her well in the color TV decision, it blinded her to the inherent difficulties of UHF television and, especially, intermixture. She did not foresee those problems. The color and UHF decisions were peripheral, however, to her ETV campaign, and it was, in fact, the issue with which she both made her most lasting public service contribution and successfully established a national political reputation.[3] Hennock was the principal moving force behind the creation of educational television, and she successfully waged considerable political and public relations campaigns to secure allocation of television channels for noncommercial, educational programming. In so doing, she also accomplished two fundamentally and personally important goals. She led a successful campaign that resulted in an FCC decision that truly and obviously benefitted the public (as opposed to corporate) interests, and she effectively made a political name for herself.

THE SEARCH FOR A CAUSE

When Hennock assumed her FCC position she had no clear-cut intentions regarding educational television. Privately, she wrote to a friend that, "Perhaps I will come out with something new, or I might be a complete flop—who knows—but I want to give myself a chance."[4] Nearly a year later, however, in early May 1949 Hennock was invited by Morris Novik to attend the annual meeting of the Institute for Education by Radio and Television (IERT) at Ohio State University.[5] The meeting was a revelation for her, as she learned first-hand from educators the problems inherent to providing educational material on radio, and the anticipated problems with television. She later disclosed that, "It was here that many of my ideas concerning educational-TV [sic] were born."[6] She became actively involved in discussions at the meeting, as indicated in letters from other participants who were impressed by "the great interest in the field of educational radio and television which you showed at Ohio State University last week."[7] Stanley Neustadt, her first legal assistant, asserted that Hennock returned from the IERT meeting with a more focused interest in educators,[8] and her newly developed commitment to educational broadcasting was immediately apparent. She commented that "I feel that it is my duty to do everything in my power to spread education over the air wherever possible and that means helping the educational institutions get more stations."[9] Indeed, in a letter to a professor of education Hennock wrote that, "It was a real education to me to attend the institute and learn the problem of the educators. . . . I have done a great deal of thinking on the subject of education in radio since my return, and feel very deeply that something should be done."[10]

Although new to Hennock, the relationship between education and broadcasting began in radio's infancy. Many of the first broadcast radio stations were licensed to educational institutions during the 1920s, although most of them were "edged out" by financial pressures, unfavorable channel assignments, interference problems, and the increasing commercialization of radio.[11] By 1934 a minority of radio stations provided exclusively educational programming. In that year the National Committee on Education by Radio (NCER) began lobbying for the reservation of frequencies exclusively for educational stations.[12] Legislation introduced before Congress, the Wagner-Hatfield Act, proposed exactly that. Acquiring considerable opposition from the commercial networks and failing to receive either congressional or Federal Radio Commission support, while simultaneously receiving curiously little support from educational broadcasters, the Wagner-Hatfield Act failed to pass and the Radio Act of 1927 eventually was replaced by the 1934 Communications Act.[13] Two things happened as a result of this near-reservation of educational channels. First, the commercial networks, perhaps recognizing the threat educational reservations posed for the loss of commercial frequencies—and hence potential affiliates—promised to provide more educational material in their programming.[14] More importantly, however, "the precedent of setting aside channels for education had been established."[15] This was a precedent of which Frieda Hennock later took full advantage.

When Hennock discovered educational television in May 1949, the timing was propitious. Just over a year into the "freeze," the commission had made little progress toward resolving television's technical problems and was in the process of scheduling hearings. On 26 May 1949 the FCC issued a public notice announcing a call for further hearings into the considerable technical problems faced by the television industry. The notice specifically asserted that, following the hearings, the FCC would create new rules that would "not only cover the contemplated use of channels in the UHF band but will also contain a revised allocation table for the present VHF band," as well as decide the future of color television technology.[16] Absent from the public notice was any mention of educational television. Given her new-found interest in educational broadcasting, Hennock recognized the need for quick action in order to ensure a place for educational television. In a statement attached to the public notice, Hennock asserted that a "multitude of other questions . . . must be solved to insure the finest development of this great new art for as many people as possible. . . . And I feel that we must patiently continue to move forward in this orderly manner. . . . We should not falter in that purpose. I therefore believe that this public notice is premature."[17] This dissent was critical to the later development of educational television. From a position of power on the commission, Hennock was able to initiate the beginnings of ETV. Richard Hull, one of the most prominent members of the National Association of Educational Broadcasters (NAEB), later asserted that "she was the one who was the hold-out, the sole dissenter, . . . and that's where the ETV reservations started from."[18]

Between May and July 1949 Hennock's vision of educational television crystallized. By July 11 she fell squarely behind reserving television channels for noncommercial use. On that date the FCC issued a *Notice of Further Proposed Rule Making*, in which it proposed its initial plan for allocating channels nationwide.[19] There was no mention of noncommercial television channels. In a lone dissent, Hennock asserted that the Notice "should include a provision for the reservation of a specified number of frequencies in the ultra-high frequency band for the establishment of a noncommercial educational television service."[20] She continued to assert that failure to make this set-aside would "result in tragic waste from the standpoint of the public interest if, at the outset of development in this field, adequate provision were not made for the realization of the almost limitless possibilities of television as a medium of visual education."[21] By this time Hennock developed a definition of educational television. She described it as a medium for providing classroom instruction, both at school and home. Viewers would literally watch lectures on television. Additionally, ETV would provide "a higher type of cultural programming."[22] By July 1949 Frieda Hennock found the issue for which she had searched since assuming her position on the FCC. For the remaining six years of her appointment, the creation and development of educational television was her primary focus.

To this end, Hennock organized a campaign to secure educational channel allocations which may be organized into three distinct phases: the Pre-ETV Hearings Phase (July 1949 to November 1950), the Hearings Phase (November 1950 to January 1951), and the Post-Hearings/Decision Phase (January 1951 to June 1955). Within each period her message remained consistent. Whether speaking to educators and women's groups, questioning witnesses, appearing on radio or television, corresponding with individuals and groups, or writing essays, her single-minded goal was the reservation of television channels for educational purposes. As Arthur Stambler noted about Hennock during this period, "She was the general [directing] . . . the hand-to-hand combat" of what would become the ETV battle.

PHASE ONE: PRE-HEARINGS (JULY 1949–NOVEMBER 1950)

As a matter of administrative policy, the FCC was required to schedule hearings during which interested parties were allowed to respond to the commission's allocation plans. Hennock's task was two-fold: to both organize witnesses to testify at the pending ETV hearings, and to build both educational and public support for her reservation plans. As fate would have it, she had plenty of time to organize the educational hearings. Between September 1949 and November 1950 the commission was consumed with two other issues related to the "freeze." The first and most tumultuous was the color TV decision, the public hearings for which ran from September 1949 to May 1950. The second issue facing the FCC was the nationwide allocation of frequencies, which was the subject of hearings from mid-October to mid-November 1950. Although time-consuming and frequently distracting, these two hearings were critical to Hennock and the development of ETV. The fifteen months devoted to the color and allocations hearings gave her the much-needed time for marshaling support for ETV. Equally as important, her participation in the color and UHF hearings enabled her to detect potential threats to her educational television plans. Like any good litigator, she mined the color and UHF hearings for both technical and industry dangers. When the ETV hearings finally opened in November 1950, Frieda Hennock was ready for the challenges.

The task of organizing the hearings fell squarely on Hennock's shoulders. Stambler asserted that, "she was the one who took upon herself, in fact [the other commissioners] left it to her, they'd have been happy if she'd done nothing. She had to get the people to testify, what to testify, how to testify, what form in which to testify, make sure they were on the issues. . . . So, yes, she had to find the witnesses, make sure they had the appropriate submissions, and so forth."[23] In correspondence, Hennock also indicated her considerable responsibilities regarding the educational hearings by writing that she was "in the midst of planning our educational television hearings and their organization demands every spare moment" she had.[24] Those whom she invited to testify at the hearings recognized the role she played in their organization, such as the individual who wrote that she would "be pleased to testify at *your* hearings on educational use of television" (emphasis added).[25] Journalists also understood her fundamental role, one of whom wrote that Hennock was "conducting practically a single-handed campaign to arouse educators and the public to the need for . . . reservation of television bands for education."[26]

As the *Notice of Further Proposed Rule Making* stipulated, however, anyone wanting to testify during hearings had to notify the FCC of their intent by 8 August 1949—less than a month after the *Notice* was issued.[27] Understanding that the future of educational television depended upon the ability of educators to persuade the FCC that they would use channels set aside for noncommercial use, Hennock realized she needed educators to contact the FCC to indicate interest in testifying before hearings. As a result, her most intensive strategies focused on both creating and maintaining educators' interests in developing noncommercial television, and cajoling them into communicating their interest. To accomplish this goal, Hennock used several methods of communicating her messages, particularly written correspondence. For instance, on literally the same day the *Notice* was publicly issued, Hennock embarked on a letter-writing campaign in which she alerted interested parties "that it [would] be necessary for the educators to file their comments by August 8, 1949, in order to be allowed to appear at the hearings. I urge you to get all of them interested in filing timely comments so that they may appear and testify in behalf of educational television."[28] Richard Hull, president of the NAEB, responded to her appeal by sending an urgent letter to all members asking them to show their "appreciation of Commissioner Hennock's efforts in our behalf" by notifying the national office of their interest in educational broadcasting.[29] A second form letter was created by Hennock's office to respond to correspondents who commented on her first ETV dissent.[30] In this letter she asserted that she felt "very strongly that educators have a responsibility to utilize the tools for mass communication in the cause of education. . . . It is to guard against early preemption of available spectrum space that I urged upon the commission the advisability of reserving television channels for the exclusive use of educational institutions."[31] Hennock also encouraged educators to "keep thinking about this great new problem child, television, and how you educators can get right into the thick of it. I will always be glad to hear any new ideas you have on the subject." Hennock's efforts were successful. By late August 1949 she reported that "several educational organizations have filed formal proposals for an educational broadcasting service and will participate in those hearings."[32]

Hennock's work behind the scenes also included working with the Joint Committee on Educational Television (JCET). Formed that August 1949 as a result of Hennock's appeal for educators to contact the FCC,[33] the JCET was a group comprised of seven educational organizations, most notably the American Council on Education, the National Education Association, the National Association of Educational Broadcasters, and the Association of Land Grant Colleges and Universities.[34] The JCET's goal was to unify the influence and energies of these seven organizations under one banner and lead the appeal for ETV reservations. Although she did not participate directly in the creation of the JCET, Hennock eventually played an active role in directing its strategies. It was she who suggested that Brigadier General Telford Taylor, former FCC counsel and Nuremberg Trial attorney, should represent the JCET at the ETV hearings.[35] Similarly, late-night strategy sessions regarding the JCET were held at Hennock's Washington, D.C. home.[36]

Preaching the gospel of educational television more directly, Hennock made several speeches to educators during the period between April and October 1950.[37] In each of these appearances she chided her audiences for their past failures to support educational broadcasting while simultaneously exhorting them to support her campaign for noncommercial channels. Referring to the failure of educational radio to maintain its presence during the 1920s and 1930s, Hennock scolded educators by asserting that, "Education once sold its broadcasting birthright for a mess of pottage. You can't let that happen again!"[38] She questioned members of the Institute for Education by Radio: "Where are the titans of our educational system now that the time has come for you to demand your rightful place in the television picture?"[39] Just two weeks later Hennock asserted that, "The cultivated and the educated have always been the first to complain about what gets on the air, but their affirmative contributions have been niggardly, to say the least."[40] Hennock made it clear that educators were partly to blame for their "mess of pottage."

Hennock assured educators, however, that the rewards would be many if they actively supported educational television. She appealed to educators' ability to extend their pedagogical touch to ever-larger groups of people. "It is quite clear that insofar as adult education is concerned, television will provide a classroom without physical boundaries. You can reach right into the home of every person sufficiently interested to tune in" she promised them.[41] She encouraged educators to share her vision that educational television could be utilized for "the preservation of our democratic ideals. . . . A people well informed is a people that can enjoy peace and plenty."[42]

Attaining these lofty goals could only be reached if the educators pressed for them, Hennock assured her audiences: "We at the FCC cannot and will not impose from above our own individual ideas of what American broadcasting should be like."[43] Indeed, she challenged educators to take responsibility for their own desires, explaining that they had to make their wishes clearly known to the FCC. "You must come out swinging,"[44] she pugilistically exhorted her followers, to "make the strongest showing possible" before the FCC.[45] In speech after speech, Hennock encouraged educators to clearly communicate their desires to the FCC. Noticeably absent from these speeches are indications of how educators would pay for the costly television equipment, particularly regarding the color TV and allocation issues pending before the FCC, or even *what* they would broadcast. The financial obstacles caused by relying on public monies to pay for television station construction and programming costs could wait until a later date. Instead, Hennock's first priority was to simply persuade educators to demand that the FCC allocate channels strictly for noncommercial programs. The choices were clear, she promised: "Education has the choice of now sitting down to the first course of a sumptuous repast, or later coming in as a beggar for its crumbs."[46]

Although Hennock rightly perceived educators to be the credible proponents of educational television before the FCC, she similarly understood the potential influence of women's professional organizations. Unusual for the time period, the women to whom she spoke—like Hennock herself—bridged the public and private worlds. As such, they had the unique ability to understand both the influence of television programming on family and home life, as well as the machinations of the industry and its regulation. Before an audience composed of the National Association of Women Lawyers, Hennock spoke both of the uses of radio and television to "keep the tired husband and the too energetic children happy . . . without undue strain on [the wife/mother's] part," while simultaneously citing legal code from the Communications Act of 1934.[47] Following a lengthy explanation of both the codified responsibilities of the FCC and the influence commercial broadcasters had over air time, Hennock explained to her audience the importance of reserving channels for educational television. "If we are to prevent television from assuming the characteristics of our aural broadcasting system," she encouraged her listeners, "we must introduce some new blood. This would . . . prove a great stimulus for the production of better programs."[48] Similarly, before the New York Women's Advertising Club, Hennock praised its members for having "the unequaled opportunity to raise TV to far greater heights of public service. . . . As women in the commercial television industry you have an intimate knowledge of its problems and play a large part in its development."[49] Recalling similar messages directed toward educators, she both chided advertisers for their irresponsible programming and encouraged them to support educational programming, which was "the best weapon our democracy has."[50]

Although appealing to the influential abilities of educators and women's organizations was a necessary strategy, Hennock well understood the concept of "public interest" and its centrality to the FCC's governance of the broadcasting industry. Indeed, one of her fundamental motivations in developing ETV was public interest. Consequently, she also created messages intended to reach the general American public, although these were much fewer in number than the considerable number of speeches and letters written to more directly effectual groups. Of course, the most efficient way to communicate to the largest numbers of people possible was mass communication, and Hennock utilized the print media to attempt to persuade Americans to support ETV. In late November 1950 Hennock telegrammed John Crosby, a syndicated columnist whose home paper was the New York *Herald Tribune*, urging him to write a column about the upcoming hearings. She specifically urged that television, "as one of the nation's greatest natural resources . . . not become a grab-bag for commercial stations alone," and she advised him of her need for "all the letters and telegrams [she could] get . . . so that they can be presented at the hearings."[51] Crosby responded with a column that appeared in several newspapers during the first week of the hearings, including one on 28 November 1950.[52] The public response was virtually immediate, with hundreds of letters pouring in from around the country. One citizen wrote wondering whether his young son would ever be able to view television programs "not dictated by commercial considerations? If the answer is 'no,' then my government will have neglected its duty to me and my son."[53] Another correspondent declared that, "If one citizen's approval can help you and John Crosby to lift the U.S. above the mental level of Howdy-Doody, here it is."[54]

PHASE TWO: THE HEARINGS (NOVEMBER 1950–JANUARY 1951)

By the time the ETV allocation hearings commenced on 27 November 1950, Hennock amassed more than sixty witnesses to testify in support of noncommercial television, including four senators, one member of the House of Representatives, the Commissioner of the U.S. Office of

Education, several university presidents, many university professors, presidents of labor and civic organizations, the former president of the NBC network, and numerous others.[55] She also received the silent support of President Harry Truman.[56] In less than eighteen months on the FCC, Hennock developed such a passion for the possibilities of educational television that she was able to motivate hundreds of supporters and organize the hearings in order to guarantee allocations of noncommercial television channels. Her accomplishments are particularly noteworthy in the light of the opposition she faced from fellow commissioners, the broadcasting industry, and the prevailing philosophies of contemporary intellectuals.

Even before developing a strong position regarding educational television, Hennock was isolated by the other six commissioners. Arthur Stambler explained that one reason for this segregation was a result of the sexist attitudes[57] of the other commissioners toward Hennock: "She was strident and insensitive, particularly to men. Men do not like to be lectured by ladies, and she was always lecturing [the other commissioners]."[58] Further, their dislike for her was also motivated by her insistence on challenging the status quo at the FCC. "She had a lot of contrarian in her," Stambler explained, "And it wasn't just personal. She wasn't just strident, and harpy, and lecturing them. She wouldn't go along. She wouldn't play the game. She wasn't the 'hail fellow, well met' [type]. . . . And she took positions on many issues that they were unhappy with."[59] As India Edwards explained to President Truman, Hennock "worked under great difficulties and in the face of opposition and prejudice."[60] It should not be surprising, then, to learn that she received little support for noncommercial channel reservations from her fellow commissioners. Although Chairman Wayne Coy occasionally encouraged educators to participate in the television hearings,[61] as did Commissioner Walker,[62] there is little evidence to suggest that they—or any of the remaining four commissioners—actively supported channel set-asides for educational television.[63] Indeed, at least one of Hennock's contemporaries recognized that "the majority of the commission does not agree with her" position on ETV.[64]

If the other commissioners failed to support Hennock behind-the-scenes, *Broadcasting*, the industry trade magazine, overtly opposed her ETV fight. *Broadcasting* was (and still is) perceived to be the voice of the industry, and its opposition to the Freeze in general was well-known.[65] Beginning in August 1949, the magazine consistently linked educational television with Hennock. Indeed, throughout the following months, stories on Hennock and educational television were often one and the same.[66] Such concentrated attention on Hennock and ETV culminated in an editorial in which the editor, Sol Taishoff, wondered why there was "No Opposition?" to the ETV hearings, "Comr. [sic] Frieda Hennock is quarter-backing the educational strategy. The FCC proceedings have been virtually *ex parte*, since no witnesses have been cross-examined by representatives of the nation's broadcast interests, who have invested so heavily in the visual medium. So Comr. [sic] Hennock has been making touchdowns in every quarter."[67] Taishoff represented Hennock as cheating commercial interests out of their right to question witnesses when, in fact, they had ample opportunity to signal their interest to the FCC. Indeed, Stanley Neustadt revealed that *Broadcasting* magazine, "hated her, period, for almost everything she stood for. But they certainly hated her for ETV. . . . [The magazine] was very conservative, and it essentially represented the view of what it thought was the broadcasting industry. Broadcasters were against it, Taishoff was against it. . . . But they sure didn't like Frieda Hennock. She was unpredictable to them. And she got attention."[68] Hence, Hennock faced formidable opposition from both her fellow commissioners as well as members of the broadcasting industry as represented by *Broadcasting* magazine.

On a broader scale, Hennock also faced opposition in the form of a philosophy communicated by a small group of vocal intellectuals who were disturbed by the development of mass culture in the United States. Dwight Macdonald defined mass culture as an article produced "solely and directly for mass consumption" [69] and decried the development of a mass culture that "exploit[s] the cultural needs of the masses . . . is manufactured for mass consumption by technicians . . . and is not an expression of . . . the common people themselves."[70] Clement Greenberg described the development of mass culture as a response to the needs of the masses who, "discover[ed] a new capacity for boredom . . . [were] insensible to the values of genuine culture, [and were] hungry nevertheless for the diversion that only culture of some sort can provide."[71] As Richard Pells concluded, these and other intellectuals deplored the media for giving "people just what they wanted: leisure activities that were 'easy to assimilate,' that promised diversion and relaxation but not 'disturbance' or 'insight.' "[72] Some intellectuals, however, viewed the mass media with considerably less hostility. David Manning White, for instance, believed the media held out "the greatest promise to the 'average' man [sic] that a cultural richness no previous age could give him [sic] is at hand."[73] Indeed, White specifically addressed the ability of educational television to provide alternatives to sponsored programming. "As educational television networks develop throughout the states there will be few communities in America where the audiences do not have their choice any evening between Berle or Bach, Godfrey or Goya, the '$64,000 Question' or a discussion of Thucydides' historical method."[74]

Hennock's vision of television closely aligned with White's. Although she rarely directly criticized the content of commercial programming, her position could be detected by looking at her insistence that "TV develops in such a way as to become an important force for intellectual and cultural betterment."[75] Before the New York Women's Advertising Club, she urged the audience to imagine what it would be like if Shakespeare could "become as vibrant as any contemporary dramatist and compete for listener attention with any murder mystery and western."[76] Fearful of repeating the mistakes of educational radio, and driven by the enormous intellectual and cultural opportunities television offered, Hennock immersed herself in the process of making "an affirmative effort to make provision to ensure that educators will be able to make full use of television."[77]

Hence, it was in this atmosphere that the educational television hearings began in Washington, D.C. on 27 November 1950. Having assembled an impressive number of people to testify, it now fell on Hennock's shoulders to ensure that their testimony communicated the importance of reserving television channels for ETV. Not one to sit idly by while others testified, she was an active participant in the hearings, and used them to accomplish two fundamental goals: she promoted ETV whenever possible, and became its most ardent champion when the idea was threatened. Indeed, transcripts of the hearings indicate the lengths to which Hennock would go to further the ETV goal.

Hennock was single-minded; the reservation of noncommercial channels was the only goal in sight. The means to the end were virtually limitless, and once an individual was on the witness stand, it didn't matter if she or he was friend or foe as long as the testimony eventually furthered ETV. On the one hand, the manner in which she questioned witnesses revealed her biases. If the witness' testimony was favorable but too vague or too technical, she might lead the person to a more succinct testimony by asking, "Is there any question in your mind about the necessity of television as an educational medium and its importance?"[78] If she perceived the witness to be hostile to her plans, she would unleash her considerable legal skills. It is not surprising that her substantial talents were used to discredit the testimony of people like Frank Stanton, President of CBS, or Richard Salant, attorney for CBS, or Kenneth Baker, President of the National Association of Broadcasters, all of whom strongly opposed noncommercial set-asides.[79] It is surprising to find her criticizing her own witnesses or fellow FCC co-workers. During NAEB President Richard Hull's testimony, she severely chastised him for showing any interest in providing commercially-sponsored programming on an educational channel.[80] While FCC General Counsel Harry Plotkin questioned other individuals, Hennock objected to both the tone and substance of his questions, and took him to task for both.[81]

Her behavior was matched by her use of questions to stipulate key points, and there were many points to make. During the course of the two months of testimony, Hennock ensured that several things were made very clear to her fellow commissioners. First, commercial stations often preempted educational programming in favor of sponsored shows.[82] Second, as a result of this practice, relegating educational programming to the whims of commercial broadcasters was unacceptable.[83] Further, a third point Hennock stressed was the error in allowing educational stations to provide sponsored programming, believing they would become too concerned with the size of viewing audiences provided to advertisers. As she put it to a witness, "How are you ever going to be a purely educational station if you keep worrying about the number of people you have listening to you?"[84]

As frequently as she made points about what noncommercial television shouldn't be, Hennock also stressed the possibilities of ETV, provided educators were given enough time to gather funding and build stations.[85] In an example of a question becoming a position statement, she asked a witness if he believed that educational

channels might be assigned to commercial interests and that they might be gobbled up in the most important areas and the best frequencies might be gone by the time you have gone through all this, and since you are in this to render a service to this great Nation [sic] and to help keep it a great Nation [sic], that the least you can expect is cooperation, a reservation of these channels to give you an opportunity to come in and do a job for the people of this country and have these channels held on to for you so that is your home, so that you can look forward to getting into that home and get the money and the backing to do so. Is that what you want us to do?[86]

The reference to the "great service" finally comes down to Hennock's fundamental belief in the capacity for television to be a tremendous teaching medium. Throughout the hearings she consistently questioned educators about the types of programming they would provide, and they wishfully responded that they would instruct students of all ages in subjects such as the creative arts, introductory psychology, American history, government, business, literature, and medical courses.[87] Through her questions and/or attacks, Hennock made it clear that the reservation of channels would not be a waste of frequency space; the channels would be put to good use.

Not content to rely on the impressions witnesses made on fellow commissioners, Hennock continued her campaign in the public arena.[88] She made at least two nationally broadcast appearances during the hearings period. On 28 November 1950, she was a guest on the ABC radio program "Town Meeting of the Air," during which she participated in a debate centering on "Who should be responsible for education on television?" Speaking to both studio and national audiences, Hennock used this opportunity to make several persuasive appeals for support for ETV. She criticized the radio networks by asserting that "our commercial broadcasters [never] have accepted or ever will accept the full responsibility for educating our listening and viewing public."[89] In a statement sounding like a modern-day sound bite, Hennock also claimed that television could "be put to better use as an electronic blackboard than as an electronic billboard, bringing roadside advertising messages into the home."[90] On 21 January 1951 she was Eleanor Roosevelt's guest on NBC's "Mrs. Roosevelt Meets the Public," during which she promoted channel reservations by arguing that "educational-TV [sic] will be an investment in our country's future that will pay dividends for generations to come."[91] Hennock later wrote to Mrs. Roosevelt expressing her deep appreciation for allowing her "the opportunity to explain to your large and faithful television audience my views concerning the reservation of television channels for educators."[92]

Consistent with her broadcast appeals, Hennock also used the print media to continue her ETV campaign. In a guest editorial for *The Saturday Review of Literature*, she convincingly outlined her arguments supporting noncommercial television.[93] For *Variety* she boldly predicted that television could "become one of the greatest forces America [had] ever known for personal improvement, mass public education, and a resulting rise in our general standard of living."[94] Finally, *Broadcasting* magazine, which strongly opposed the reservations, printed a year-in-review essay in which Hennock lauded the future of educational television.[95] Simultaneously, *Broadcasting* sent out warning signals to the broadcasting industry, indicating that Hennock's campaign was achieving success. Editor Sol Taishoff asked why there was "No Opposition?" to Hennock's carefully orchestrated hearings and public campaign, and chastised the industry for failing to "join the issue."[96]

When the hearings were adjourned on 30 January 1951 Hennock had accomplished an amazing feat. Thousands of letters supporting educational set-asides indicated the success of her public campaign. During eleven of the fourteen days of hearings, dozens of proponents of educational television testified on its behalf. In November 1950 and January 1951, Senator John Bricker of Ohio introduced two senate resolutions supporting ETV.[97] While Hennock may have won her fight in the court of public opinion, as indicated in a *Broadcasting* article,[98] the battle was not yet over. Although she continued her public campaign over the next two months, the time drew near to make a decision about reserving television channels for educational purposes.

PHASE THREE: POST-HEARINGS/DECISION (JANUARY–JUNE 1951)

Although during the hearings Hennock concentrated most of her efforts on carefully examining witnesses, and strictly limiting her public appearances, this behavior changed as soon as the hearings adjourned. Her public appearances quickly resumed the same maddening pace as before. The fact the hearings had occurred was immediately apparent through the content of her addresses. In addition to frequent references to the hearings, she often incorporated ideas presented during testimony. Hence, her post-hearing speeches demonstrate the development of new arguments in support of educational television. For instance, in several speeches she made repeated analogies to television frequencies as a natural resource. "There is no question but that the television spectrum is one of our greatest natural resources," she told the Women's National Democratic Club and, as such, ought to be treated in a similar fashion as national forests.[99] Another theme that similarly ran through several post-hearing speeches was the importance of television to maintaining and elevating America's cultural tastes. She encouraged one audience to consider television as "an unparalleled instrument for spreading knowledge, enlightenment and culture throughout the United States" by making "every American a student of national affairs, of history, of culture and art."[100]

Yet a third message added to her post-hearing repertoire of arguments supporting ETV was a focus on the ability of educational television to promote democracy and, hence, combat totalitarianism. In the context of the early 1950s, with Russian, Chinese, and Korean communism looming on the horizon and McCarthyism festering, this was a formidable argument to make. "Through education," she declared, "we have developed the world's greatest democracy. . . . [But] modern man [sic] requires modern techniques of learning."[101] One of those modern techniques, of course, was educational television. She concluded by stating that "A reservation of television channels for educational purposes will be a major factor toward strengthening our educational system and our democratic institutions. In advocating such a reservation, I believe I am advocating the preservation of our sacred American heritage."[102] Moreover, if educational television was the greatest communicator of democratic ideals, it was similarly useful in revealing the evils of non-democratic systems. "In a world of crisis where democracy is threatened by totalitarianism seeking to draw a curtain of ignorance before the minds of men [sic], there is nothing more deserving of our attention and effort than education," she illuminated.[103]

Although these themes run steadily through all of Hennock's post-hearing speeches, she reserved special messages for educators. As she told members of the Institute for Education by Radio and Television, the same organization from whom she first learned about educational broadcasting, "One thing is clear—this warning I must make—the fight for educational television is by no means over. It has just begun!"[104] In a series of speeches, Hennock reminded educators that they must accept the responsibility of educational television and work at its development,[105] they must provide extensive programming,[106] all of which had to be stimulating.[107] Furthermore, educators could not let the costs of building stations and developing programs distract them,[108] and must make budgetary room for educational television.[109]

While her speeches were made to limited audiences, Hennock remained publicly visible. Her addresses were usually covered by both the popular and trades presses; the *New York Times* frequently reported Hennock's activities,[110] and *Broadcasting* monitored virtually every move she made.[111] Further, Hennock published essays in the *Journal of New York State Education*, *The Commercial and Financial Chronicle*, and *Educational Outlook*.[112] Finally, on 10 June 1951 she appeared on NBC's "Meet the Press," at the opening of which she was introduced as "the most controversial figure on the commission."[113] During the program Hennock was questioned by *Broadcasting* editor Sol Taishoff, who blatantly reminded her when her term expired. She responded by reminding him that the "air waves belong to the people . . . and this educational reservation is [to serve the public interest], and that is more important than anything else we can do in my opinion."[114]

By the time Hennock appeared on "Meet the Press," however, the FCC had made its decision regarding channel reservations for noncommercial use. As part of its overall television assignments plan, on 22 March 1951 the commission set aside approximately 10% of television frequencies for noncommercial stations.[115] Although Hennock was "in complete agreement with the commission's action in finally adopting the principle of indefinitely reserving television channels for noncommercial educational purposes,"[116] she was simultaneously deeply disappointed at the commission's failure to reserve the twenty-five percent of channels for which she lobbied. "By failing to provide education with its rightful share of the television spectrum," she wrote, "the commission . . . runs the risk of stunting the growth of educational-TV [sic] in the formative days of its infancy and of forever retarding the future of our entire educational system."[117] She continued, "the commission has grievously erred in not providing education with the reservations it needs and deserves and that, in so doing, it has worked an injustice to the public interest."[118]

Though disappointed by the decision, she continued to press for educational television. Through correspondence she encouraged educators to respond to FCC requests for comments regarding its television assignments.[119] As already mentioned, months after the FCC decision she encouraged educators through public addresses to take their responsibilities seriously, and she kept the educational television issue before the public through appearances such as the one on "Meet the Press." The day after that appearance, on 11 June 1951, President Truman nominated Hennock for a Federal judgeship.[120] Her attentions turned away from ETV and toward organizing a campaign to secure the judicial position. Four months later, having withdrawn her nomination, Hennock returned to her FCC duties. The battle for educational reservations, however, was over. Although victorious in that campaign, the remainder of her four years on the commission were spent fighting to protect the concept of educational television and furthering its development.

Hennock's efforts to further ETV continued long after publication of the FCC's *Sixth Report and Order*. Her prediction to the IERT in 1951 that the ETV fight had "just begun" was an accurate assessment. She continued to fight a multi-front battle to promote the development of educational television, the most critical of which was persuading educational institutions and local governments to take advantage of the reserved channels and initiate educational programming. This required extensive traveling on Hennock's part, as she toured the country speaking to local community organizations. Throughout 1952 and 1953 Hennock's journeys ranged from San Francisco to Houston to Atlantic City. As she later explained, somewhat defensively, to a Congressional subcommittee, her extensive travels were intended to endorse and further educational television, "If a commissioner spends weekends with a little briefcase and a lit-tle suitcase traveling all over the country, trying to stimulate interest in educational television and getting applications in to protect those chan-nels . . . if that is not spending Government money in the public interest, I would like to know what is."[121] Wherever she traveled, Hennock stressed the point that educators and government leaders had to get start-ed on educational programming. *"[T]he fundamental point,"* she urged the American Association of School Administrators, *"is the importance of getting started, of going on the air* [emphasis added]."[122]

Hennock's insistence that educational programming get underway was motivated by both an understanding and a fear that, despite the FCC's *Sixth Report and Order*, the educational reservations were always threat-ened. Certainly commercial broadcasters, who so completely dominated radio and were attempting to achieve mastery over television, made their opposition to noncommercial reservations very clear to the Government. Failure to take advantage of educational set-asides validated commercial broadcasters' complaints, voiced loudly during the ETV hearings, that educators would not be able to raise the money necessary to start a tele-vision station, thereby wasting a valuable broadcasting resource.

The threat to ETV was similarly manifested in a rumor that began floating through the broadcast industry soon after the *Sixth Report and Order* was released, which claimed that the *Order* had a one-year dead-line for educational channel requests. If the one-year deadline was not met, the channel would become a commercial channel. Educators, of course, could not arrange financial support for noncommercial stations in so short a period of time, hence the rumor was intended to both dis-courage them from attempting to get noncommercial licenses while simultaneously reinforcing the commercial broadcasters' claims that educators were ill-prepared to operate television stations. True to her devotion to ETV, Hennock took the lead position in quelling this rumor. "[T]his harmful misconception has . . . largely been the result of a will-ful campaign of misunderstanding and doubt that has been waged by the enemies of educational television," she told Senator Tobey and the Senate Committee.[123] Hennock went on to assert that other members of the commission, notably Commission Chair Walker and Commissioner Bartley, perpetuated the notion that a deadline existed. She contended, however, that the commission "set these 242 educational channels aside for an indefinite period and placed no specific time limitation of any kind upon their use. There is not a single word in the commission's decision about such a definite time limitation or 'deadline' as it might be called."[124] Hennock's points were well-taken. Shortly after the hearings she explained that "the effect of the Senate hearings on the Commission cannot be underestimated. There was a strong unanimity of opinion supporting the reservations from every senator present."[125] True to her demand that ETV channels get underway, however, she concluded that "it would be most unfortunate (as has too often happened before) if the resulting initiative and momentum are lost and if only small capital is made out of such a firm display of public support as has been manifested [by the Senate Committee] in the last few days."[126] The battle regarding the deadline was won when the FCC issued a public notice on 11 May 1953 which stated unequivocally that "a belief that the reservation of television channels for noncommercial educational use will expire on 2 June 1953" was "*not* the case; such reservations continue *indefinitely*."[127]

Although frequently forced to take a defensive position to protect the development of educational television, Hennock, ever the politician, recognized the need to make offensive moves to nurture its growth as well. The single greatest obstacle to the progress of ETV was the lack of funding for building television stations and producing and/or purchasing programming. In 1952 Hennock persuaded Benjamin Abrams, President of the Emerson Radio and Phonograph Corporation and a major television manufacturer, to create a fund from which the first ten ETV stations on the air would get $10,000 each.[128] Hennock went on to act as the intermediary between Abrams and eligible television stations, as when she informed Abrams that KETC in St. Louis was on the air and whom he should contact to make the $10,000 award.[129] She similarly pursued support from the Ford Foundation for the development of educational television.[130] Recognizing the second most difficult problem facing educational programmers, that of producing and/or acquiring quality programming, she contacted individuals regarding ways in which noncommercial stations could share programs by distributing kinescopes of locally produced shows.[131]

EPILOGUE: "I LED THE FIGHT FOR THE RESERVATION OF THE 252 EDUCATIONAL CHANNELS"[132]

When Frieda Hennock joined the FCC in 1948, she had no clear vision of what she wanted to accomplish. As a politically astute person, however, she understood the importance of creating a niche for herself; of finding a "white horse." This she found in educational television programming. Barely a year after joining the commission, she became the standard-bearer for the cause of noncommercial channel allocations, and devoted the next two years to creating demand for educational programming, organizing both the ETV hearings and most of its witnesses, dissenting against unfavorable FCC decisions, and rallying educators, women's organizations, and the general public to follow her lead. Hennock was so single-minded in her desire to witness the creation of educational television, that she assumed the major responsibility of orchestrating many of the events necessary to achieving that end.

The public service accomplishment represented by the ETV reservations were matched by the political currency Hennock collected as a result of the campaign. Countless peers recognized the fundamental influence she exerted over the development of educational reservations. Letters written to support her federal judgeship nomination focused on Hennock's "invaluable campaign,"[133] and "untiring efforts in support of education's need."[134] When Hennock's FCC appointment expired in 1955, dozens of congratulatory letters hailed her "almost single-handed victory."[135] As one correspondent put it,

> I share the gratefulness of your host of friends for the splendid contribution which you have made to the cause of educational television. You would be the first to argue that there is still a long way to go to attain the status which educational television rightly deserves, but you most certainly can, with pardonable pride, claim to be the most outspokenly constructive crusader in the history of the entire educational television movement.[136]

During the testimonial dinner honoring her tenure at the FCC, Hennock was praised by some of the highest members of federal and state government recognizing her significant accomplishments regarding educational television. Senator Estes Kefauver served as the dinner's Master of Ceremonies, and Senators Warren Magnuson, Herbert Lehman, and Wayne Morse made remarks during the event. Although unable to attend, former President Harry Truman, New York Governor Averell Harriman, former Senator and Governor Edwin Johnson, and Eleanor Roosevelt were among the noteworthy politicos sponsoring the dinner.[137] Even as late as 1995 Reed Hundt, then Chair of the FCC, proclaimed "Long Live Frieda Hennock" and recognized her as one commissioner who "saw that the public property of the airwaves should and could be used as a free medium for improving our culture and educating our children."[138] Hennock's political instincts were right when she selected educational television to be her "white horse," and she capitalized well on them.

NOTES

An earlier version of this chapter appeared in *Historical Journal of Film, Radio and Television*, 18(3), 1998.

1. I. Keith Tyler to Burt Harrison, Series 1/Box 6/Folder 16, Burt Harrison Papers, Public Radio Oral History Project Series, National Public Broadcasting Archive, University of Maryland, College Park, MD, (hereafter cited as Harrison Collection).

2. I. Keith Tyler to Jim Robertson, Series 1/Box 3/Folder 12, Robertson Collection.

3. The centrality of educational television to Hennock's FCC career is clearly evidenced by the amount of material devoted to it in her archives (the Schlesinger Library at Radcliffe College and the Truman Presidential Library). Virtually all of the documents contained in the Truman archive relate to Hennock's efforts toward educational television. The Schlesinger collection holds a considerable amount of personal documents, but professional material is devoted almost exclusively to ETV. There is comparatively little material relating to UHF, and almost none regarding the color television decision.

4. FBH to Fraser, 6 September 1948, Box 1/Folder 18, Frieda Hennock Simons Collection, Schlesinger Library, Radcliffe College, Cambridge, MA (hereafter cited as FHS).

5. Morris Novik to Burt Harrison, Series 1/Box 6/Folder 3, Harrison Collection. See also I. Keith Tyler to Burt Harrison, Series 1/Box 6/Folder 16, Harrison Collection; Richard Hull to Burt Harrison, Series 1/Box 5/Folder 16, Harrison Collection; Richard Hull to Jim Robertson, Series 1/Box 2/Folder 6, Robertson Collection.

6. FBH speech, Educational Television: An Opportunity or a Responsibility, 5 May 1951, 8/104, FHS.

7. Broderick to FBH, 17 May 1949, 2/ Cor-Bo, FBH.

8. Personal interview with Mr. Stanley Neustadt, 16 May 1996 (hereafter cited as Neustadt interview).

9. FBH to Brower, 17 May 1949, 2/Cor-Bo, FBH.

10. FBH to Tyler, 17 May 1949, 8/Cor-Tu, FBH.

11. Erik Barnouw, *The Golden Web* (New York: Oxford University Press, 1968) p. 23; Willard D. Rowland, "The Meaning of 'Public Interest' in Communications Policy, Part I: Its Implementation in Early Broadcast Law and Regulation," *Communication Law and Policy* 2: 363–396.

12. Christopher Sterling and John Kittross, *Stay Tuned: A Concise History of American Broadcasting* (Belmont, CA: Wadsworth Press, 1990), p. 159.

13. The philosophy of the Wagner-Hatfield Act was incorporated into the Communications Act of 1934. It is inherent to Section 307(a), which required the Federal Communications Commission to investigate the need for reserving radio frequencies for noncommercial, educational use. See also Erik Barnouw, *The Golden Web*.

14. Ibid.

15. Sterling and Kittross, p. 160.

16. "FCC Announces Plans for Further Television Proceedings," FCC 49–693, 26 May 1949.

17. Ibid.

18. Richard Hull to Burt Harrison, Box 5, Folder 16, Harrison Collection.

19. *Notice of Further Proposed Rule Making*, FCC 49–948, 11 July 1949.

20. Ibid.

21. Ibid.

22. Topical Outline for Commissioner Hennock's Informal Talks, undated, 7/97, FHS.

23. Ibid.

24. FBH to Poole, 29 September 1950, 4/45, FHS.

25. Gordon to FBH, 29 November 1950, 4/Cor-Go, FBH.

26. Dorothy Brandon, "Blackboard of Future?" *New York Herald Tribune*, 14 May 1950, section 2, p. 4. See also "Speak Now, or Forever. . . , " *NEA Journal* 39 (November 1950), p. 618.

27. The FCC later changed the deadline for filing comments from 8 August 1949 to 26 August 1949. FBH to Abbot, 3 August 1949, 1/Cor-A, FBH.

28. FBH to Bartlett, 14 July 1949, 1/Cor-Ba, FBH. Several duplicate copies of the exact same letter were found throughout Hennock's correspondence files (e.g., FBH to Carson, 14 July 1949, 2/Cor-Ca, FBH).

29. Hull to National Association of Educational Broadcasters members, 21 July 1949, 4/Cor-Hu, FBH.

30. For example, see FBH to Abbot, 3 August 1949, 1/Cor-A, FBH.

31. Ibid.

32. FBH to Carpenter, 29 August 1949, 2/Cor-Ca, FBH.

33. Richard Hull to Jim Robertson, Series 1/Box 2/Folder 6, Robertson Collection.

34. Telford Taylor, "Finding a Place for Education on TV," *New York Times*, 28 January 1951, Sec. 6, p. 9.

35. I. Keith Tyler to Burt Harrison, Series 1/Box 6/Folder 16, Harrison Collection. See also "Educators Name Taylor," *Broadcasting*, 13 November 1950, p. 90.

36. Richard Hull to Jim Robertson, Series 1/Box 2/Folder 6, Robertson Collection.

37. FBH speech to the 37th Annual Schoolmen's Week, 20 April 1950; FBH speech to the Institute for Education by Radio, 4 May 1950; FBH speech to the Symposium on the Regulation of Radio and Communication, 17 May 1950; FBH speech at the Dedication of Studios at WKBW, 27 October 1950, all found at 8/104, FHS.

38. FBH speech, 37th Annual Schoolmen's.

39. FBH speech, Institute for Education by Radio.

40. FBH speech, Symposium on the Regulation.

41. FBH speech, 37th Annual Schoolmen's.

42. FBH speech, Dedication of Studios.

43. FBH speech, Institute for Education by Radio.

44. Ibid.

45. FBH speech, 37th Annual Schoolmen's.

46. Ibid.

47. Frieda Hennock, "The Free Air Waves, An Administrative Dilemma," *Women Lawyers Journal* 36 (Fall 1950), pp. 5–6.

48. Ibid., p. 29.

49. FBH speech, New York Women's Advertising Club, 15 November 1950, 8/104, FHS.

50. Ibid.

51. FBH to Crosby, 21 November 1950, 2/Cor-Co, FBH.

52. John Crosby, "Get the Educators in There Pitching," *Washington Post*, 28 November 1950, p. 15B. Correspondence to Hennock indicated readers saw the same column in the *Boston Globe* and the *New York Herald Tribune*.

53. Janssen to FBH, 27 November 1950, 12/Public Opinion Mail-J, FBH.

54. Spillman to FBH, 27 November 1950, 13/Public Opinion Mail-S, FBH. There are dozens of such letters in boxes 1–9 and 12–13 of the FBH.

55. U.S. Congress, Senate, Official Report of Proceedings before the Federal Communications Commission, 82nd Congress, 1st session, 27 November 1950–8 December 1950 (Volumes 87-94), 22 January 1951–30 January 1951 (Volumes 95–100), hereafter cited as Official Report. See also an undated document reviewing key witnesses and their testimony in 1/Misc. Lists, FBH.

56. After a visit with President Truman on 1 September 1949, Hennock wrote to him that "it was inspiring to know how you felt about the great media of mass communications and their possibilities for the good of the people." FBH to Harry Truman, 1 September 1949, Box 121/Folder General File (Ha–He), Harry S. Truman Presidential Library (hereafter cited as HST).

57. I described these attitudes as sexist, not Mr. Stambler.

58. Personal interview with Mr. Arthur Stambler, 16 May 1996 (hereafter cited as Stambler interview).

59. Ibid.

60. Edwards to Truman, 10 April 1951, 121/ General File (Ha–He), HST.

61. "Coy Talk," *Broadcasting*, 2 August 1948, p. 54.

62. "Education Goal," *Broadcasting*, 10 July 1950, p. 64.

63. Although R. Franklin Smith argues that both FCC commissioners and staff members believed that Hennock's importance was overstated, and that there was consistent commission support for ETV, I believe this position represents a reconstruction of the past. *Broadcasting* magazine, no supporter of ETV, consistently singled out Hennock for her support of noncommercial television. If other commissioners actively supported the proposal, they would have been the subject of criticism as well.

64. "School Stations," *Broadcasting*, 29 August 1949, p. 26.

65. For instance, *Broadcasting* regularly published articles that questioned the FCC's wisdom regarding the "freeze," such as " 'Freeze' in Vain?," *Broadcasting*, 6 November 1950, p. 52.

66. For example, see "School Stations," p. 26; "FCC Let-Up Period," *Broadcasting*, 25 September 1950, p. 36; "Education's Place in TV Considered," *Broadcasting*, 23 October 1950, p. 82; "NAEB Sessions," *Broadcasting*, 2 October 1950, p. 44; "Public Service Role," *Broadcasting*, 20 November 1950, p. 57.

67. "No Opposition?" *Broadcasting*, 4 December 1950, p. 46.

68. Personal interview with Mr. Stanley Neustadt, 16 May 1996, (hereafter cited as Neustadt interview).

69. Dwight Macdonald, "A Theory of Mass Culture," *Mass Culture: The Popular Arts in America*, ed. Bernard Rosenberg & David Manning White (Glencoe, IL: The Free Press, 1957), p. 59.

70. Ibid, p. 60.

71. Clement Greenberg, "Avant-Garde and Kitsch," *Mass Culture: The Popular Arts in America*, ed. Bernard Rosenberg & David Manning White (Glencoe, IL: The Free Press, 1957), p. 98.

72. Richard H. Pells, *The Liberal Mind in a Conservative Age: American Intellectuals in the 1940s and 1950s.* (New York: Harper & Row Publishers, 1985), p. 223.

73. David Manning White, "Mass Culture: Another Point of View," *Mass Culture: The Popular Arts in America*, ed. Bernard Rosenberg & David Manning White (Glencoe, IL: The Free Press, 1957), p. 17.

74. Ibid, p. 19.

75. Frieda Hennock, "My First Year," *Variety*, 27 July 1949, p. 43.

76. FBH speech to the New York Women's Advertising Club, 15 November 1950, 8/104, FHS.

77. *Notice of Further Proposed Rule Making*, Separate Views of Commissioner Hennock, FCC 49–948, 11 July 1949.

78. Official Report, 1950, Volume 87, p. 15859.

79. Stanton testimony, Official Report, 1951, Volume 100; Salant testimony, Official Report, 1951, Volume 102; Baker testimony, Official Report, 1951, Volume 98.

80. Official Report, 1950, Volume 93, p. 16953.

81. During the course of the hearings there were several tense moments during which Hennock attacked Plotkin regarding the questions he asked witnesses. Official Report, 1950, Volume 89, pp. 16128–16129, and pp. 16170–16171. These exchanges were also reported in "Educators Take Up Torch," *Broadcasting*, 4 December 1950, p. 55+.

82. For example Official Report, 1950, Volume 87, p. 15840.

83. For example Official Report, 1950, Volume 88, pp. 15928–15931.

84. Official Report, 1950, Volume 93, p. 16953.

85. Educators' difficulty in raising money to build stations was a point Hennock stressed frequently throughout the hearings. See for example, Official Report, 1950, Volume 90, p. 16323+.

86. Official Report, 1950, Volume 89, p. 16152.

87. Official Report, 1950, Volume 87, p. 15842; Volume 89, p. 16104, 16112; Volume 90, p. 16142.

88. By January 1951, other ETV supporters were also beginning to use the print media to communicate their concerns. See, for instance, John Crosby, "The Time is Now," *New York Herald Tribune*, 10 December 1950; Earl James McGrath, "Safeguarding Television Channels for Education," *School Life* 33 (January 1951): p. 51; and Telford Taylor, "Finding a Place for Education on TV," *New York Times*, 28 January 1951, sec.6, p. 9.

89. Frieda Hennock, ABC broadcast, *Town Meeting of the Air*, "Who Should Be Responsible for Education on Television?" 28 November 1950. Transcript of program found in 15/152, FHS. Hennock's personal statement, prepared prior to the program and containing virtually the same content as the program's transcript, is in 8/104, FHS.

90. Ibid.

91. A rough draft of Hennock's comments is in 9/116, FHS.

92. FBH to Roosevelt, 24 January 1951, 8/Cor-Ro, FBH.

93. Frieda Hennock, "TV Conservation," *The Saturday Review of Literature* 33 (9 December 1950): pp. 22–23.

94. Frieda Hennock, "The 3 R's on TV," *Variety*, 3 January 1951. A copy of this article was also found in 1/11, FHS.

95. "Hennock, Webster," *Broadcasting*, 1 January 1951, p. 36.

96. Taishoff, "No Opposition?" p. 46.

97. "School TV Stations Sought by Bricker," *New York Times*, 30 November 1950, p. 52; The Bricker Resolution, 19/156, FHS.

98. "Public's Views," *Broadcasting*, 12 February 1951, p. 57.

99. Frieda Hennock speech to the Women's National Democratic Club, 1 February 1951, 8/104, FHS. She made similar arguments regarding television channels as a natural resource in addresses to the Adult Educational Council of Philadelphia, 15 February 1951; American Association of School Administrators, 20 February 1951; the Sixth Annual Michigan Radio-Television Conference, 3 March 1951; and the Eighth Annual Community Institute of Mamaroneck-Larchmont, 19 March 1951, all in 8/104, FHS.

100. FBH speech, Eighth Annual Community Institute. Similar themes concentrating on television as an agent of high culture to the Women's National Democratic Club, Adult Educational Council, American Association of School Administrators, Sixth Annual Michigan, Federation of Jewish Women's Organizations, 18 April 1951; and to the Mills School, 8 June 1951, all in 8/104, FHS.

101. FBH speech, Adult Educational Council.

102. Ibid. Similarly patriotic themes are found in speeches to Women's National

Democratic Club, American Association of School Administrators, Eighth Annual Community Institute, Federation of Jewish Women's Organizations.

103. FBH speech, Mills School. Similar indication of television's usefulness to combat totalitarianism are found in addresses to Women's National Democratic Club, American Association of School Administrators, Eighth Annual Community Institute, Federation of Jewish Women's Organizations.

104. FBH speech, Institute for Education by Radio-Television.

105. FBH speeches, Adult Educational Council, Sixth Annual Michigan, Eighth Annual Community Institute, Mills School.

106. FBH speeches, Sixth Annual Michigan, Institute for Education by Radio-Television.

107. FBH speech, Institute for Education by Radio and Television.

108. FBH speech, Sixth Annual Michigan

109. FBH speeches, American Association of School Administrators, Sixth Annual Michigan.

110. For examples see "Television Hailed as National Asset," *New York Times*, 2 February 1951, p. 29; "TV Education Backed," *New York Times*, 16 February 1951, p. 27; and "Warns Public on TV," *New York Times*, 20 March 1951, p. 33.

111. For examples see "Program Appeal," *Broadcasting*, 5 February 1951, p. 70; "Michigan Meet," *Broadcasting*, 12 February 1951, p. 27; "Public's Views," *Broadcasting*, 12 February 1951, p. 57; "Honor Hennock," *Broadcasting*, 12 February 1951, p. 70; "Freedom to View," *Broadcasting*, 19 February 1951, p. 60; and "Hennock Talk," *Broadcasting*, 26 February 1951, p. 56.

112. Frieda Hennock, "TV-Problem Child or Teacher's Pet?" *Journal of New York State Education* (March 1951): 397-400; Frieda Hennock, "Educational Opportunities in Television," *The Commercial and Financial Chronicle* 173 (15 March 1951), pp. 10+; Frieda Hennock, "Television and Teaching," *Educational Outlook*, May 1951, pp. 199–203.

113. Frieda Hennock, NBC broadcast, "Meet the Press," 10 June 1951. Preparatory material for the appearance may be found in 7/97, FHS.

114. Ibid.

115. *Third Report and Order*, 41 FCC 158. See also "TV Expansion Plan Maps 2,000 Outlets," *New York Times*, 23 March 1951, p. 23.

116. Hennock Dissent, *Third Report and Order*, 41 FCC 588.

117. Ibid, p. 589.

118. Ibid.

119. For example, see FBH to Renne, 20 April 1951, 7/Protest Letters, FBH.

120. Warren Moscow, "Truman Promotes Medina," *New York Times*, 12 June 1951, p. 1.

121. U.S. Congress, House, Interstate and Foreign Commerce Committee, Hearings for the Investigation of Regulatory Commissions and Agencies, 85th Cong., 2nd sess., p. 2374 (hereafter cited as House, Hearings for the Investigation).

122. Address to the American Association of School Administrators, 19 February 1953, 8/105, FHS.

123. Draft of Statement by Commissioner Hennock before Senator Tobey and Senate [Foreign and Interstate Commerce] Committee, 9 April 1953, 7/100, FHS.

124. Ibid.

125. Hennock to Tannenwald, 22 April 1953, 8/Corresp-Ta, FBH.

126. Ibid.

127. "Educational Television Channel Reservations," FCC Public Notice 90136, 11 May 1953, 9/122, FHS.

128. House, Hearings for the Investigation, p. 2376. See also Hennock address, "Educational TV: An Unusual Opportunity for the Set Manufacturing Industry," undated, 7/98, FHS.

129. Hennock to Abrams, 18 October 1952, 1/Corresp-A, FBH.

130. Tannenwald to Katz, 8 January 1953, 3/32, FHS. The Ford Foundation later became one of the most significant sources of financial support for educational broadcasting.

131. Hennock to Abramson, 31 October 1955, 6/76, FHS.

132. U.S. Congress, House, Hearing Before the Special Subcommittee on Legislative Oversight, 86th Cong., 2nd sess., 1958, p. 4255.

133. Mazer to Truman, 12 June 1951, 4/53, FHS.

134. Broderick to Wheatley, 18 July 1951, 5/61, FHS.

135. Cohn to Hennock, 23 July 1955, 5/64, FHS.

136. Dameron to Hennock, 24 July 1955, 5/63, FHS.

137. Program for the Testimonial Dinner, 9/119, FHS.

138. "Long Live Frieda Hennock," Address by Reed Hundt to Women in Government Relations, 24 August 1995.

Conclusion

Let's give a toast to Frieda
Tonight and every night she's the Queen
There's no one greater than this crusader
For the best on your TV Screen[1]

On Wednesday evening, 20 July 1955, a host of government dignitaries met at the Shoreham Hotel in Washington, D.C. to honor Frieda Hennock,[2] who was retiring from the FCC. Her New Deal approach to communications regulation was an anachronism in the Eisenhower administration, so her friends and colleagues met to laud her accomplishments and bid her farewell. The guests were welcomed by India Edwards, the chair of the Women's Caucus of the Democratic National Committee and the woman who played a pivotal role in Hennock's appointment to the FCC. Senator Estes Kefauver served as master of ceremonies. The guest of honor arrived fashionably late, sweeping to the dais in her floor-length fur wrap. All eyes were on her, and the rest of the evening was spent lauding "Queen" Frieda's accomplishments.

The ETV campaign was something of a distant memory for Hennock, a hard fight she won four years earlier that served as the last of the major decisions made by the Federal Communications Commission during the "freeze." It was a period during which she took frequently unpopular positions regarding the color system, UHF allocation, and educational television, opinions that form the crux of Frieda Hennock's participation in the FCC's 1948 "freeze" judgments and represent rulings that had the greatest long-term impact on television broadcasting in the United States.

They are clear examples of how Hennock's personal characteristics played a role in the development of public policy.

EPILOGUE: BEYOND THE "FREEZE"

In seven years serving on the commission, however, these were not the only decisions in which Hennock participated. Indeed, she joined in hundreds of rulings ranging from granting broadcast licenses to establishing regulatory policy. Many decisions were considerably more mundane, such as the fairly routine decisions regarding broadcast licensing. Others were more complex and resulted in long-lasting, and usually controversial, policies that governed the broadcast industry. There were several other decisions in which Hennock joined that deserve mention as they provide further evidence of either the role her political motivations played in her FCC positions, the centrality of her devotion to serving public interests, or both.

The Fairness Doctrine

One case in which Hennock's politics played a significant role was the 1948 policy that became known as the Fairness Doctrine, which was one of the first major decisions on which she participated. It was also one of the most controversial decisions the FCC ever made. In 1940 the commission created a rule that was known as the Mayflower Doctrine[3] which, simply stated, prohibited radio broadcasters from "editorializing" on their stations; they were not allowed to express opinions on the air. The belief that this policy violated the First Amendment by restricting broadcasters' freedom of speech grew during the 1940s until, in 1949, the FCC revised its Mayflower Doctrine by allowing broadcasters to express opinions as long as it was done fairly.[4] This decision was released on 1 June 1949, only 11 months after Hennock joined the commission. Her strongly worded, albeit short, opinion was an indication of the lone dissenting position she would usually take over the next seven years. The Fairness Doctrine, she asserted, was "foolhardy." The foundation of her dissent rested on two arguments. First, the commission's belief that "a high standard of impartiality"[5] was required of broadcasters was correct, but the FCC would be unable to monitor and ensure such a standard was consistently achieved. Failure to guarantee fairness, Hennock believed, required that the commission ban editorializing completely, as that was the only way to ensure "the proper use of radio in the public interest."[6]

Hennock's strong position against editorializing was motivated by both

personal and public interests. Her devotion to the Democratic Party likely played a role in this decision. Throughout the 1930s a variety of radio
personalities, most notably Father Coughlin, routinely and fiercely
attacked President Franklin Roosevelt on the radio. But her position
against allowing radio station owners to express opinion over the air may
have been rooted in a fear of the potential power of radio to assert influence over the public's lives. As Commissioner Clifford Durr remarked in
1948, "the soundest idea uttered on a street corner or even in a public
auditorium cannot hold its own against the most frivolous or vicious idea
whispered into the microphone."[7] Hennock agreed with Durr and, believing that it was impractical for the commission to monitor "fairness," she
argued that editorializing ought to be banned.

The ABC/UPT Merger

Hennock participated in a similarly prominent case involving the
merger of ABC and United Paramount Theaters (UPT), which was decided by the FCC on 9 February 1953.[8] There were several issues before the
commission in this case involving the renewal and transfer of broadcast
licenses between Paramount Television Productions, Balaban & Katz
Corporation, and the Allen B. DuMont Laboratories, Inc. The larger issue
at stake, however, was the proposed merger between American
Broadcasting Company and United Paramount Theaters.[9] The alliance
between the two companies would be mutually beneficial. UPT stood to
increase its audience by making its vast movie library available as television programming. ABC would benefit by having access to UPT's financial resources, which would enable the network to develop programming,
acquire affiliates, and lure advertisers. Approved by the commission, the
merger set the precedent of allowing the motion picture industry *entre*
into the broadcasting business at the corporate level.

Frieda Hennock strongly opposed the commission decision and wrote
a thirty-seven page dissent detailing her complaints with the majority
judgment.[10] Her exhaustive dissent may be abbreviated to three central
arguments, all of which revolve around her devotion to serving the public's interest. First, Hennock believed the merger violated the antitrust
policies established in the 1941 Chain Broadcasting Rule, in which NBC
was forced to divest itself of either the Red or Blue networks because
their joint operation constituted unfair competition.[11] In her view, ABC/
UPT would have an unfair competitive advantage over the other three
television networks. Her antitrust concerns were closely linked to her
strong disapproval of allowing the motion picture industry to gain footing

in the television industry, her second major complaint. As she wrote in 1953, "it must be anticipated that this merger will serve as a forerunner for other similar vast concentrations of control over the mass media. This must result in depositing control of these media, as well as the vital source of programming for them, in fewer and more powerful hands."[12] She was particularly concerned about the ability of too few individuals and/or companies to control the flow of ideas through television. She decried corporate attempts to further control the mass media and thereby limit the voices that could find expression.

Characteristically, her third major argument asserted that the majority decision did not clearly explicate exactly *how* the merger would serve the public interest, although it clearly outlined how it would serve both ABC and UPT. Hennock argued that the public interest would not be served by the merger, but would instead be facilitated by ensuring "diversification of control among multiform interests [which would] bring about greater freedom of access to communications facilities that gives . . . fuller meaning and scope to our nation's and each individuals freedom of speech, viewpoint, and conscience."[13] Indeed, the position she took against the ABC/UPT merger was consistent with her support of educational television, which she perceived as a medium for the communication of ideas alternative to those presented in mainstream, commercial television. It was also indicative of her growing distrust of the corporate giants, such as RCA, NBC, and CBS, who, in reality, dictated the development of the television industry. Although the FCC had not yet been forced to reconsider its selection of the CBS color system when the ABC/UPT merger was considered, it was clear by February 1953 that the television industry simply ignored the commission's color decision and followed their own path. From Hennock's perspective, the merger served only to exacerbate the wide-ranging influence corporations already had over the industry. Moreover, the more power the corporations enjoyed the less influence the public could assert in the industry except as audience members.

Multiple Ownership

Hennock's position on multiple ownership of radio and television stations was motivated by public interests. The FCC limited the number of radio and television stations an individual and/or company could own in an effort to "implement the Congressional policy against monopoly and in order to preserve competition."[14] The conflict among commissioners and with the broadcast industry revolved around how many stations con-

stituted too many. In November 1953 the commission reevaluated its policy and decided that no one could own more than seven AM, seven FM,
and seven TV stations (two of which had to be UHF).[15] Hennock believed
there was a fundamental flaw in the commission's reasoning, in that it set
national limits on the station ownership without considering the damag-
ing influence an individual or company might have by owning seven stations within a particular region. As she stated, such an arrangement "may
often have a more deleterious effect on competition and constitute a more
stifling concentration, than the ownership [of stations] scattered throughout the United States."[16] When considered in the light of her positions
regarding educational television, diversity in programming, and a deep
distrust of communication corporations, her strict limits on multiple ownership of stations were also related to a desire to open broadcasting, and
particularly television broadcasting, to a wider range of people than simply the corporations. Indeed, her position on multiple ownership was
another attempt to serve public interests.

Frieda Hennock's interests in serving both personal and public goals
were manifested through these and other decisions. She invariably represented the minority opinion on commission judgments and, throughout
seven years of FCC decisions, she issued one dissent after another. Her
constant challenges were costly, though. Indeed, her relationship with the
other six commissioners was tense and strained as a result of both personality conflicts and administrative issues. As one of her legal assistants
explained, "she was strident and insensitive—particularly to men. Men do
not like to be lectured by ladies, and she was always lecturing the [men].
. . . [But] it wasn't just personal. She wasn't just strident, and harpy, and
lecturing them. She wouldn't go along, she wouldn't play the game. . . .
And she took positions on many issues that they were unhappy with."[17]
Hennock's years on the commission, while personally satisfying, were
not altogether pleasant experiences.

1951 FEDERAL JUDGESHIP NOMINATION

For a brief period it appeared as if her commission career would be cut
short when she was nominated by President Truman in June 1951 to fill
the vacancy left by Judge Alfred C. Coxe who retired as the U.S. District
Judge for the Southern District of New York.[18] It was a position she
longed to hold. She received considerable support, particularly from divi-
sional bar associations and possibly from the broadcasting industry,
whom some believed wanted her constant challenges to their supremacy
removed from the FCC. But her selection was quickly contested. The day

after her nomination was announced the New York City Bar Association (NYCBA) declared that she was "totally unqualified to be a United States District Judge [and would] vigorously oppose confirmation of her nomination."[19] A few days later the American Bar Association (ABA) similarly decided to oppose Hennock's nomination.[20] Accustomed to gathering supporters for a political fight,[21] Hennock spent July, August, and September of 1951 preparing witnesses and herself to testify before the Senate Judiciary Committee regarding her nomination.[22]

The complete story regarding Hennock's nomination is unclear.[23] Judging by her own testimony before the Judiciary Committee,[24] however, six issues formed the basis of the ethical complaints against her nomination. Three of the issues are so small that their insertion into the debate seems trivial.[25] The remaining three were probably taken more seriously. The first involved *Hennock versus Silver*, the lawsuit Hennock filed against her former law partner Julius Silver in 1934, in which she asserted that Silver defrauded her of fees she should have received as a result of the firm's representation of Edwin Land and the invention of his "polaroid" camera.[26] The second allegation related to the accusation that Hennock placed a private wager that Franklin Roosevelt would seek a third presidential term in 1940 which, a bar association argued, resulted in a felony violation when she subsequently voted in the same presidential election. Hennock admitted to the wager, although she claimed that it was arranged by her broker. She went on to assert that "a private wager is not a crime under the laws of New York State."[27] "I am not aware," she continued, "of any person being prosecuted on the basis of the tortured interpretation suggested by the Bar Association here."[28] The third, and probably most serious, grievance against Hennock alleged an "improper relationship" between Hennock and Judge Ferdinand Pecora.[29] Although Hennock and Pecora seemed to have had a close friendship,[30] there is no direct evidence to suggest that theirs was an "improper" one.[31] Nonetheless, the accusation was serious enough to have weighed heavily against Hennock.

By the end of October 1951 Congress adjourned without confirming Hennock's appointment. Profoundly disappointed, she informed President Truman that "the sound development of television [which was her] major concern . . . on the commission" prevented her from accepting a recess appointment. Truman "reluctantly deferred" to her decision.[32] While her friends rallied around her decision, especially praising that she would remain "in the field to uphold and fight for the cause of Educational Television [sic],"[33] they similarly recognized that "she was terribly disappointed that she wasn't appointed as a federal judge."[34]

While the high point of Hennock's political career occurred in March 1951 when the FCC approved her plan to reserve television channels for educational broadcasting, the low point surely occurred just seven months later when she asked President Truman to withdraw her nomination for a federal judgeship.

Hennock's inability to achieve this appointment was her greatest political failure. She returned her attentions to the commission in late 1951 with a reinvigorated devotion to ETV, for now her political future truly rested on this significant issue. Having secured the reservations prior to the federal judgeship nomination, she began traveling around the country trying to persuade university administrators and community leaders to support noncommercial television and commit the financial resources necessary to building ETV stations. She later told a Congressional sub-committee investigating agency expense accounts that she spent her "weekends with a little briefcase and a little suitcase traveling all over the country, trying to stimulate interest in educational television and getting applications in to protect those channels. . . . [If] that is not spending Government money in the public interest, I would like to know what is."

POST–FCC

Hennock's post–FCC life was active. After she left the commission in July 1955 she joined the Washington, D.C. law firm of Davies, Richberg, Tydings, Beebe & Landa to practice telecommunications law.[35] In April 1956 she married William H. Simons, a prominent real estate developer in Washington. She then turned to practicing law on her own, sharing an office with Mr. Simons. Her independent law career was quite successful. Both her connections to the FCC and the knowledge of the communications industries she acquired while serving on the commission left her particularly well-suited to practicing communications law. Unfortunately, Hennock did not enjoy a less-hectic professional life, and more settled personal life, for many years after leaving the FCC. In the spring of 1960 she developed a brain tumor and, nine days after surgery to remove the tumor, she died on 20 June 1960. She was fifty-five years old, and was buried with her mother and father in the New Mount Carmel cemetery in Queens, New York.

ASSESSMENT: FRIEDA B. HENNOCK AND THE FEDERAL COMMUNICATIONS COMMISSION

Hennock's tenure on the FCC represents an intersection of broadcasting history, policymaking and regulatory history, and women's history. Hennock played a central role in the regulatory development of television. Perpetually the minority voice promoting policies to serve public interests, Hennock was one of the very few "dissident voices that happened to positions on the FCC."[36] Her nonconformist positions were motivated partially by her desire to help people.

One of her overriding concerns throughout the color television debacle was the tremendous cost the public would have to bear. During the hearings she consistently demanded to know how the public would be affected by each of the competing color systems, what the costs would be, and how quickly the public would get color television. Hennock believed the CBS "incompatible" system simply did not serve the public interest. Millions of Americans in "TV cities" had already purchased black-and-white television sets when the color hearings began in September 1949. During the nine months of the hearings thousands more sets rolled off assembly lines and into homes, thereby exacerbating the dilemma of people whose sets would be rendered virtually useless if the CBS system was selected as the industry standard. Engineers who promised adaptors and converters missed the more fundamental point, according to Hennock, since consumers would be expected to spend more money on an already-costly piece of equipment.

Her concerns regarding public interests were similarly manifested during the allocation hearings, in which she pressed for both the UHF assignments as well as the development of the technical infrastructure necessary for UHF, all of which were necessary for the nationwide television system the American public demanded. Unfortunately, the UHF allocation hearings represent one of Hennock's misdirected decisions, as she failed to take heed of industry warnings that the ultra high frequencies were considerably more problematic than the VHF frequencies. The UHF misstep illuminates the same mistake politicians before and since Hennock have made, which is to be so completely devoted to achieving one political aim that threats to its success are overlooked.

Her greatest achievement was the campaign to secure channel reservations for educational television which, in her mind, would accomplish two important goals. First, it would democratize education in the United States by delivering educational material to the entire country via television programming. Second, it would provide a much-needed alternative to network-provided commercialized programming. The public would be served in both cases. Hennock passionately carried her ETV message throughout the country, whether through delivering speeches to a wide variety of audiences, making radio and television appearances, publishing magazine articles, visiting potential ETV sites, or browbeating witnesses during the color television and allocations hearings. She fundamentally believed in the power of education; her own personal experiences were testament to the ability of education to lift an individual out of poverty into a life of wealth, prestige, and power. Her belief in education left her disgusted with the debris she saw littering the television programming landscape, filled with nothing more than the antics of Milton Berle, Howdy-Doody, and violent detective shows. She wanted to bring culture and education to the American public through television.

Hennock was not completely altruistic, however. She was not the entirely self-sacrificing person that feminine socialization teaches women to be nor did she engage in "feminine politics." Her FCC decisions were also strongly motivated by her own political ambitions. This is particularly the case regarding the positions she took during the "freeze." Frieda Hennock was an astute politician who understood the importance of finding an issue with which she could make a positive name for herself, for with that prominence came the likelihood of access to greater political power. She similarly understood the attention she drew in the politically prominent appointment as the first woman appointed to a federal agency and the first women at the FCC; missteps would be costly. Educational television was a political godsend under the historical circumstances and she quickly adopted it as her "white horse." Public education was a subject considered appropriate for a woman to tackle since it necessarily involved nurturing the minds of children; it was a subject that people could interpret as "naturally" important to a woman. Hennock attacked the campaign for educational television with a fervor (albeit political) that seemed "natural" for a woman bent on saving the minds of the American public.

Educational television represented Hennock's political aspirations, and its development and ultimate success influenced other decisions she made during the "freeze." During the color television hearings it became clear to Hennock that the CBS "incompatible" color system represented a significant threat to the development of educational television. Its technical incompatibility with existing television technology created even more difficulties for educational broadcasters, who already faced considerable financial troubles. Educational broadcasters faced considerable difficulty getting the funding to build and equip ETV stations. Once the CBS color system was selected the entire industry, including ETV, was expected to convert all of their equipment and begin broadcasting in color. The cost of the equipment was prohibitive for potential educational broadcasters who did not have network contracts that ensured income and, hence, the ability to pay for color technology. Moreover, an ETV broadcaster who might have managed to acquire color equipment would have had a very difficult time developing an audience since no television sets would receive their transmissions. On the other hand, the RCA "compatible" color system was not a menace to ETV. This was one of the principal reasons she supported the RCA color system, despite the fact that it was years away from public availability. Three years after the majority of the commission selected the CBS "incompatible" color as the industry standard, it reversed its position and established the RCA system as the operating standard. It appeared to be a vindication for Hennock, who seemed to presciently understand three years earlier that the RCA system was the best. Her position was not particularly insightful, but was motivated by a personal political desire to protect educational television.

Hennock's emphasis on serving both personal and public interests served her well in the color television decision, yet these same motivations resulted in a considerably less astute position regarding the UHF allocation decision. The timing of the allocation hearings was significant. Unlike the color hearings, during which Hennock was able to successfully divide her time between attending the hearings and directing the ETV campaign, the allocation hearings were held just one month before the ETV hearings. Hennock was distracted by last-minute preparations for the ETV hearings, including preparing witnesses and developing defenses against the anticipated attacks against ETV. These preoccupations interfered with both her attentions at the allocation hearings as well as her attendance; consequently, she did not devote her full attention to understanding the significant issues that threatened UHF: the inherent problems of transmissions, industry reluctance to manufacture transmitters and receivers, and intermixture. Witnesses at the allocation hearings clearly warned all of the commissioners about these problems. Hennock, in particular, failed to see the bigger picture. She simply pushed the problems aside by assuming that all of the problems could be resolved through industry cooperation and then turned her attention to what she believed was the more important issue, which was asserting educational broadcasters' rights to both VHF and UHF channel allocations. When the commission delivered its allocations decisions, she fully supported intermixture. Once again her devotion to serving both public and personal interests through the establishment of educational television guided her decision-making.

In a broader historical context, Hennock's tenure on the commission coincided with some of the most significant decisions made by the agency, particularly regarding the evolution of policies guiding the development of the television industry. Surprisingly little research has focused on the "freeze," despite its momentous impact on the future of television. The issues at stake during the four years of the "freeze," including the technical, political, and economic aspects of allocating frequencies and setting broadcast standards, as well as the corporate intrigues, had a significant and lasting impact on the future of the industry. And while the 1948 Freeze proved politically beneficial for Hennock, it was a regulatory nightmare.

FCC decisions made during the "freeze," and comprehensively released in the *Sixth Report and Order*, were costly. The color television decision is a case in point. In an effort to bring color television to the public as quickly as possible, the majority of the commission voted to implement a technology that violated the agency's own technical standards and, hence, was incompatible with every television set in the country's living rooms. Further, the FCC failed to fully recognize RCA's dominance over the manufacturing industry and its associated ability to effectively dismiss the agency's decision favoring CBS color. Its failure resulted in the FCC creating a situation in which its own credibility and authority were challenged by the industry giant.

While the commission recovered fairly quickly from the ill-conceived color decision, its UHF allocation judgment was disastrous. The commissioners, including Hennock, were too eager to find an easy solution to a complex problem that would mollify too many people. Intermixing VHF and UHF channel assignments limited the development of television in the United States, rather than serving as the catalyst of its growth. Setting aside UHF frequencies for television proved to be a theoretical response to the problem of insufficient television frequencies and gave the public the illusion that TV could develop unfettered from technical constraints. When the commission intermixed VHF and UHF, however, the theoretical promise was bumbled. The limited number of VHF channels allocated to a community were quickly snapped up by licensees who, in turn, were generously courted by the television networks. Since many towns and cities received only two VHF assignments, those two channels were quickly licensed and their owners promptly affiliated with one of the two most powerful networks: NBC or CBS. This left ABC and DuMont to battle over affiliation with the third station that eventually opened in a market, often on a UHF channel. The end result was that the commission's VHF/UHF intermixture decision limited both the development of television in the United States and reinforced the dominance of NBC and CBS.

From a broader perspective, the action of "freezing" television licensing in 1948 created an artificial barrier to the growth of television, which resulted in a licensing logjam when the moratorium was lifted in 1952. Television was in its infancy when the commission issued the "freeze." There were only fifty television stations on the air and only fifty more under construction, there were only about 7 million television sets in American homes, and the networks provided extremely limited programming choices. When the "freeze" was lifted in 1952, there were many more million sets in homes, the networks had developed full programming schedules, but there were still only 100 television stations on the air. Not surprisingly, the commission was deluged with license requests. In many cases two or more individuals requested the same VHF channel assignment, which required the Broadcast Bureau of the agency to hold hearings to determine who should receive the coveted channel. The logistics of coping with thousands of license requests caused the commission to cut corners, to assign licenses without adequate review or, as was often the case, to re-allocate frequencies. From a licensing perspective, it took the FCC more than ten years to clear the mess left by the "freeze."

The only positive decision to come out of the "freeze" was the reservation of noncommercial channels, and even that did not develop as intended. The fact that the majority of the educational set-asides were in the UHF band doomed ETV to a difficult childhood. The prodigious efforts of Frieda Hennock, the Joint Commission on Educational Television, the Institute for Education by Radio and Television, the Ford Foundation, and eventually even FCC Chair Newton Minow, kept educational television alive but not necessarily thriving. It was only after federal legislation created the mechanism for financial support that public television began to flourish. Taken as a whole, then, the 1948 "freeze" must be deemed a regulatory failure. The FCC's attempts to resolve problems only created a different set of difficulties. And throughout the entire ordeal, the public was the least served of all of the participants.

But the 1948 "freeze" served Frieda Hennock well, as did her entire tenure at the Federal Communications Commission. Hennock's political hopes were partially realized in educational television. During her life her contemporaries recognized the significance of her contribution. She was known throughout the country, and particularly among government officials, as principally responsible for the development of educational television. Although its path did not follow the same route envisioned by Hennock, her work established the foundation on which our current system of public broadcasting stations is built; the road to the 1967 Public Broadcasting Act and the creation of the Corporation for Public Broadcasting would have been considerably more difficult—if not impossible—without the noncommercial reservations for which Hennock campaigned and achieved.

Until now ETV is the only issue for which Hennock received attention. The little academic research that focused on Hennock is directed toward her ETV work.[37] As recently as 1995, former FCC Chair Reed Hundt exclaimed "Long Live Frieda Hennock" as he decried the sad state of television programming and longed for the kind of educational television Hennock supported.[38] But Frieda Hennock was much more than just a single accomplishment. She was a complex person who attempted to navigate the difficult terrain of being a politically ambitious woman during a period of changing sociocultural attitudes toward women. She came of age during the Progressive and New Deal eras of American history when women began to flex their political muscles, and she was among the second generation of New Deal women who followed the likes of Frances Perkins into politically powerful positions in Washington, D.C. [39] She joined the commission as an outsider, and remained as such throughout her tenure. First and foremost she was a woman, the first female commissioner in an agency that existed (in one form or another) for over twenty years and had developed a culture of male authority. Her six male colleagues administered industries completely dominated by men. Once installed at the commission, she challenged the status quo by developing independent positions that were motivated either by public or political interests but were not, in any case, directed by a sense of submission to male authority; she certainly was not one of the "three-piece suit men" of either the commission or the broadcast industry it oversaw. Sometimes her positions were politically astute and publically beneficial; sometimes they weren't.

Above all, Hennock continued the political legacy started by women of the New Deal, who demonstrated that they could ably serve in powerful political positions. The combined desires of serving both public and personal political interests enabled Hennock to serve with distinction at the FCC, and to develop the lasting legacy of educational television in the United States. She is an important reminder of what a woman can accomplish if given half a chance and, more importantly, the degree to which an individual can effect change.

NOTES

1. "To Frieda," Program for the Testimonial Dinner to the Honorable Frieda B. Hennock, 20 July 1955, Box 9/Folder 119, Frieda Hennock Simons collection, Schlesinger Library, Radcliffe College, Cambridge, MA (hereafter cited as FHS).

2. Program for the Testimonial Dinner, 9/119, FHS.

3. In the Matter of The Mayflower Broadcasting Corporation and The Yankee Network, Inc., 8 FCC 333 (16 January 1941).

4. In the Matter of Editorializing by Broadcast Licensees, 13 FCC 1246.

5. Ibid, p. 1270.

6. Ibid.

7. Clifford Durr, "The Voice in Democracy: Radio Frequencies Are Not Private Property," *Vital Speeches of the Day* 14 (1 May 1948): p. 443. Frieda Hennock replaced Commissioner Durr after he refused a second term on the FCC.

8. In the Matter of the Applications of Paramount Television Productions, Inc. et al., 17 FCC 264, 9 February 1953. Hereafter cited as Paramount Television Productions.

9. In 1948 the United States Supreme Court ordered Paramount (and all movie distribution companies) to divest themselves of their theater chains (U.S. v. Paramount, 334 U.S. 131). United Paramount Theaters was the new, and completely independent, company formed to oversee the theaters that once belonged to Paramount Pictures. UPT held a significant library of Paramount movies that would be very useful for television programming.

10. Paramount Television Productions, 17 FCC 365–402.

11. Federal Communications Commission, *Report on Chain Broadcasting* (Washington, D.C.: GPO, 1941).

12. Paramount Television Productions, 17 FCC 381.

13. Ibid, p. 380.

14. In the Matter of the Amendment of the Rules and Regulations Relating to Multiple Ownership of AM, FM, and Television Broadcasting Stations, 18 FCC 288, 25 November 1953.

15. Ibid.

16. Ibid, p. 299.

17. Telephone interview with Mr. Arthur Stambler, 16 May 1996.

18. Warren Moscow, "Truman Promotes Medina," *New York Times*, 12 June 1951, p. 1; "Judge Medina Promoted," *New York Times*, 12 June 1951, p. 28; "The Federal Judgeships," *New York Herald Tribune*, 12 June 1951, p. 22.

19. "City Bar to Oppose Hennock Selection," *New York Times*, 13 June 1951, p. 17. See also Sonia Stein, "Everybody Happy About Frieda?" *Washington Post*, 17 June 1951, Sec. 6, p. 1.

20. "Hennock Nomination Opposed by U.S. Bar," *New York Times*, 28 June 1951, p. 16.

21. See Box 5, Folders 59 and 60 in FHS for several letters between Hennock and others regarding their support of her nomination. See also Hennock's list of support she received from bar associations, organizations, judges, attorneys, educators, and private individuals for the nomination, 19/155, FHS.

22. Hearings Before the Committee on the Judiciary for the U.S. District Judge for the Southern District of New York, U.S. Senate, 28 September 1951–13 October 1951. (There are six volumes of hearings testimony regarding

Hennock's appointment, four of which are available on microfiche in Federal Depository libraries. The remaining two volumes are sealed at the National Archives). A wide variety of bar associations supported Hennock's nomination, including the New York Women's Bar Association, two Federal Bar associations, and the Federal Communications Bar Association ("Frieda Hennock," Box 38, Notable American Women Archive, Schlesinger Library, Radcliffe College).

23. The Senate Judiciary Committee documents regarding the Hennock nomination, held in the National Archives in Washington, D.C., are not available until fifty years have passed since the hearings were held. Hence, they will not be available for research until 2001.

24. The notes from which Hennock likely read during her confirmation hearing are located in 19/158, FHS. Since transcripts of her testimony to the Judiciary Committee are unavailable for review, it is impossible to verify that this is the exact information she provided.

25. The first regarded whether Hennock was a *partner* or an *associate* with Choate, Mitchell and Ely, the accusation being that Hennock unethically presented herself as a partner in the firm when, in fact, she was an associate. The second issue questioned whether Hennock's nomination was supported by John W. Davis, a pre-eminent New York attorney. The third issue questioned why Hennock allegedly refused to be interviewed by the County Lawyers Association of New York. Hennock's responses to these allegations may be found in FHS 19/155.

26. "Hennock v. Silver," 19/155, FHS; "Hennock v. Silver," 19/158, FHS.

27. "The Election Bet," 19/155, FHS.

28. Ibid.

29. "Personal Issues," 19/155, FHS. Ferdinand Pecora rose to national prominence as a special Congressional investigator of the 1929 Stock Market Crash. He served as a Justice on the New York Supreme Court from 1935–1950, at which time he resigned his judgeship to run for mayor of New York City (an election bid he lost).

30. Mrs. Selena Sheriff, Hennock's niece, affirmed that Judge Pecora frequently attended dinners and special occasions in Frieda Hennock's home (personal interview with Selena Sheriff, 7 April 1999). Further, although there are several references to "the Judge" in letters to Hennock from friends, none of them suggest an "improper relationship."

31. India Edwards' claim that it was an extra-marital affair.

32. Hennock to Truman, 30 October 1951, Box 121/Folder:General Files/Ha-He, HST-Secretary's Files, Harry S. Truman Presidential Library, Independence, MO, (hereafter cited as HST); Truman to Hennock, 31 October 1951, 121/General Files Ha-He, HST-Secretary's Files, HST.

33. Gordon to Hennock, 9 November 1951, 5/62, FHS.

34. Morris Novik to Jim Robertson, Series 1/Box 3/Folder 1, Jim Robertson Collection, Public Broadcasting Oral History Project, National Public Broadcasting Archive, University of Maryland, College Park, MD.

35. Abrams to Hennock, 12 July 1955, 5/64, FHS.

36. Robert McChesney, *Telecommunications, Mass Media, & Democracy: The Battle for the Control of U.S. Broadcasting, 1928–1935* (New York: Oxford University Press, 1993), p. 250.

37. Susan L. Brinson, "Frieda Hennock: FCC Activist and the Campaign for Educational Television," *Historical Journal of Film, Radio, and Television* 18(3): 411–429; Henry Morgenthau, "Dona Quixote: The Adventures of Frieda Hennock," Television Quarterly 26(2): 61–73; Cary O'Dell, *Women Pioneers in Television: Biographies of Fifteen Industry Leaders* (Jefferson, NC: McFarland & Co., 1997); R. Franklin Smith, "Madame Commissioner," *Journal of Broadcasting* 12 (1967-1968): 69–81.

38. Reed Hundt, "Long Live Frieda Hennock," speech delivered to the Women in Government Relations, 24 August 1995, *http://www.fcc.gov/Speeches/Hundt/spreh524.txt*.

39. Susan Ware, *Beyond Suffrage: Women in the New Deal* (Cambridge, MA: Harvard University Press, 1981).

Works Cited

ARCHIVES

Owen Brewster collection, Bowdoin College, Brunswick, ME.
Brooklyn Law School, institutional file on Frieda B. Hennock, Brooklyn, NY.
Mary Dewson collection, Schlesinger Library, Radcliffe College, Cambridge, MA.
India Edwards collection, Harry S. Truman Presidential Library, Independence, MO.
Federal Communications Commission Archives, National Archives and Records Administration, College Park, MD.
Susan Brandeis Gilbert collection, Brandeis University, Waltham, MA.
Burt Harrison collection, Public Radio Oral History Project Series, National Public Broadcasting Archive, University of Maryland, College Park, MD.
Frieda B. Hennock collection, Harry S. Truman Presidential Library, Independence, MO.
Frieda B. Hennock, Senate Files 80B-A3 Interstate and Foreign Commerce Committee, Executive Nominations: Frieda Hennock, National Archives and Records Administration, Washington, D.C.
Ruth Cowan Nash collection, Schlesinger Library, Radcliffe College, Cambridge, MA.
Jim Robertson collection, Public Broadcasting Oral History Project,

National Public Broadcasting Archives, University of Maryland, College Park, MD.

Eleanor Roosevelt collection, Franklin D. Roosevelt Presidential Library, Hyde Park, NY.

Franklin D. Roosevelt collection, Franklin D. Roosevelt Presidential Library, Hyde Park, NY.

Frieda Hennock Simons collection, Schlesinger Library, Radcliffe College, Cambridge, MA.

Robert A. Taft collection, Manuscript Division, Library of Congress, Washington, D.C.

Harry S. Truman collection, Harry S. Truman Presidential Library, Independence, MO.

GOVERNMENT DOCUMENTS

Congressional

U.S. Congress. House. Committee on Appropriations. Hearings Regarding Goodwin B. Watson, William E. Dodd, Jr., and Robert Morss Lovett, 78th Congress, 1st sess.

U.S. Congress. House. Hearing Before the Special Subcommittee on Legislative Oversight. 86th Cong., 2nd sess., 1958.

U.S. Congress. House. Interstate and Foreign Commerce Committee. Hearings Before the Subcommittee on Communications of the Committee of Interstate and Foreign Commerce, Color Television, 83rd Cong., 1st sess., March 1953.

U.S. Congress. House. Interstate and Foreign Commerce Committee. Hearings for the Investigation of Regulatory Commissions and Agencies, 85th Cong., 2nd sess., April 1958.

U.S. Congress. House. Representative Charles Vursell of Illinois speaking against Frieda B. Hennock nomination to the FCC, 80th Cong., 2nd Session. *Congressional Record*, 1 June 1948, p. 6816.

U.S. Congress. Senate. Senator Albert Hawkes of New Jersey speaking for Frieda Hennock nomination to the FCC, 80th Cong., 2nd sess. *Congressional Record*, 17 June 1948, p. 8619.

U.S. Congress. Senate. Senator Owen Brewster of Maine speaking for Frieda B. Hennock's nomination to the FCC, 80th Cong., 2nd sess. *Congressional Record*, 19 June 1948, p. 9169.

U.S. Congress. Senate. Senator Ball of Minnesota speaking against Frieda B. Hennock's nomination to the FCC, 80th Cong., 2nd sess. *Congressional Record*, 19 June 1948, pp. 9168–9169.

U.S. Congress. Senate. Committee on the Judiciary. Frieda B. Hennock: Hearings for the U.S. District Judge for the Southern District of New York Before the Committee on the Judiciary, 82nd Cong., 1st sess., September–October 1951.

U.S. Congress. Senate. Interstate and Foreign Commerce Committee. Status of UHF and Multiple Ownership of TV Stations. Hearings Before the Subcommittee on Communications of the Committee of Interstate and Foreign Commerce, 83rd Cong., 2nd sess.

U.S. Congress. Senate. Official Report of Proceedings before the Federal Communications Commission, 82nd Cong., 1st sess., 1949–1950.

U.S. Congress. Senate. Senate Interstate Foreign Commerce Committee. Report of the Advisory Committee on Color Television, 81st Cong., 2nd sess.

Federal Communications Commission

"Commission to Consider Applications for UHF Television Stations Proposing No Local Programming." 54 FCC 991.

"Educational Television Channel Reservations." FCC Public Notice 90136, 11 May 1953.

"FCC Announces Plans for Further Television Proceedings." FCC 49–693, 26 May 1949.

Federal Communications Commission. *First Annual Report of the Federal Communications Commission*. Washington, D.C.: GPO, 1936.

Federal Communications Commission. *Third Annual Report of the Federal Communications Commission*. Washington, D.C.: GPO, 1937.

Federal Communications Commission. *Fourth Annual Report of the Federal Communications Commission*. Washington, D.C.: GPO, 1939.

Federal Communications Commission. *Fifth Annual Report of the Federal Communications Commission*. Washington, D.C.: GPO, 1940.

Federal Communications Commission. *Sixth Annual Report of the Federal Communications Commission*. Washington, D.C.: GPO, 1940.

Federal Communications Commission. *Seventh Annual Report of the Federal Communications Commission*. Washington, D.C.: GPO, 1941.

Federal Communications Commission. *Thirteenth Annual Report of the Federal Communications Commission.* Washington, D.C.: GPO, 1947.

Federal Communications Commission. *Fourteenth Annual Report of the Federal Communications Commission.* Washington, D.C.: GPO, 1948.

Federal Communications Commission. *Nineteenth Annual Report of the Federal Communications Commission.* Washington, D.C.: GPO, 1954.

Federal Communications Commission. *Twentieth Annual Report of the Federal Communications Commission.* Washington, D.C.: GPO, 1955.

Federal Communications Commission. *Report on Chain Broadcasting.* Washington, D.C.: GPO, 1941.

First Report of the Commission, 41 FCC 4. (1 September 1950).

In the Matter of Amendment of the Commission's Rules Governing Color Television Transmissions. *Report and Order*, 41 FCC 658, 20 January 1954.

In the Matter of the Amendment of the Rules and Regulations Relating to Multiple Ownership of AM, FM and Television Broadcasting Stations. 18 FCC 288, 25 November 1953.

In the Matter of the Applications of Paramount Television Productions, Inc. et al. 17 FCC 264, 9 February 1953.

In the Matter of the Commission's Rules Governing Color Television Transmissions. 41 FCC 658, 17 December 1953.

In the Matter of Editorializing by Broadcast Licensees. 13 FCC 1246, 1948.

In the Matter of the Mayflower Broadcasting Corporation and The Yankee Network, Inc. 8 FCC 333, 16 January 1941.

Notice of Further Proposed Rulemaking, 41 FCC 948, 11 July 1949.

Second Report of the Commission, 41 FCC 111, 10 October 1950.

Sixth Report and Order of the Commission, 41 FCC 148, 11 April 1952.

Third Report and Order of the Commission, 41 FCC 158, 20 June 1951.

Reports and Publications

McMillin, Lucille Foster. *Women in the Federal Service.* Washington, D.C.: U.S. Civil Service Commission, 1941.

U.S. Department of Commerce. Bureau of the Census. *Statistical Abstracts of the United States, 71st Edition.* Washington, D.C.: Government Printing Office, 1950.

U.S. Department of Commerce. Bureau of the Census. Historical *Statistics of the United States, Part I*. Washington, D.C.: Government Printing Office, 1976.

U.S. Department of Commerce. Bureau of the Census. *Historical Statistics of the United States, Part II*. Washington, D.C.: Government Printing Office, 1976.

Women in the Federal Service, 1923–1947, Part 1: Trends in Employment. Washington, D.C.: U.S. Civil Service Commission, 1949.

Women in the Federal Service, Part 11: Occupational Information. Washington, D.C.: U.S. Civil Service Commission, 1950.

Legislation

Communications Act of 1934, 48 Stat. 1064, 47 USC 151.

Coolidge's message to Congress, H.R. Doc. 483, 69th Cong., 2nd sess., 7 December 1926.

Radio Act of 1912, 37 Stat. 302, 13 December 1912.

Radio Act of 1927, 44 Stat. 1162, 23 January 1927.

Wireless Ship Act of 1910, 36 Stat. 629, 24 June 1910.

PERSONAL INTERVIEWS

Personal interview with Selena Sheriff, 7 April 1999.

Personal interviews with Mr. Stanley Neustadt, 16 May 1996; 12 February 1998; 27 April 1998.

Personal interview with Mr. Arthur Stambler, 16 May 1996.

JUDICIAL SOURCES

Glendening v. Glendening, 29 NE 2nd 926 (1939), 19 NYS 2nd 693 (1939), 22 NE 2nd 169 (1939), 10 NYS 2nd 17 (1939).

Hoover v. Intercity Radio, 52 AppDC 339, 286 Fed 1003.

NBC v. U.S. 319 US 190 (1943).

Radio Corporation of America et al. v. United States et al., 95 F. Supp. 660.

U.S. Attorney General William J. Donovan to Secretary of Commerce and Labor Herbert Hoover, 35 Ops Att'y Gen 126.

U.S. v. Paramount, 334 U.S. 131.

U.S. v. Zenith Radio Corp., 12 F2d 614.

PRESS ARTICLES

"ABC of Radio and Television." *Broadcasting*, 30 March 1953, p. 89.

Beatty, J. Frank. "The Color Triangle." *Broadcasting*, 27 February 1950, p. 53.

"The Big Fight." *Newsweek*, 30 October 1950, p. 54.

"Boro Woman Lawyer Named to FCC Post." *Brooklyn Eagle*, 25 May 1948, p. 1.

Brandon, Dorothy. "Blackboard of Future?" *New York Herald Tribune*, 14 May 1950, section 2, p. 4.

Brittin, Frank L. "Ultra-High Frequency TV Stations Due in 1952 . . ." *Popular Mechanics*, October 1951, p. 228.

Carson, Saul. "On the Air: Color Controversy." *New Republic*, 13 November 1950, p. 22.

"CBS Color Gets the Nod." *Newsweek*, 11 September 1950, p. 65.

"CBS Color Video Favored by Board." *New York Times*, 2 September 1950, p. 17.

"CBS Color Video Starts Nov. 20; Adaptors Needed by Present Sets." *New York Times*, 12 October 1950, p. 6.

"City Bar to Oppose Hennock Selection." *New York Times*, 13 June 1951, p. 17.

"Closed Circuit." *Broadcasting*, 21 December 1953, p. 5.

"Color Climax." *Time*, 23 October 1950, p. 66.

"Color Enigma." *Time*, 11 September 1950, p. 73.

"Color Television Again Under Study." *New York Times*, 19 February 1950, Sec. 3, p. 9.

"Color TV Inquiry Set." *New York Times*, 16 March 1953, p. 22.

"Color TV Is Stopped Cold." *Business Week*, 27 October 1951, p. 21.

"Color TV Shelved as a Defense Step." *New York Times*, 20 October 1951, p. 1.

"Coy Talk." *Broadcasting*, 2 August 1948, p. 54.

Crater, Rufus. "TV Faces Crisis." *Broadcasting*, 13 September 1948, p. 21.

———. "Television Freeze." *Broadcasting*, 4 October 1948, p. 22A.

———. "TV Processing." *Broadcasting*, 20 September 1948, p. 21.

——— and Larry Christopher. "TV Expansion." *Broadcasting*, 27 September 1948, p. 21.

Crosby, John. "Get the Educators in There Pitching." *Washington Post*, 28 November 1950, p. 15B.

———. "The Time is Now." *New York Herald Tribune*, 10 December 1950.

"Death of Color TV." *Business Week*, 30 December 1950, p. 24.

"DuMont Challenges Wilson on Color TV." *New York Times*, 21 October 1951, p. 47.

"Education Goal." *Broadcasting*, 10 July 1950, p. 64.

"Education's Place in TV Considered." *Broadcasting*, 23 October 1950, p. 82.

"Educators Take Up Torch." *Broadcasting*, 4 December 1950, p. 55+.

Eklund, Laurence. "Portia on the FCC." *The Milwaukee Journal*, 1 September 1948, p. 18.

Engel, Leonard. "Should You Buy Color Television?" *The Nation*, 11 November 1950, p. 430.

"FCC Asked to Suspend All TV Grants Until Hearings Are Held on Hill." *Broadcasting*, 19 April 1954, p. 48.

"FCC Favors CBS Color." *Broadcasting*, 4 September 1950, p. 4.

"FCC Let-Up Period." *Broadcasting*, 25 October 1950, p. 38.

"FCC Planning TV Future." *New York Post*, 30 October 1949, p. T6.

"The Federal Judgeships." *New York Herald Tribune*, 12 June 1951, p. 22.

"The First." *Time*, July 7 1948, pp. 92, 94.

"Freedom to View." *Broadcasting*, 19 February 1951, p. 60.

Freeman, William. "Video Set Sales Decline at Stores." *New York Times*, 22 October 1950, Sec. 3, p. 3.

"'Freeze' in Vain?" *Broadcasting*, 6 November 1950, p. 52.

"Freeze of New VHF's Asked by UHF Stations." *Broadcasting*, 24 May 1954, p. 119.

"Frieda Barkin Hennock." *Cyclopedia of American Biography*, Vol. H. (New York: James T. White & Co., 1952), p. 337.

"Frieda Hennock Simons Dead." *New York Times*, 21 June 1960, p. 33.

"Getting the UHF Story." *Broadcasting*, 12 April 1954, p. 134.

"Girl Lawyer Wins Point." *New York Times*, 28 April 1928, p. 21.

Gould, Jack. "High Court Backs CBS Color Video." *New York Times*, 29 May 1951, p. 1.

———. "Public, TV Industry Stirred by FCC Ruling on Color." *New York Times*, 13 October 1950, p. 1.

———. "The Crisis in UHF." *New York Times*, 18 April 1954, Sec. II, p. 9.

———. "Television in Color." *New York Times*, 22 October 1950, Sec. II, p. 11.

———. "Time for Action." *New York Times*, 29 January 1950, sec. 2, p. 11.

Hatch, Mark. "FCC Lady Member Gives Her Views on Color TV Muddle." *Boston Sunday Post*, 22 October 1950, p. A4.

Hennock, Frieda. "Educational Opportunities in Television." *The*

Commercial and Financial Chronicle, 173, 15 March 1951, pp. 10+.

———. "My First Year." *Variety*, 27 July 1949, p. 43.

———. "Television and Teaching." *Educational Outlook*, May 1951, pp. 199–203.

———. "The 3 R's on TV." *Variety*, 3 January 1951.

———. "TV Conservation." *The Saturday Review of Literature*, 33, 9 December 1950, pp. 22–23.

——— "TV-Problem Child or Teacher's Pet?" *Journal of New York State Education*, March 1951, pp. 397-400.

"Hennock Heard." *Broadcasting*, 14 June 1948, p. 21.

"Hennock in Balance." *Broadcasting*, June 22, 1948, p. 22+.

"Hennock Nomination Opposed by U.S. Bar." *New York Times*, 28 June 1951, p. 16.

"Hennock Reiterates Plea for All-UHF; Sterling Challenges at NARTB Panel." *Broadcasting*, 31 May 1954, p. 63.

"Hennock Talk." *Broadcasting*, 26 February 1951, p. 56.

"Hennock, Webster." *Broadcasting*, 1 January 1951, p. 36.

"Hill Readies List of Witnesses on UHF." *Broadcasting*, 5 April 1954, p. 52.

"Honor Hennock." *Broadcasting*, 12 February 1951, p. 70.

"Is CBS Stuck with Color?" *Business Week*, 21 October 1950, p. 49.

"Johnson Lauds FCC." *Broadcasting*, 15 May 1950, p. 62.

"Judge Medina Promoted." *New York Times*, 12 June 1951, p. 28.

"Lady Commissioner." *Broadcasting*, June 28, 1948, p. 25.

MacLeod, John. "The Woes and Triumphs of a Lady Advocate." *American Weekly*, September 5, 1948, p. 12.

"Madam Commissioner." *Broadcasting*, 31 May 1948, p. 44.

McConnell, Chris. "NFL on Fox Highlights UHF Shortcomings." *Broadcasting*, 17 October 1994, p. 60.

———. "UHF Spectrum: Telcom's New Hot Property," *Broadcasting*, 29 July 1996, p. 20.

McCrary, Tex and Jinx Falkenburg, "New York Close-Up." *New York Herald-Tribune*, 15 June 1950, p. 31.

McGrath, Earl James. "Safeguarding Television Channels for Education." *School Life*, 33, January 1951, p. 51.

"Members of FCC Clash on UHF Issue." *New York Times*, 28 May 1954, p. 30.

"Michigan Meet." *Broadcasting*, 12 February 1951, p. 27.

Millspaugh, Martha. "Miss Commissioner Hennock." *Baltimore Sun*, 8 August 1948, p. A5

Montanari, Val. "First Woman Member of FCC Makes Impression on Senators With Frankness." *Washington Post*, 5 July 1948 , p. 2.

Moscow, Warren. "Truman Promotes Medina." *New York Times*, 12 June 1951, p. 1.

Murphy, Herbert. "FCC Still Holding Off on Color Decision." *Barron's*, 10 April 1950, p. 11.

"NAEB Sessions." *Broadcasting*, 2 October 1950, p. 44.

"New Company Shows Video Color to FCC." *New York Times*, 21 February 1950, p. 46.

"New York Woman Is Named to FCC, Would Be First on the Board." *New York Herald-Tribune*, 24 May 1948, p. 1.

"Potter Subcommittee Meets, Sees Public Hearings on UHF Troubles." *Broadcasting*, 8 March 1954, p. 46.

"Program Appeal." *Broadcasting*, 5 February 1951, p. 70.

"A Promising New Era Begins for Television." *Life*, 17 September 1951, p. 63.

"Public Service Role." *Broadcasting*, 20 November 1950, p. 57.

"Public's Views." *Broadcasting*, 12 February 1951, p. 57.

"School Stations." *Broadcasting*, 29 August 1949, p. 26.

"School TV Stations Sought by Bricker." *New York Times*, 30 November 1950, p. 52.

"Senate UHF Hearing Again Postponed; New Date May 19." *Broadcasting*, 10 May 1954, p. 55.

"Senate Unit Launches Radio-TV Study." *Broadcasting*, 1 March 1954, p. 51.

Shuster, Alvin. "Video Expansion in U.S. Imperiled." *New York Times*, 19 April 1954, p. 41.

"Speak Now, or Forever. . . . " *NEA Journal*, 39, November 1950, p. 618

Stein, Sonia. "Everybody Happy About Frieda?" *Washington Post*, 17 June 1951, Sec. 6, p. 1.

———. "FCC Approves CBS System for Color TV." *Washington Post*, 12 October 1950, p. 1.

Sugrue, Patricia. "Frieda Hennock, Attorney, Is Dead." *The Washington Post*, 21 June 1960, p. B4.

Taishoff, Sol. "No Opposition?" *Broadcasting*, 4 December 1950, p. 46.

Taylor, Telford. "Finding a Place for Education on TV." *New York Times*, 28 January 1951, Sec. 6, p. 9.

"Television Chaos." *New York Times*, 18 October 1950, p. 32.

"Television: Green Light to Black and White." *Time*, 31 March 1947, p. 70.

"Television Hailed as National Asset." *New York Times*, 2 February 1951, p. 29.

"Truman Picks Lady Lawyer for FCC Post." *New York Journal-American*, 24 May 1948, p. 1.

"TV: Answers to Some Questions on What UHF Means to TV Set Owners." *Consumer Reports*, June 1952, p. 305.

"TV Color's Future: 7 Who Rule." *U.S. News and World Report*, 27 October 1950, p. 34.

"TV Education Backed." *New York Times*, 16 February 1951, p. 27.

"TV Expansion Plan Maps 2,000 Outlets." *New York Times*, 23 March 1951, p. 23.

"TV Freeze." *Broadcasting*, 11 October 1948, p. 28.

"Twinkle, Flash & Crawl." *Time*, 28 November 1949, p. 49.

"2 Television Manufacturers Sue to Halt CBS Color Broadcasts." *New York Times*, 18 October 1950, p. 1.

"UHF Group Formed to Plan Senate Hearing Strategy." *Broadcasting*, 26 April 1954, p. 52.

"UHF Outlets." *Broadcasting*, 9 March 1953, p. 5.

"Ultra High Frequency: The Promised Land of TV?" *Business Week*, 9 August 1952, p. 42.

"Upper UHF Operation Begins This Week, Target Dates Show." *Broadcasting*, 9 February 1953, p. 58.

"'Upstairs' TV." *Newsweek*, 6 October 1952, p. 68.

"Video Set Owners Get Reassurance." *New York Times*, 23 October 1950, p. 25.

"Warns Public on TV." *New York Times*, 20 March 1951, p. 33.

"Why UHF Operators Want Another Freeze." *Broadcasting*, 3 May 1954, p. 52.

"Woman Is Counsel for 2 as Slayers." *New York Times*, 3 May 1928, p. 7.

"Woman Lawyer Named to Commission Post." *Radio Daily New York City*, 25 May 1948, p. 1.

"Woman Nominated as Member of FCC." *New York Times*, 25 May 1948, p. 29;

"Youngest Portia Uses Her Charm." *New York City American*, 24 June 1929.

Zoglin, Richard. "Murdoch's Biggest Score." *Broadcasting*, 6 June 1994, p. 54.

RADIO/TELEVISION PROGRAMS

Frieda Hennock, ABC broadcast, Town Meeting of the Air, "Who Should Be Responsible for Education on Television?" 28 November 1950.

Frieda Hennock, NBC broadcast, *"Meet the Press,"* 10 June 1951. Manuscript provided by the Manuscript Division of the Library of Congress.

SCHOLARLY SOURCES

Amott, Teresa and Julie Matthaei. *Race, Gender, and Work: A Multicultural Economic History of Women in the United States.* Boston, MA: South End Press, 1991.

Antler, Joyce. *The Journey Home: Jewish Women and the American Century.* New York: The Free Press, 1997.

Auerbach, Jerold S. "From Rags to Robes: The Legal Profession, Social Mobility and the American Jewish Experience." *American Jewish Historical Quarterly*, 66(2) (December 1976): 249–284.

————. *Unequal Justice: Lawyers and Social Change in Modern America.* New York: Oxford University Press, 1976.

Barnouw, Erik. *The Golden Web.* New York: Oxford University Press, 1968.

————. *A Tower in Babel.* New York: Oxford University Press, 1966.

Baum, Charlotte, Paula Hyman, and Sonya Michel. *The Jewish Woman in America.* New York: The Dial Press, 1976.

Benjamin, Louise. "Radio Regulation in the 1920s: Free Speech Issues in the Development of Radio and the Radio Act of 1927." Ph.D. dissertation, University of Iowa, 1985.

————. "Working It Out Together: Radio Policy from Hoover to the Radio Act of 1927." *Journal of Broadcasting and Electronic Media*, 42 (Spring 1998): 221–236.

Berrol, Selma. "Education and Economic Mobility: The Jewish Experience in New York City, 1880–1920." *American Jewish Historical Quarterly*, 65(3) (March 1976): 257-271.

————. "From Compensatory Education to Adult Education: The New York City Evening Schools, 1825–1935." *Adult Education*, 26(4) (1976): 208–225.

————. "Public Schools and Immigrants: The New York City Experience." *American Education and the European Immigrant: 1840–1940*, Bernard J. Weiss, ed. Urbana, IL: University of Illinois Press, 1982: 32.

Bilby, Kenneth. *The General: David Sarnoff and the Rise of the Communications Industry.* New York: Harper & Row Publishers, 1986.

Brinson, Susan L. "Frieda Hennock: FCC Activist and the Campaign for

Educational Television." *Historical Journal of Film, Radio and Television*, 18(3) (1998): 411–429.

Brumberg, Stephan F. Going to America, *Going to School: The Jewish Immigrant Public School Encounter in Turn-of-the-Century New York City*. New York: Praeger Special Studies, 1986.

Cowan, Neil M. and Cowan, Ruth Schwartz. *Our Parents' Lives: The Americanization of Eastern European Jews*. New York: Basic Books, Inc., Publishers, 1989.

Douglas, Susan. *Inventing American Broadcasting, 1899–1922*. Baltimore, MD: The Johns Hopkins University Press, 1987.

Ellmore, R. Terry. *Broadcasting Law and Regulation*. Blue Ridge Summit, PA: Tab Books, Inc., 1982.

Emery, Walter B. *Broadcasting and Government: Responsibilities and Regulations*. Michigan State University Press, 1971.

Erickson, Don. *Armstrong's Fight for FM Broadcasting: One Man vs. Big Business and Bureaucracy*. Tuscaloosa, AL: The University of Alabama Press, 1973.

Ewen, Elizabeth. *Immigrant Women in the Land of Dollars: Life and Culture on the Lower East Side, 1890–1925*. New York: Monthly Review Press, 1985.

Feingold, Henry A. *A Time for Searching: Entering the Mainstream, 1920–1945*. Baltimore, MD: The Johns Hopkins University Press, 1992.

Flannery, Gerald V. and Peggy Voorhies, "Frieda Hennock." *Commissioners of the FCC: 1927-1994*. Gerald V. Flannery, ed. Lanham, MD: University Press of America, 1994: 96–98.

"Frieda B. Hennock." *Current Biography-1948*, New York: H.W. Wilson, 1948: 278–280.

Friedman-Kasaba, Kathie. *Memories of Migration: Gender, Ethnicity, and Work in the Lives of Jewish and Italian Women in New York, 1870–1924*. Albany, NY: State University of New York Press, 1996.

Gabaccia, Donna. *From the Other Side: Women, Gender, and Immigrant Life in the U.S., 1820–1990*. Bloomington, IN: Indiana University Press, 1994.

Garvey, Daniel E. "Secretary Hoover and the Quest for Broadcast Regulation." *Journalism History*, 3 (Autumn 1976): 66–69.

Glanz, Rudolf. *The Jewish Woman in America: Two Female Immigrant Generations 1820–1929*. New York: KTAV Publishing House, Inc., 1976.

Glenn, Susan A. *Daughters of the Shtetl: Life and Labor in the Immigrant*

Generation. Ithaca, NY: Cornell University Press, 1990.

Goldberg, Albert I. "Jews in the Legal Profession: A Case of Adjustment to Discrimination." *Jewish Social Studies*, 32 (1970): 148–161.

Greenberg, Clement. "Avant-Garde and Kitsch." *Mass Culture: The Popular Arts in America*. Bernard Rosenberg & David Manning White, eds. Glencoe, IL: The Free Press, 1957.

Halpern, Ben. "The Roots of American Jewish Liberalism." *American Jewish Historical Quarterly*, 66 (September 1976): 190–214.

Hazlett, Thomas. "The Rationality of U.S. Regulation of the Broadcast Spectrum." *Journal of Law and Economics*, 33 (April 1990): 133–175.

Hennock, Frieda B. "The Free Air Waves, An Administrative Dilemma." *Women Lawyers Journal*, 36 (Fall 1950): 7.

Herring, James and Gerald Gross. *Telecommunications: Economics and Regulation*. New York: McGraw-Hill, 1936.

Horowitz, Robert B. *The Irony of Regulatory Reform: The Deregulation of American Telecommunications*. New York: Oxford University Press, 1989.

Howe, Irving. *World of Our Fathers*. New York: Harcourt Brace Jovanovich, 1976.

Hyman, Paula. "Culture and Gender: Women in the Immigrant Jewish Community." *The Legacy of Jewish Migration: 1881 and Its Impact*. David Berger, ed. New York: Brooklyn College Press, 1983

Kahn, Frank J. *Documents of American Broadcasting*. Englewood Cliffs, NJ: Prentice-Hall, 1984.

Krasnow, Erwin G. *The Politics of Broadcast Regulation*. New York: St. Martin's Press, 1973.

Lipsitz, George. "The Meaning of Memory: Family, Class and Ethnicity in Early Network Television." *Cultural Anthropology*, 4 (1986), 355–387.

Lopata, Helena Znaniecki. *Polish Americans: Status Competition in an Ethnic Community*, Englewood Cliffs, NJ: Prentice-Hall, Inc., 1976.

Macdonald, Dwight. "A Theory of Mass Culture." *Mass Culture: The Popular Arts in America*, Bernard Rosenberg & David Manning White, eds. Glencoe, IL: The Free Press, 1957.

MacDonald, J. Fred. *One Nation Under Television: The Rise and Decline of Network TV*. New York: Pantheon Books, 1990.

Marcus, Jacob R. *The American Jewish Woman, 1654–1980*. New York: KTAV Publishing House, Inc., 1981.

Markowitz, Ruth Jacknow. *My Daughter, The Teacher: Jewish Teachers in the New York City Schools*. New Brunswick, NJ: Rutgers University Press, 1993.

Mass Culture: The Popular Arts in America, Bernard Rosenberg & David Manning White, eds. Glencoe, IL: The Free Press, 1957.

McChesney, Robert W. *Telecommunications, Mass Media, and Democracy: The Battle for the Control of U.S. Broadcasting, 1928–1935*. New York: Oxford University Press, 1993.

Moore, Deborah Dash. "Assimilation of Twentieth Century Jewish Women." *Jewish Women in America: An Historical Encyclopedia, Vol. 1*. Paula E. Hyman and Deborah Dash Moore, eds. New York: Routledge, 1997: 92–101.

———. *At Home in America: Second Generation New York Jews*. New York: Columbia University Press, 1981.

Morgenthau, Henry. "Dona Quixote: The Adventures of Frieda Hennock." *Television Quarterly*, 26(2): 61–73.

National Health Assembly, *America's Health: A Report to the Nation, Official Report*. New York: Harper & Brothers Publishers, 1949.

O'Dell, Cary. *Women Pioneers in Television: Biographies of Fifteen Industry Leaders*. Jefferson, NC: McFarland & Co., 1997.

Pells, Richard H. *The Liberal Mind in a Conservative Age: American Intellectuals in the 1940s and 1950s*. New York: Harper & Row Publishers, 1985.

Perry, Elisabeth Israels. *Belle Moskowitz: Feminine Politics and the Exercise of Power in the Age of Alfred E. Smith*. New York: Oxford University Press, 1987.

Powe, Lucas A. *American Broadcasting and the First Amendment*. Berkeley, CA: University of California Press, 1987.

Ray, William B. *FCC: The Ups and Downs of Radio-TV Regulation*. Ames, IA: Iowa State University Press, 1990.

Roosevelt, Eleanor. *It's Up to the Women!* New York: Frederick A. Stokes Co., 1933.

Rowland, Willard D. "The Meaning of 'The Public Interest' in Communications Policy, Part I: Its Origins in State and Federal Legislation." *Communication Law and Policy*, 2 (1997): 309–328.

Rowland, Willard D. "The Meaning of 'The Public Interest' in Communications Policy, Part II: Its Implementation in Early Broadcast Law and Regulation." *Communication Law and Policy*, 2 (1997): 363–396.

Seeber, Frances M. "Eleanor Roosevelt and Women in the New Deal: A

Network of Friends." *Presidential Studies Quarterly*, 20 (Fall 1990): 707–717.

Shapiro, Edward S. *A Time For Healing: American Jewry since World War II*. Baltimore, MD: The Johns Hopkins University Press, 1992.

Smith, Maryann Yodelis. "Frieda Hennock." *Notable American Women, The Modern Period: A Biographical Dictionary*. B. Sicherman and C.H. Green, eds. Cambridge, MA, 1980: 332–333.

Smith, R. Franklin. "Madame Commissioner." *Journal of Broadcasting*, 12 (1967–1968): 69–81.

Sobel, Robert. *RCA*. New York: Stein and Day, 1986.

Sorin, Gerald. *A Time for Building: The Third Migration 1880–1920*. Baltimore, MD: The Johns Hopkins University Press, 1992.

Sterling, Christopher H. and John M. Kittross. *Stay Tuned: A Concise History of American Broadcasting*. Belmont, CA: Wadsworth Publishing Co., 1990.

Stone, Daniel. "Jewish Emigration from Poland Before World War II," *Polish Americans and Their History: Community, Culture, and Politics*. John J. Bukowczyk, ed. Pittsburgh: University of Pittsburg Press, 1996: 91–120.

Thompson, Kristin and David Bordwell. *Film History: An Introduction*. New York: McGraw-Hill, 1994.

Ware, Susan. *Beyond Suffrage: Women in the New Deal*. Cambridge, MA: Harvard University Press, 1981.

———. *Holding Their Own: American Women in the 1930s*. Boston: Twayne Publishers, 1982.

Weatherford, Doris. *Foreign and Female: Immigrant Women in America, 1840–1930*. New York: Facts on File, Inc., 1995.

Weinberg, Sydney Stahl. "Longing to Learn: The Education of Jewish Immigrant Women in New York City, 1900–1934." *Journal of American Ethnic History*, 8(2) (Spring 1989): 108–126.

———. *The World of Our Mothers: The Lives of Jewish Immigrant Women*. Chapel Hill, NC: The University of North Carolina Press, 1988.

White, David Manning. "Mass Culture: Another Point of View." *Mass Culture: The Popular Arts in America*. Bernard Rosenberg & David Manning White, eds. Glencoe, IL: The Free Press. 1957.

SPEECHES

Durr, Clifford. "The Voice in Democracy: Radio Frequencies Are Not

Private Property." *Vital Speeches of the Day*, 14 (1 May 1948): 444.

Hundt, Reed. "Long Live Frieda Hennock." Address to Women in Government Relations, 24 August 1995.

Index

About the Author

SUSAN L. BRINSON is an Associate Professor of Communication at Auburn University, where she teaches such subjects as broadcast history, media law, and gender communication.